Brian,

Happy Christ[...]   !

Lots of love
Aidan, Sophia xxxx

MUSIC
OF THE
SCOTTISH REGIMENTS

*Her Royal Highness The Princess Royal, Colonel-in-Chief, The Royal Scots (The Royal Regiment)
From the portrait by June Mendoza RP, ROI, commissioned by the regiment and reproduced here by
kind permission of the Trustees of the Regimental Museum*

MUSIC
OF THE
SCOTTISH REGIMENTS

COGADH NO SITH
(WAR OR PEACE)

DAVID MURRAY

Mercat Press
www.mercatpress.com

Dedicated by gracious permission
to
Her Royal Highness Princess Anne, The Princess Royal
Colonel-in-Chief, The Royal Scots (The Royal Regiment)

The Spartans moved slowly, and to the music of many flute players, who played, not as an act of religion, but in order that the army might march evenly and in true measure, and that the line might not break.
Thucydides, *The Peloponnesian War*, Book V (401 BC).

© D.J.S. Murray 1994, 2001

First published in 1994, The Pentland Press Ltd.
This edition published 2001
Mercat Press
53 South Bridge
Edinburgh
EH1 1YS
www.mercatpress.com

ISBN 1 84183 026 7

Printed in the United Kingdom by Cromwell Press

CONTENTS

~

LIST OF ILLUSTRATIONS

~

PREFACE

~

In attempting to trace the history and evolution of military music in the Scottish regiments, the researcher soon finds that there is no centrally held corpus of previous work on the subject to which he can refer and that, consequently, he has no alternative but to trawl through the regimental sources, published and unpublished, perforce ignoring the many tempting byways which the process reveals. This is not to claim that there has been no previous interest taken in the subject. There has; but such work as has been published is in the vast majority of cases the product of enthusiasts who, through no fault of their own, have had little practical experience and who, in the case of the Highland bagpipe in particular, tend to view the subject through romantic eyes, a very different viewpoint from that of the piper striving to keep his pipes in order in a winter bivouac. And if the majority of those who write have little experience of running a regimental pipes and drums or military band in peace or war, far less have they themselves ever led a marching column over the plains of India or anywhere else. It is from this latter standpoint that this book has been written.

My thanks and appreciation must go in the first place to my friend and comrade Lieutenant-Colonel Angus Fairrie, Curator of the Queen's Own Highlanders Museum Collection, for unstinted help and advice, and for ready access to the riches of the regimental museum in Fort George. Major Richard Powell, late Royal Logistic Corps, a fellow enthusiast for military music in all its forms, has also given me much help and has thrown the resources of his unrivalled collection of published sources open to me. Colonel The Honourable W.D. Arbuthnott MBE, then Regimental Secretary of The Black Watch (Royal Highland Regiment) – whose red hackle I once wore with pride – gave me invaluable help in confirming that the 1st Battalion kept up its military band, albeit sorely reduced in numbers, during the Great War. Lieutenant-Colonel G.P. Wood MC placed his unique knowledge of his beloved Argyll and Sutherland Highlanders freely at my disposal, as did Lieutenant-Colonel Alasdair Scott-Elliot, Regimental Secretary of that distinguished regiment. Colonel S.W. McBain, Regimental

Secretary of The Royal Scots (The Royal Regiment) – I first played 'Dumbarton's Drums' at the head of a Young Soldiers Company of the 'Scots Royals' – also gave invaluable help in the later stages of the book. Thanks to the kindness of Lieutenant-Colonel J.M.L. Fleming, and with much assistance from Major W. Shaw, I spent happy hours browsing through the photographic archives of the Royal Highland Fusiliers. Major D.H. White of the Gordon Highlanders was equally forthcoming. Colonel Colin Hogg and Lieutenant-Colonel David Ward of the King's Own Scottish Borderers went to much trouble to provide me with a wide range of information and illustrations.

Brigadier John Paley CBE MC, then Commandant of the Abu Dhabi Defence Force, allowed me to prove my theories about the value of military music in the indoctrination and initial training of young soldiers. The late Major Raja Sher Altaf Khan, a former Commandant of the Pakistan Army School of Music, gave me a fascinating insight into the social pressures on musicians in the old Indian Army and painted a very different picture from that described in the memoirs of *quondam* sahibs. The late Lieutenant-Colonel Sam Rhodes, Director of Music, Scots Guards, and late of the Royal Scots, explained to me how the valves on a brass instrument worked as, well-fortified internally, we watched the Edinburgh Tattoo from the Half Moon Battery one cold and windy night. With the late Lieutenant-Colonel David McBain, Director of Music, Royal Horse Guards, and also of the Royal Scots, he gave me an insight into the austere life of a bandsman after the Great War and the heavy responsibilities of a bandmaster and director of music in the days when excellence was regarded as normal and the absence of censure constituted praise. The Army School of Piping has been both a refuge and a tower of strength during the period of gestation of this book, and Major John Allan MBE and Major Gavin Stoddart MBE BEM, the present Director of Army Bagpipe Music, together with the late Pipe Major Angus MacDonald MBE, have described in detail the life of a regimental pipe major in the post-war army and allowed me a glimpse behind the immaculate façade of the Scots Guards in which all three had served.

Lieutenant-Colonel L.M.B. Wilson MBE has allowed me to

take advantage of his research into the music of the former
Queen's Regiment – whose treatment at the hands of the
authorities all right-minded soldiers must deplore – and for
access to this mine of information I am truly grateful. Colonel
I.H. McCausland, Regimental Secretary of the Royal Green
Jackets made available the regiment's early bugle resources, to
which I hope I have done justice in the text. Chapter sixteen
could not have been written without the help of Major C.L. Pape
of the Regimental Headquarters of the Devon and Dorset
Regiment; Lieutenant-Colonel E.J. Downham, The Queen's
Lancashire Regiment; Major A.F.W. Astle, The 22nd (Cheshire)
Regiment; Colonel R.K. May, The King's Own Royal Border
Regiment; Major C.P.T. Rebbeck, the former Gloucestershire
Regiment; Major P.J. Ball, the former Duke of Edinburgh's
Royal Regiment; Major J.S. Knight, the former Queen's Own
Hussars; and Colonel C.J. Dale, The Royal Anglian Regiment.

For military folklore over nine decades I am indebted first to
my father, Captain James Murray, Queen's Own Cameron
Highlanders, who enlisted in 1905 at the age of sixteen and who
served before the Great War with the 2nd Battalion in South
Africa, Hong Kong, North China – where he saw the funeral of
the notorious Empress Dowager, Tsü Hsi – and India. My
revered piping tutors, Pipe Major Robert Reid, 7th (Blythswood)
Battalion Highland Light Infantry – renowned as 'The Brig'ton
Slashers', equally formidable in peace or war – and Pipe Major
William Ross, Scots Guards were wont to reminisce once lessons
were over. Friends and comrades in the Cameron Highlanders
who regaled me over thirty years and three continents with tales
– sometimes lurid and always graphic – of soldier life between
the wars, were Pipe Majors Norman Scott and Donald Allan,
who spoke of cantonment life in Burma, India and the Sudan.
Serjeant James Fergie described the life of a military bandsman
on tour 'sure of bringing off a girl in every quarter'. Captain
John MacLellan MBE and Pipe Major Evan MacRae BEM had
been lively Enlisted Boys in the 1930s.

The late Lieutenant-Colonel Douglas Pope, Director of
Music, Coldstream Guards, and sometime Bandmaster of the
Cameron Highlanders, took time to foster the interest of an
insignificant junior officer in his band and its music, as did
Bandmaster Douglas Start and, latterly, Bandmaster Walter

Babbs. Mr William Thorburn, former Keeper of the National War Museum of Scotland and the late Mr William Boag, former Assistant Keeper, were always ready to share their incomparable fund of knowledge of military music in its widest sense, while, shortly before his untimely death, the latter authorised the use of his own unpublished work on the history and evolution of the drum and its music.

I owe thanks to Mr Stephen Wood, Keeper of the National War Museum of Scotland and Mr Charles Burnett, Curator of Fine Art. Mrs Edith Phillips, Librarian at the National War Museum of Scotland, has also given me much assistance in finding and making available the majority of the illustrations, as well as allowing me to browse at my leisure along the libraary shelves in my search for source material. Mr Douglas Anderson, the well-known military artist, has allowed me to use illustrations from his private collection. He has also shared information with me, as has Monsieur Jean-Pierre Maingam, to whom I am greatly indebted for much knowledgeable advice and help on Continental military music in general, and that of France, where the military musical inheritance is cherished, in particular. To my editor, Camilla James, I am further indebted for helpful criticism and friendly advice, and for her lively interest in what is essentially a specialised subject.

Many of those mentioned above are now in well-earned retirement or have otherwise moved on. Sadly, several – good friends all – have now joined the great majority. This book records their many contributions, and to them I remain forever indebted. To those left out for reasons of space or through inadvertence, I extend my thanks and appreciation.

But without the practical help and encouragement of my friend and former Commanding Officer, Lieutenant-Colonel Niall Baird OBE, this book could never have appeared. My wife and indefatigable research assistant, Rosemary, has been an unfailing source of support and encouragement throughout the period during which it has been written, and over the years has gracefully borne with her husband's arcane and obscure musical interests.

DJSM
Herriotshiels
June 2001

ACKNOWLEDGEMENTS

~

The excerpts from *The Bugle Horn Major's Companion* and *The Drum Major's Manual* are included by kind permission of Messrs George Potter & Co, Aldershot.

The bugle calls are published under British Crown Copyright 1993/MOD and are reproduced with the permission of the Controller of Her Britannic Majesty's Stationery Office.

DEFINITIONS

~

A military band consists of woodwind and brass instruments with a percussion section forming part of the band. A corps of drums consists of flutes in Bb and F, bugles in Bb, side, bass, and tenor drums and cymbals. Several bell lyra or vertical glockenspiels are sometimes included. Its members are referred to as 'drummers' regardless of instrument. A pipes and drums has Highland bagpipes and a similar percussion section to the corps of drums less cymbals and bell lyra. Pipers and drummers are referred to as such.

92nd Highland Regiment, Piper and Drummer, Edinburgh Castle, 1846
One of a series of photographs taken when the 92nd, better known as the Gordon Highlanders, was stationed in Edinburgh Castle. The piper wears the dress of the rank and file, with shoulder belt and broadsword. Distinctive uniforms for pipers were yet to come. The drummer's coatee is laced along the seams with the regimental lace of the 92nd. As was the practice at the time, the drum is slung very low with the drum carriage round the drummer's neck. Carried thus, the drum was said to be easier to play.
(National War Museum of Scotland)

CHAPTER I
THE ORIGINS OF MILITARY MUSIC
~

The origins of military music derive from the demands of war itself. From earliest times until the invention of radio as a means of communication, it had three principal functions: to pass orders and give signals in battle; to regulate the military day in camp and garrison; and 'to excite cheerfulness and alacrity in the soldier'.

Throughout the ages, battle has retained certain characteristics which have not been eliminated even in this modern age of satellite communications and sophisticated weaponry. The impressions most vividly implanted in the minds of the participants have been those of noise, slaughter and, above all, confusion. Not much can be done about the noise of battle, which has to be endured, or the slaughter, with which each soldier must come to his own terms. But given an adequate degree of foresight and planning, with timely information, confusion ought to be, if not avoidable, at least controllable. Yet the elements of confusion are inherent in battle itself. They arise from what Karl von Clausewitz, the nineteenth-century Prussian military thinker, called 'the friction of war'. As he explained: 'Everything in war is simple, but the simplest thing is difficult. Difficulties accumulate, and produce a friction which is inconceivable unless one has seen war.'[1]

This confusion, apparently inseparable from battle and, indeed, from war, extends from the higher echelons of command, where decisions can only be based on the information available, however flawed and incomplete, right down to the lower levels at which the actual fighting is done; that is, to the tactical as well as to the strategic level.[2] 'No operations plan will ever extend with any sort of certainty beyond the first encounter with the hostile main force,' according to Field Marshal Graf Helmut von Moltke, another of Prussia's thinkers on war and one of its most successful practitioners.[3] What von Moltke meant was that the initial orders for any operation of war must cover as many eventualities as can be foreseen and anticipated.

Once contact with the enemy's main force is made, however, such orders will have to be amended, because 'the more energetic and resourceful the enemy, the more difficult it will be to predict the course of events'.[4]

It is when those amended orders have to be passed on to the troops in contact with the enemy that confusion at the tactical level is most likely to arise, the orders, perhaps, having to deal with a totally unexpected situation, the implications of which are clearer at the higher levels than on the ground. Added to the difficulty of passing orders quickly and unambiguously in such a situation in the days, still within living memory, before a reliable radio had reached the forward troops, was the superficially simpler one of distinguishing friend from foe. Yet from the continuing efforts to solve those two puzzles have evolved not only the distinctive military costumes we call uniform, but also the whole corpus of military music, from the relatively simple tunes in basic marching rhythms, to the more complex codes of signals sounded on the bugle and trumpet, and, in former days, also beaten on the drum.

The old, deep-shelled wooden drum, beaten in the rudimental style with heavy wooden drumsticks, provided at least a partial solution to this problem of control, particularly when beaten in unison. Therefore, it was necessary to provide the commander of the lowest major tactical unit, the infantry battalion of ten companies, with a sufficient number of drums, and the men to beat them.

The companies were simply administrative sub-units. In battle, the battalion was 'told off' – organised – into eight equal divisions, each of two platoons, each platoon commanded by an officer with a serjeant to assist him. The platoons, in turn, were told off into three 'firings', so that the fire of the battalion would be equally distributed along its front. The principle was that at any one time one of the three would be firing; the second would be loading; and the third would be loaded and ready to fire. The establishment – the authorised strength – of each company included two drummers, making twenty in all. It was through these drummers that the battalion commander controlled its actions and reactions, not only in battle, but also in bivouac, camp or garrison.

The instrument they played was called a snare drum because the cords of gut which lay against the lower head, or skin, of the drum resembled a poacher's snare. It was sometimes called the side drum because it was carried canted to the right, so that the upper skin was set at an angle to the body. Such early military drums were made of wood. The wood had to be available in large sheets and had to be capable of being bent without splitting and of standing up to hard usage in bad weather. The shell of the drum was cylindrical, and to hold its shape it had to be braced internally with hoops. Where the two ends joined, they were secured by nails, hence the nail board pattern still to be seen on bass and tenor drums. These old drum shells might be up to thirty inches in depth, and eighteen in diameter.

The heads were made of cured animal skins. 'Shall some wee fellow who beats a sheepskin take the right hand of me who am a musician?' expostulated an eighteenth-century soldier piper when ordered to take his place to the left – the junior side – of a drummer. Much thicker than the synthetic heads now in use, they were durable and resistant to puncture, as well as less likely to split in wet weather than the later much thinner skin, or even plastic, heads. The head on which the drumsticks beat is called the batter head; the lower, against which the snares rested, is the snare head. Snares were in general use by the beginning of the eighteenth century. They raise the tone of the drum by about one octave, and produce a crisper sound. The wooden drumsticks with which the drum was played were much thicker than those currently in use. With such an instrument, only open rolls could be played, so the beatings, by modern standards, sound simple and unsophisticated. Played well by skilled drummers, massed drums of the period sound impressive and, indeed, inspiring. In the words of the old Scots song:

Dumbarton's drums beat bonny, O,
And I'll leave a' my freens and my Nancy, O,
And I'll bide nae mair at hame, but I'll follow wi' the drum,
And whene'er it shall sound, I'll be ready, O.[5]

The drum itself is a very ancient instrument, its warlike

connotations going back to classical times. The drummers themselves were always men somewhat apart, their roles and functions bringing them into frequent contact with their commanders and other senior officers. In the days when warfare was arguably more civilised, and certainly more leisurely, that is, up to and including the Crimean War of 1854–1856, it was often the case that communication had to be established between the opposing armies. Matters of common interest to both sides might have to be discussed, terms offered or rejected, prisoners exchanged and complaints laid about violations of the Laws and Usages of War on Land with restitution demanded or refused, rather as the English and Scottish Wardens of the Marches in the Border country would meet to settle outstanding issues and disputes between the wild Border folk on both sides of the frontier between the two countries. In war, a drumbeat signal signified that such a meeting was desired.

The drummers had to be trained, led and commanded: enter then the drum major, who makes his entry about the end of the sixteenth century and who was well established by the middle of the seventeenth when all the regiments of Cromwell's Army of occupation in Scotland had one on their strength. For a time, indeed, there was a drum major general, who appointed all the drummers to the Army at a flat rate of six shillings – 30p – per head, but he disappears in 1706. The three regiments of foot guards and the Royal Regiment – later the Royal Scots – were the only units to have the drum major paid by the public; in other regiments he was paid by deductions from his drummers' pay, which can hardly have added to his popularity. But that, then, was the custom of the Service; and by the mid- to late seventeenth century the drum major and his drummers were an integral and very important part of every battalion of the line, including those raised in Scotland.

Over the years – centuries almost – a complex code of drum signals had been evolved and refined. It covered most of the eventualities which might arise in camp, on the march, and in battle. By the middle of the eighteenth century, all tactical functions and evolutions could be regulated by means of a well understood and well-rehearsed system of rhythms and beatings whose significance was appreciated by all, at least in theory. Muskets were loaded, volleys fired and bayonets fixed and unfixed, all according to orders conveyed through drumbeat signals transmitted by the drummers, who were stationed in the centre of the line with the commanding officer, usually the lieutenant-colonel, and in two groups on either flank of the battalion. The system covered the evolutions necessary for the battalion to change formation from column, when the eight tactical divisions stood one behind the other, into the line in which they stood side by side when engaging infantry, or the square in which cavalry attacks were 'received' and, in most cases, repulsed, provided that the soldiers stood firm and kept their heads.

For its time, it was a very practical system, technically simple, easy to understand and efficient over the distances involved. The drummers were key communications men, as the buglers were later to become, their position being analogous to that of the modern radio operator. Drummers were usually enlisted as boys, because the handling of the heavy wooden drumsticks required supple wrists and strong arms and because the number and complexity of the beatings and signals demanded instant recall and quick reaction. A muddled, indistinct or mistaken signal could throw the whole battalion into that very state of confusion which it was the purpose of the system to prevent.

The drum also had its part to play in the in the solution of that perennial problem which has dogged armies for centuries, and which even the current advanced state of battlefield technology seems unable to prevent: the identification of friend or foe. In the same way as drumbeat signals were evolved for tactical control on the battlefield so did beatings with national connotations appear. These were necessary as even though from time to time efforts had been made to dress all members of a unit in the same way, formal uniform did not become general until 1645 when the New Model Army, the reformed and reorganised Army of Parliament, took the field against the Royalists.

The New Model's twelve regiments of infantry, eleven of cavalry and one of dragoons, were uniformly dressed in red coats with different facings. Until then, the mass of the soldiery had fought in the clothes they had worn at home, each side distinguished only by its field mark: a handkerchief tied round one arm, a sprig of leaves in the hat or a coloured sash; and by its field or password. All these methods were clearly unsatisfactory, and cases of disaster caused by failure to recognise which side was which in the heat of battle were common in all wars.

Why red? One source claims that by this time the red coat was the mark of the English soldier, and suggests that it derives from the fact that King James I of England, had been King James VI of Scotland until succeeding to the English throne in 1603. The Royal Standard of Scotland, which is a red lion on a yellow ground and red faced yellow had been the livery of the House of Stuart and the uniform of the Scottish Army.[6] This is possible, because at this time the Scots Army, trained by veterans of the Thirty Years War on the principles of King Gustavus Adolphus of Sweden, the Lion of the North, was fighting on the Parliamentary side.

But even when national uniforms became standard, they were never an infallible guide to the identity of the wearers. In the eighteenth century, the French, Saxons, Austrians and some Italians wore white, while Britain shared red with the Swiss, the Danes, the Hanoverians and the Irish regiments in the service of her enemy, France. In any case, a few nights in bivouac in the rain soon reduced everyone to a uniform mud colour. National flags and Regimental Colours and Standards did not always fly out, and were equally susceptible to rain and mud, so were kept cased until the moment of truth: 'Uncase the Colours! The line will advance!'

As a result, visual signals of identification tended to be less effective in practice than aural signals, which could be heard and recognised by everyone.

Like all forms of music that are learned and passed on by ear, these national drum beatings tended to become garbled with the passage of time. It fell to King Charles I to draw the attention of all his drummers to the state of the 'English March', long heard with apprehension on the continent of Europe as it announced the approach of English troops. King Charles had the score duly published. Whatever the drummers of 1632 thought of it, to a modern drummer the score is all but unreadable, although in the last decade it has been deciphered and recorded.[7]

While a drummer would have been expected, as a matter of course, to remember and reproduce all the signals in his own side's system, his general military knowledge would be expected to include the more frequently used signals of the enemy. At the Battle of Breitenfeld in September 1632, Sir Robert Munro, commanding a battalion of Scots mercenaries in the Swedish service, found himself alone with his drummer in a dense fog of chalk dust and cannon smoke. He was able to rally friends and scare off foes by telling his drummer to beat the 'Scots March', realising that it would be well known to both sides through long familiarity.

By extension, the negotiations and courtesies between opposing sides led to the formulation of a code of internationally understood drum beatings. The last battle on British soil, which finally crushed the Jacobite rising of 1745, took place on Culloden Moor near Inverness in April 1746. The bulk of the Jacobite Army consisted of what was left of the Highland clans that had come out in support of Prince Charles Edward Stuart, but the disciplined core was provided by small detachments from the British mercenary units in the service of France. It was those soldiers, Irish and Scots, who covered the flight of the Prince and the clansmen before the dragoons of the Duke of Cumberland's victorious Army.

But when their sorely wounded commander, Brigadier Stapleton, ordered his drummers to beat the 'Chamade', all Cumberland's men knew what it meant: a request for a parley, a stay of operations, so that terms of surrender might be discussed. As regular soldiers formally enlisted into the French Army, Stapleton's men – he died of his wounds – were entitled to be regarded not as rebels, but as prisoners of war, which meant, in effect, that they were treated with marginally less brutality than the unfortunate captured rebels.

It was after the Battle of Culloden that there reappeared in the British Army an instrument which had not been heard for forty years. This was the fife. It is said that the contingent of Hessians hired to augment the government forces during the suppression of the '45 Rebellion brought with them a band of fifers and drummers, and that their music so impressed the Duke of Cumberland that he ordered the fife to be reintroduced into the British Army.[8] The fife of the period was a simple cylindrical wooden instrument with a mouth hole or embouchure and six finger holes, in fact, a primitive flute.

The fife is of almost equal antiquity to the drum. Like the drum, it is believed to have originated in the Orient, and so might have been brought to Europe by the Crusaders. In its earliest form, it appears to have been played like a recorder – or a practice chanter – but later it came to be treated as a transverse instrument, one blown at right angles. In the course of time, one key was added, but essentially the semitones were produced by cross fingering, and the octave by overblowing.

This was the instrument made famous by the Landsknechten, the Swiss and German mercenaries of the fifteenth and sixteenth centuries. The oldest march for the fife is said to date from 1462, and there are others dating from the next century. In those days, the fife was the companion instrument to the drum, and it was the custom, in the Free Companies which hired themselves out to the highest bidder, to station a drummer and a fifer beside their battle flag or standard. These two, the drummer and the fifer, were called the 'Spiel' or 'Spil', and to this day in the German Bundeswehr the drummers and the fifers are called the '*Spielleute*', and, when playing as a corps of drums, as the '*Spielmannzug*'.

The fife and drum thus became associated with the basic tactical sub-unit, as until the early eighteenth century each company in the infantry and troop in the cavalry had its own flag, carried by the ensign and the cornet respectively. In older times, these had been the names of the flags themselves – ensign being a corruption of the older ancient, hence Shakespeare's Ancient Pistol, who was, in fact, a junior officer. Later, an infantry flag was called a colour and that of the cavalry a standard in the regiments of horse and a guidon in the dragoons.

These flags served a purpose. They indicated the centre of the line and served as 'markers' from which the line could take up its dressing, in other words straighten itself out, and on which the soldiers, horse and foot, could rally when in disorder. In such an event, the attention of the soldiers was drawn to the position of the colour by the fifer and drummer sounding a rallying call, 'The Point of War', which is still played and beaten as a salute by both corps of drums and pipes and drums. The cavalry equivalent, the 'Rally', still appears in the current manual *Trumpet and Bugle Calls for the Army*.

The fife, however, was always ancillary to the drum, the

instrument of command, as the bugle later became. In the majority of the standing or professional armies that the emerging nation states of the seventeenth century had begun to maintain once it became clear that their national interests could not be adequately served by hired bodies of mercenaries like the Landsknechten. Only one or two fifes were allowed to each battalion, whereas the scale of drummers was usually two to each company, totalling some twenty in the battalion, experience having shown that ten companies were the maximum which could be trained and administered by one man in peace, or commanded by one man in war.

In the British service, the fife had disappeared by 1692 in favour of the hautbois, the ancestor of the modern oboe, which had apparently replaced it in the esteem of colonels of regiments and others interested in such matters. The hautbois, too, had come out of the East, and a very similar instrument, loud and with a piercing tone, exists today in the *zurna* of the Turkish Army's traditional Mehter Band, and in the *surnai*, whose strident but invigorating tone resounds through every bazaar in the Northern towns of Pakistan. But, for forty years, the 'Cheerful Fife' disappeared from the British service until it was reintroduced about 1749.

Like all musical instruments, the simple six-holed fife is difficult to play well, needing constant practice, but at least it was capable of producing a tune which the soldiers could recognise. It was thus a great improvement on the drum. In some cases the significance of a beating could only be deduced from the number of 'flams', or taps, which followed one, two or three rolls. A misheard beating could result, for instance, in the wrong people reporting to the wrong place. The fife tunes came to be associated with certain beatings and certain events, and, in time, the tunes came to be known by the event or function the drum beating was meant to notify. And not only that, the tunes also came to be associated with the Army which played them, so that when troops of the different coalitions formed from time to time in the eighteenth century were camped together, they heard and picked up the different tunes; hence we have the 'Prussian Assembly', the 'Bavarian Reveille', the 'Saxon Tattoo', and so on. The fife, therefore, became the instrument associated with the relatively settled life in camp or garrison, the drum with the training area and war.

The training area of the eighteenth century was the 'Field of Exercise', and most garrison towns had one adjacent to the castle, citadel or fortress, or a short march away. Until the Great War, the Review Ground in Holyrood Park, beside the Palace, was used as a training area by the troops of the garrison of Edinburgh Castle. It was about half an hour's march away, and one of the sights of the city was that of the garrison battalion marching down the Royal Mile headed by the pipes and drums, with the military band behind, each playing in turn.

The drill of the eighteenth century was a battle drill, based on the formations and evolutions required to enable the battalion to manoeuvre quickly in close order, the soldiers shoulder to shoulder, and to engage the enemy at the very short ranges imposed by the limitations of the flintlock musket. The system reached its most advanced stage of development in the Prussia of the 1730s and 40s, and it was the Prussian system which other nations sought to emulate.

The Prussian system, devised for the plains of Central Europe, transformed each battalion into a flexible and manoeuvrable fire unit, capable of firing controlled volleys either on the move or at the halt, while performing the appropriate evolutions swiftly, smoothly and without crowding or confusion in the ranks. This demanded a steady and regular marching pace, with each of the eight divisions keeping its proper station and each soldier his correct position in the ranks, maintaining his dressing by the directing flank and not hurrying the rate of marching. The object was to be able to deploy quickly from the column in which the battalion moved, into the line, echelon, or square formation in which it fought, so as to bring the maximum number of muskets to bear at any one time and at any stage in the deployment.

Although the ultimate aim, and one unlikely ever to be achieved, was for the battalion to perform all the evolutions in step and time without any help from outside sources, in practice it was necessary for the drums to beat some sort of marching rhythm, known as the cadence, while the troops were manoeuvring in training. Each nation had its own cadence for beating the time and keeping the step, and this was yet another aid to the identification of friend or foe. There are also early marches lovingly recorded in manuscript by musicians long dead. They date from the middle and later decades of the eighteen century, an important period in the history of military music.

Although the fifers and drummers were wont to march in step while playing, nobody else did until Prince Leopold of Anhalt Dessau reintroduced the cadenced step into the Prussian Army about 1730. Marching in step had not been the practice since Roman times, and even then it would appear that the Romans only marched in step on ceremonial occasions. Prince Leopold – 'Der alte Dessauer' – had been the Drill Master of the Prussian Army in the days of King Frederick William, father of Frederick the Great. His Army was at the heart of Frederick William's interests, and he bequeathed his son a first-class fighting machine, trained for the field by Prince Leopold, who was not merely a barrack square martinet but also a fighting general of merit. He devised and codified the battle manoeuvres and increased the rate of musket fire by substituting iron ramrods for the wooden ones originally in use.

Out of all this deliberation on tactics came three marching speeds. In the British Army, these were defined as follows:

The Ordinary Time

Military philosophers of the eighteenth century – the Age of Reason – had concluded that battle evolutions gained in effectiveness if performed in time to the rhythm of the heartbeat, and for this bizarre reason all musket exercises and drill movements were carried out at the speed of seventy-two counts to the minute. At the time, this was very practical, as the soldier in every Army went into battle carrying all his possessions and provisions on his back and was incapable of moving quickly without debilitating effort. It was also possible to maintain this speed when manoeuvring over rough ground, and seventy-two paces to the minute was also the normal rate of progress on the line of march, sensible enough, given the load the soldiers carried and the state of the unmade roads along which they wended their weary way. For this reason, a day's march in the eighteenth century was rarely more than ten or twelve miles and often less.

Ordinary time survived, in the British Army only, as the Slow

March, where it was used when marching past the saluting base on ceremonial occasions. It ceased to be taught to recruits in 1992. Drill with the rifle and what is known as foot drill – e.g. turnings at the halt – were also performed with pauses between movements based on a rhythm of seventy-two beats to the minute.

The Quick Step

This was carried out at one hundred and eight paces to the minute. It was used when forming line from column on the right or left of the leading division. During such evolutions control was very easily lost, and it was disastrous for a battalion to be caught by enemy cavalry while in the process of deploying. These evolutions were therefore carried out as quickly as was consonant with control. The Quick Step was also used by small parties on good roads, and it survived as a marching pace until marching itself fell into disuse as a means of military progression. Marching tunes designed to be played at one hundred and eight to the minute were also called quicksteps, and the term is still occasionally used in this connection.

The Quickest Step

At one hundred and twenty paces to the minute, the Quickest Step was used when a company or battalion had to change its direction, by wheeling when in line to face in a different direction. This could be achieved by wheeling forwards, backwards, to the left or to the right about, on the right or left flanks or on the centre of the battalion, the division, or the platoon, the men in those positions being known as the 'pivots'. Direction could also be changed by diagonal or oblique marching to the right or left, the delightfully archaic word of command still in use in the decade before the Great War being 'left shoulders forward' when the line was to reform facing the right, and 'right shoulders forward' when the opposite was required.

As time went on, and new and improved weapons dictated different tactics, the rates of march were progressively increased. Today, in the British Army only the foot guards use the Ordinary Step or Slow March, although the occasional ceremonial sentry can be seen moving in slow and stately time in the Russian Army, and those of Russia's former satellites. The

Ordinary Step might well have originated in Russia; the *Parademarsch* – the goose step – of the old German Army certainly did. Combining the dual functions of looking impressive when well done and of giving the leg, thigh and stomach muscles a thorough workout, the *Parademarsch* telescoped hours of normal marching into a very short time. The French Foreign Legion also retains the Ordinary Step, if it can be called that, but at the faster speed of eighty-eight paces to the minute. The tradition derives, it is said, from the former Régiment de Hohenlohe into which foreigners had been enlisted and from which the Legion claims descent.

The Quick Time of one hundred and eight paces to the minute was the regulation rate of march in the British Army in the days when the soldier carried upwards of sixty pounds in full marching order with ammunition – the usual load in the Great War. This worked out at three miles per hour, or two and a half allowing for the regulation halt of ten minutes in the marching hour. It was a practical rate on good roads, both for the marching troops and for the bands that accompanied them.

Today, the Quickest Time of one hundred and twenty beats to the minute is the normal marching speed in most armies and was the drill pace of the British Army. While the battalions of the infantry of the line and the foot guards march past on ceremonial occasions at one hundred and sixteen, and the Highland regiments at one hundred and twelve, although one hundred and eight is nearer the mark. The light infantry and Green Jackets – the old Rifles – go past at the accelerated pace of one hundred and forty to the minute, as do the chasseurs of the French Army.

In discussing marching speeds and their musical implications it has to be borne in mind that until the general introduction of metalled roads at the end of the eighteenth century, marching in step was confined to the parade ground. What passed for roads then were little better than cart tracks, and when an Army moved, such roads as did exist were required for the guns of the artillery and the 'train', the ration and forage waggons and the baggage, which in the case of the senior commanders could amount to several coaches, drays and pack-animals, as well as their domestic employees, cooks, valets and even barbers, not to mention the occasional mistress.

Therefore, the infantry were compelled to move more or less across country on a broad front, taking bogs, marshes, streams and hedgerows in their stride. True, the drums might thunder out a marching cadence and the fifes squeak bravely as the battalions moved off from their camp or bivouac sites, but once clear, all the drums were unbraced. The term 'unbraced' means that the lugs on the tension cords were slackened so that the tension on the heads was released, making them less likely to split or puncture during the march, which might be across rough country. The adjutant was the battalion's staff-officer, to whom the detailed running of the battalion was delegated. One drummer was detailed to accompany him, and his drum was kept braced up in case any signals had to be beaten. Those appropriate to the line of march were, among others, 'Halt'; 'March'; 'Slower in front'; and so on – it being a perennial characteristic of all military movement, either on foot or in vehicles, that however steadily the march proceeds in front, the rear will always be hurrying to keep up. The other drummers slung their drums over their shoulders with what are now called the 'dress ropes'. These swing underneath the snare head. The correct term is the 'back carriage', and the ropes were used primarily for this purpose until the eclipse of the marching bands after World War II.

Notes

1. 'On War', iii, 1832, Major General Karl von Clausewitz, tr Howard and Paret, in *Warrior's Words*, Peter G. Tsouras (Cassell 1992).
2. *It Doesn't Take a Hero*, General Norman Schwartzkopf, Commander-in-Chief of the Coalition forces, (BCA,1992). In this is included his personal narrative of the Gulf War of 1991 and records his anger on discovering that certain units had reported that they had captured enemy localities, which they had not in fact reached, despite the advanced navigation systems with which they were equipped.
3. Field Marshal Helmut Graf von Moltke, in *Warrior's Words*, Peter G. Tsouras (Cassell, 1992).
4. Marshal of the Soviet Union Mikhail N. Tukhachevsky 1924 in *Warrior's Words*, Peter G. Tsouras (Cassell, 1992). Tukhachevsky was executed in the purge of the Red Army instituted by Stalin in 1937.
5. Quoted in John Buchan's novel *The Free Fishers* (1934). The lovely Scots ballad sung today under the title 'Dumbarton's Drums' bears no relation either to the tune or the sentiments of the march.
6. W.Y. Carman, *British Military Uniforms* (Hamlyn Publishing Group, 1968).

7. The contemporary score of the English March has been transcribed by James Blades, a member of the Guild of Ancient Fifes and Drums, a group of professional orchestral players and talented amateur musicians who share an enthusiasm for the music of fife and drum as played in the British Army since 1750, the year after the reintroduction of the fife.

8. *The Hessians March*: The Aberdeenshire ballad 'Where Gaudie runs' is sung to the tune once known as 'The Hessians March'. John Ord, in his *Bothy Songs and Ballads*, describes the song as the anthem of Aberdeenshire folk wherever they foregather. *Ord's Bothy Ballads and Songs* (John Donald Publishers).

CHAPTER II
THE SOLDIERS' DAY

~

By the middle of the seventeenth century, bodies of professional soldiers were emerging, organised on a national basis under clearly defined hierarchies, controlled by formal systems of discipline and rationed and paid relatively regularly – payment being in coin and not in plunder. Operational plans became correspondingly more ambitious and led, in turn, to increased demands on the troops. The success of these more elaborate plans depended to an increasing extent on an enhanced standard of training, based on a progressive programme and on regular musters of the soldiers for the purpose of improving their individual and collective efficiency. This further depended on a regular daily routine so that all the component units, horse and foot, were available at stated times for 'Exercise', as training was called at the time.

The difficulty was the establishment of a uniform time throughout the Army in the field. Carriage clocks were rare and expensive; pocket-watches could stop; and both needed regular winding. In any case, even in the last quarter of the eighteenth century the standard of education was low, which meant that not every soldier could tell the time. Uniformity of time and, therefore, of routine and procedure, could only be established by means of a code of plainly audible and easily recognisable signals, emanating from the headquarters of the force and designed to indicate to the units under command what they had to do.

Routine matters were logical enough. The principal problem facing commanders at all levels, from the general in command to the captains of companies, was that of keeping the soldiers under control. To this end, the roll was called four times a day at a parade at which each and every soldier had either to answer to his name, or to be otherwise accounted for – on guard, in hospital or, rarely, on leave.

The first roll call was at Reveille, when the soldiers had to rise from their beds, wash, shave, and, until 1808, plait their long hair – 'A plait for a plait!' was the morning cry – and, on great days of parade, powder their resulting coiffure. The sentries on the gates and on the walls ceased challenging those approaching their post with 'Halt! Who comes there?', and the night routine was succeeded by the daytime procedures. The soldiers had also to dress themselves in the uniform ordered for the day, ready for the main event of the morning.

This was the Assembly, or Troop, when the soldiers paraded under arms for inspection and roll call. The Colours, King's and Regimental, were displayed by trooping them along the ranks, after which the soldiers were marched off to drill or other training. The guards for the next twenty-four hours were inspected and marched to their place of duty; this was the procedure known as 'guard mounting'. These camp and garrison guards could involve a significant number of the soldiers. Several might be commanded by a junior officer.

After the drill, the soldiers were dismissed to cook their midday meal, their dinner. It was the only meal for which rations were issued. The rations consisted of bread, meat and a measure of spirits, beer, or wine, for which a deduction was levied from the soldier's pay. Otherwise, they fended for themselves.

The soldiers then had to fill in the rest of the day as best they could. Some might work, either on the land, or as labourers on building sites; those employed on repairing the fortifications or on making roads were paid extra. Those who had learned a trade before enlisting might find work among the factories and shops of the town. There were also lots of odd jobs to be done around the camp or garrison, the 'fatigues', for which the fife tune played to summon the fatiguemen was the intriguingly named 'Roundheads and Cuckolds, Come Dig!'. It was officially 'The Pioneers March'. The pioneers were the battalion's own tradesmen – carpenters and blacksmiths – who worked under the direction of the quartermaster, the officer, promoted from the ranks, who was responsible for the day-to-day administration of the battalion.

To recall everyone to the billets, barracks, or camp and to make sure that there were no stragglers or absentees, a parade was held at the end of the working day at which the roll was called yet again. This was Retreat; the term has no connection with the tactical manoeuvre of that name, but derives from the secondary meaning of the French *retraite*, a place of refuge or shelter.[1]

After the soldiers had returned to their camp or garrison, those not on guard were allowed to seek what entertainment the place offered, usually in the taverns and drink shops in which the soldiers were fleeced of their scanty pay. The 'women of the camp', the military counterparts of the 'ladies of the night', also featured prominently in the off-duty activities after dark, and not only the wretched drabs, whores and part-time prostitutes who formed the majority of the female camp followers. It has never been possible to keep girls away from soldiers, or vice versa. Not only girls: 'A bottle and kind landlady cures all again'; so ends 'How Stands the Glass Around?', a popular song with the soldiers in the wars of the eighteenth century.[2]

Inevitably, however, the good times had to come to an end, and at Tattoo the soldiers had to drink up, tear themselves away and return to their tents or billets, where the roll was called for the last time and lights and fires were extinguished. The sentries began challenging whoever approached their posts; and peace ostensibly descended and reigned until Reveille next morning.

Those four occasions became ceremonies in their own right. They were notified by music, in which a prescribed series of beatings for the drums and tunes for the fifes were played round the lines of tents in camp, or through the streets in garrison. At Tattoo, for instance, the drums beat and the fifes played for half an hour. At the first beat of the drum, the liquor taps were turned off and the bungs were replaced in the barrels. The provost guard – the military police of the period – then drew a chalk line across the bung so that it could not be opened again without leaving incriminating evidence.[3] In the lingua franca of the seventeenth-century camps this process became known as 'Doe den Tap toe', hence 'Tap To' and 'Tattoo'. The soldiers had to reach their billets, tents or quarters by the time the drums and fifes ceased beating.

When effective military bands – the Bands of Musick of the late eighteenth century – began to take the field along with their parent regiments, it became the practice to have them parade and play at Tattoo, the close of the military day. The inclusion of an evening hymn dates from the later decades of the century. The custom originated in the armies of Czarist Russia, where the soldiers, conscripted virtually for life from the deeply religious peasant masses, sang a chorale as Tattoo ceased. The custom spread, first to the Catholic armies of Imperial Austria and, later, to those of Lutheran Prussia, where the beating and sounding of Tattoo ('*Der grosse Zapfenstreich*', '*Zapfenstreich*' or 'Strike Tap', deriving from the same root as 'Tattoo') developed into an impressive torchlight ceremony with all musical resources – band, fife, drum, and trumpet – taking part.

In the British Army of the eighteenth century, the musical sequences played at those four principal ceremonies of the soldier's day were known as 'The Drum and Flute Duty', an ancient and evocative title which has been resurrected in the official manual *The Drummer's Handbook*, issued in 1985. There were, however, two separate duties, the English and the Scotch. Regiments of Scottish origin played the Scotch Duty, and this was a potent factor in maintaining a sense of identity during the period in which there was little or no difference in uniform between those Scottish regiments we now call Lowland and the rest of the infantry of the line.

In 1816, the Scotch Duty was ordered to be discontinued in the interests of uniformity, and the drums and fifes of the Scottish regiments, including the Highland, duly conformed, no doubt with regret, although there was nothing particularly Scottish about the tunes which made up the Scotch Duty, at least if the only four samples to survive complete are typical of the remainder. These are the Reveille, the Retreat, the Tattoo and the General, which was the tune which was played instead of Reveille on those days on which the Army was to march to new quarters or a fresh camping ground.

As well as the formal events of the military day, administration had also to be regulated, largely as a result of what the troops got up to when they dispersed to look for forage and for food and water. There were tunes and beatings to go for wood, for water, to draw rations, to call for the non-commissioned officers on duty and for the parties detailed to carry out all the labour necessary to keep the camp and its surroundings reasonably clean.

There were also tunes and beatings associated with specific occasions. When a soldier was to be discharged in disgrace – with ignominy in Army parlance – the battalion was drawn up on parade. The adjutant read out the soldier's offences and the punishment; the serjeant major stripped the buttons and braid from his regimental coat, and the man, a soldier no longer, was marched through the ranks of his former comrades to the barrack gate, while the drums and fifes played 'The Rogues March', a jaunty little tune in 6/8 time, with none of the solemnity which it might be imagined the occasion deserved.

> Fifty I got for selling me coat,
> Fifty for selling me blanket;
> If ever I 'list for a sodger again
> The Divil shall be me Sarjint!

The reference is to the number of lashes the singer was 'awarded' for the offences of selling his coat and blanket, presumably to get money for drink.[4]

'Camp Followers', in the wider sense of the term could also disturb the peace and harmony of the battalion and the camp, and cause much trouble for a commanding officer anxious to keep matters under control. *Advice to Officers of the British Army* was published in 1782. It warns that drummers, in particular, were 'sure of bringing off a girl in every quarter. After infecting her with a certain disease, and selling her clothes, you may introduce her to the officers, your employments making a dependent on Mercury as well as Apollo,' a reference to the contemporary treatment of venereal disease. When matters did get out of hand – 'The women of the camp are pretty much in common,' according to the same source – or perhaps when the married women of the battalion mutinied at the behaviour of the sluts and bawds who hung about the lines after dark, soliciting custom, the long-suffering commanding officer might turn out the drums and fifes to play 'The Pioneers March'. When played twice, the first four bars summoned the Pioneers; the whole tune, played once, the fatiguemen; but, repeated, it was the signal to 'drum out idle women from the camp'.[5]

Although it was in this way that the 'Duty Tunes' played by the Scots regiments to mark the various events of the day originated, this system of regulating the daily occasions of the military day was in no sense peculiar to the British Army. A similar system of maintaining control had evolved in other

Continental armies. Some drum beatings from the Prussian Army of the mid-eighteenth-century period survive in a little pamphlet published in Berlin in 1777 by 'A Musician'. It includes a simple tutor for playing the drum, and gives beatings for Reveille, Church Parade, Guard Mounting, the Fire Alarm and a Dead March. Notes explain how each call is to be beaten. The Reveille is to be beaten 'steadily yet briskly, so that everyone looks forward to breakfast'; while the Tattoo is to be played 'with emphasis, so that everyone who hears it drains his tankard, and seeks his quarters'.

The sound of the drum and, to a lesser extent, the fife, being the background to the events of daily life, and in the case of the drum alone, the voice of command on the battlefield, it was but a short step to invest the drums themselves with a certain mystique. Therefore, they were prominent among the household gods of the regiment, second only to the Colours in symbolism. It was again but a short step to illustrate the veneration in which they were held by adorning them with the symbols of the regiment which appeared on the Regimental Colour. The drums were painted in the facing colour, which appeared on the collars, cuffs and lapels of the red coats, and was the field or background of the Regimental Colour. The motif of the King's Colour was the Great Union. The drums bore the royal monogram, the precedence number of the regiment to which the battalion belonged and, perhaps, some device awarded to the regiment as a mark of special distinction, such as the dragon of the 3rd Foot and the antelope of the 6th, both regiments raised in 1572 for service in Holland, but taken on to the English establishment in 1665 and 1685 respectively. Badges and devices were also awarded for distinguished service in the field, the sphinx for Egypt, the dragon for China, and the tiger or the elephant for India, although these were much later developments.

When not in use, the drums were piled in state in front of the centre of the line of tents in camp, with the Colours, in their leather cases, resting against them, all guarded by a sentry from the Quarter Guard, responsible for the security of the lines. In garrison, the drum pile was set up in the quarters occupied by the adjutant.

The drums formed the altar at divine service or church parade when the battalion worshipped in the field, the service conducted by the battalion's chaplain. This aspect of their use, and a reminder of the respect in which the drums were held, is seen today only when a battalion receives new Colours, which rest against the drum pile formed with much ceremony by the drummers, until they are handed over to the person presenting them, who in turn passes them on to the kneeling subalterns who receive them on behalf of the battalion and, nowadays, the regiment. Before that, they are consecrated with appropriate ritual, and this represents an ancient and once widespread military practice, which may well have its origins in the pre-Christian rites of the Roman Army, where an important annual event was the reconsecration by the priests of the legion's shrines and standards

Therefore, it followed that the loss of the drums to the enemy was a calamity only surpassed by the loss of the Colours, which were sometimes burned to prevent them falling into enemy hands. In October 1811, the British 34th Cumberland Regiment captured the drums, drum major's staff, band instruments and band music of their French counterparts, the French 34th of the line, at Arroyo dos Molinos in Spain. By custom, drums were regarded as legitimate prizes of war; and on the anniversary of the battle the King's Own Royal Border Regiment, heirs and successors to the old 34th, 'troop' the French drums. To 'troop' means to display something or someone by marching it or them along the ranks of the battalion drawn up in line, from the left of the line to the right, headed by the band and drums playing a slow troop. In this case, the French drums are carried by drummers wearing the uniform of 1811. Until the amalgamation of the Border Regiment with the King's Own Royal Regiment, the march of the French 34th formed part of the march past, played after 'John Peel'. In the same tradition, the Green Howards, the old 19th Foot, troop the Russian drums they captured at the Battle of the Alma during the Crimean War of 1854–1856.[6]

The drums of the 2nd Battalion of the Gordon Highlanders were left at Ostend when the battalion disembarked in October 1914 as part of the British 7th Division. There they were discovered by the Germans and were taken to Berlin and displayed as trophies of the victorious advance of the German Army. The drums remained in Germany until 1933, when they were returned to the Gordons with due ceremony, a gesture prompted more by politics than by chivalry as the Hitler regime sought to ingratiate itself with Germany's former foes.

In June 1940, the 51st Highland Division was compelled to surrender at St Valéry on the Channel coast of France. The drums of the 4th Battalion of the Cameron Highlanders were sunk in a pool outside a French farmhouse to prevent them from falling into enemy hands. They were salvaged by the farmer, hidden until the end of the war, and were eventually handed back to representatives of the 4th Camerons some years later.

In the final flowering of the British regimental system in the days between the Great War and World War II, some county regiments of the line were presented with complete sets of silver drums – bass drum, two tenor and eight side drums – by their home county, and sometimes by individuals wishing to make a gesture in memory of relatives who had served in the regiment. The drums, in some cases, were formally dedicated before being handed over.

Before leaving the fife and the drum for a while, it should be noted that the sound of the modern pipe band drum, with its plastic synthetic heads, batter head snares, rod tension and sophisticated techniques, bears little resemblance to the resonant and sonorous tone of the old, deep-shelled, rope-tension drum. The rudimental style of playing, with its open rolls, was difficult to master and needed constant practice, but its effect was arresting and profound, and can still stir the blood and lift the heart.

The influence of the modern pipe band style of drumming, in which everything is subordinated to technique alone, has led to the gradual, but now complete, erosion of the old marching style of military drumming in both the pipe and drum and the flute and drum combination. It is to the bands of foreign nations, principally the French, that we have to turn to hear military drumming in all its ancient glory. In America, too, the old style is kept alive by the many musical guilds which have made the preservation of the 'Ancient Musick' their aim, as well as by the 3rd Infantry, stationed in Washington. One such guild exists in Britain, a step in the right direction, but otherwise that sound of the drum to which our ancestors once thrilled, marched and fought has vanished from our shores, and we are the poorer.

Notes

1. In mediaeval times, many cities and towns employed fifers and drummers to play appropriate music first thing in the morning, to wake everybody up; at sunset, when the gates would be closed; and last thing at night, when domestic fires would be banked up because of the ever-present danger of fire. Towns also had their own tunes; the ' March of the Town of Bamberg', and the 'March of the Town of Worms' both date from the fifteenth century. It is tempting to think that the corresponding military ceremonies and the tradition of distinctive regimental marches might derive from those municipal customs. In the French Army, the final call of the day is not 'Lights Out' but *'Extinction des Feus'*.

In Oman in the south-east corner of the Arabian Peninsula, the gates of the city of Muskat were closed every night at sunset until 1970 on a drumbeat signal. Thereafter, citizens wishing to leave their houses for any reason had to carry a lighted lantern, and had to move in groups of less than four.

2. *'How stands the Glass around?'* The final stanza runs:
'Should next campaign
Send us to Him who made us, boys,
We're free from pain.
But should we still remain,
A bottle and kind landlady
Cures all again.'

Songs and Music of the Redcoats, Lewis Winstock (Leo Cooper, London, 1970).

3. *Army Officers Guide,* Lieutenant-Colonel Lawrence P. Crocker, United States Army.

4. *Corporal Punishment.* In the infantry, it was the duty of the drummers, supervised and trained by the drum major, to inflict sentences of corporal punishment. Flogging with the cat-o'-nine-tails was the most commonly awarded punishment for all manner of misdemeanours, however minor.

The minimum number of lashes was 25; until 1812 there was no upper limit, and sentences of up to 1,000 were not uncommon. Over the years, the maximum was steadily reduced under the pressure of public opinion, aroused by a series of cases where men had died after having been flogged. In 1846, the maximum was reduced to 50, and in 1868 flogging was abolished except for offences committed on active service.

The handle of the cat was about the length of a drumstick. From it came nine cords, each knotted three times towards the end. Pickling the cords to make them harder was forbidden, as was the employment of left-handed drummers. The drummers flogged in relays of 25 strokes. The majority were, of course, right handed, and a left-handed drummer, flogging across the weals made by the others, made the punishment more severe, which was considered to be unfair. The cat used by the Army was not the fearsome instrument of torture employed by the Navy, where flogging was carried out by the bo'suns mates, all grown men, whereas the drummers tended to be very much younger. A Navy 'dozen' was said to equal an Army 'hundred' in severity.

Flogging could only be ordered by a court martial, of which there were three levels: regimental, district, and general. The officer commanding a battalion could convene a regimental court martial, consisting of three or five officers according to circumstances, on the spot; he could confirm the sentence, on the spot; and he could order the sentence to be put into effect, again on the spot.

Jurists objected to the system on the grounds that the members of the court martial were empowered to award sentences of corporal punishment to which they themselves were not liable, on charges which they themselves framed, for offences which they, the members of the court martial, defined. There is no doubt that the system allowed a brutal, sadistic, or merely short-tempered commanding officer to do more or less as he pleased.

On the other hand, it has to be said that the soldiers of the period themselves approved of the system as the only sure method of keeping the bullies and ruffians in order, and as the only protection the more sober and quieter soldiers had against the depredations of the rougher element, a sentiment with which anyone who has had to live in a barrack-room would agree. It is also only fair to add that it was a brutal age, and that soldiers were flogged for offences for which civilians were hanged.

Corporal punishment was abolished in 1881.

5. Charles S. Ashworth

6. The Green Howards acquired their distinctive name in the days before the introduction of precedence numbers in 1751. Before then, regiments were known by the name of their colonel. At one time, both the 3rd and the 19th Foot were commanded by colonels named Howard. The 3rd wore buff facings and the 19th green. Therefore, the 3rd were called the Buff Howards and the 19th, the Green Howards.

CHAPTER III
The Six Old Regiments

~

From 1618 until 1648, Europe was devastated by the Thirty
Years War. Originally a consequence of the ostensibly religious
strife that followed the adoption of the reformed religion in
Switzerland and much of Germany, it later developed into a
blatant power struggle between the Protestant princes of
Sweden, Germany and their allies on the one hand, and on the
other the mighty Holy Roman Empire. Eventually France joined
the war on the Protestant side, for, as ever, her own reasons.
Thus it was for the French service that Sir John Hepburn of
Athelstaneford in East Lothian was permitted by King Charles I
to raise 1,220 men in Scotland. Hepburn's contingent landed at
Boulogne in 1633, and eventually came to incorporate the
remnants of the various bands of Scots mercenaries which had
been fighting for one cause or the other. Hepburn died of
wounds in 1636, but his regiment was continued in the Order of
Battle of the French Army after the Peace of Westphalia, which
brought the war to a conclusion in 1648.

There was, however, another body of Scots mercenaries
serving on the Continent at the same time. This was the Scots
Brigade in the service of the United Provinces of Holland. In
1572, what we know as the Benelux countries were under
Spanish rule. Active resistance on the part of the people of
Holland had begun earlier, but in that year the States General,
effectively the Parliament of the seventeen provinces which had
made up the Spanish Netherlands, decided to bring in mercenary soldiers to fight for their cause. They turned, naturally,
to their nearest Protestant neighbours, mainland Britain, where,
for once, the interests of Scotland and England coincided, united
as they were by a detestation of all things Spanish and Catholic
and appalled at the excesses of the Inquisition. Scotland and
England each contributed three battalions, which were to serve
their host country well and loyally until recalled to the home
country − a century later in the case of the English battalions
and two centuries later in the case of the Scots.

So it transpired that when in 1660 'The King came Home in Peace again', serving on the Continent there were the Scots and English Brigades in the Dutch service and, in France, the successors to Sir John Hepburn's regiment. There were others; and the disposal of those troops was very much in what became the Stuart tradition in which expediency and parsimony dictated the fate of the men involved, many of whom had joined the French service out of loyalty to the Stuart cause.

The colonel – 'proprietor' describes his role better – of what had been Hepburn's Regiment was now Lord George Douglas, and it was as Douglas's that the regiment was recalled to Britain in 1661 and 1666. Under regulations promulgated in 1694, the regiment's seniority was held to date from its first coming on to British pay in 1661. Douglas's thus became the senior Regiment of Foot in the British Army, although not until 1678 did the regiment return finally to the British service. In 1684, it became the Royal Regiment of Foot – 'Afoot' was the original term – which is still the subsidiary title of the Royal Scots.

Under the Commonwealth, the system adopted after the end of the English Civil War, Scotland and England had been ruled as one country; Scotland being one of the nine districts governed by a major general appointed by Oliver Cromwell, the Lord Protector. This meant that Scotland was garrisoned by English troops. When the Restoration took place, and the Commonwealth system was dismantled as a result, these troops had to be transferred to England, where barrack accommodation in which to house them was scarce. It was not until 1662 that General Morgan's English regiment, a thousand-strong, was able to vacate the Fort at Leith, outside Edinburgh, thus making it available for the accommodation of troops raised on the Scots establishment, that is, troops paid and maintained out of the revenues due to the Scots Parliament. When Scotland was finally clear of English troops, five companies were raised in Scotland, two of which were intended to garrison the castles at Stirling and Dumbarton, although it appears that all five were, in fact, sent to Glasgow after receiving their Colours at Edinburgh. The Colours were red, with a Saltire or Saint Andrew's Cross in a field azure and a thistle crowned, with this motto round the thistle: '*Nemo me impune lacessit*', or, in the vernacular, 'Wha daur meddle wi' me?'. Thus was formed the regiment which

King Charles II nominated as his Scots Regiment of Foot Guards, the predecessors of the present Scots Guards.[1]

King Charles's experiences of the Scots had not been entirely happy. His father had been executed in 1649, and the following year had seen the first attempt at restoration, when Charles had been crowned as King Charles II in the ancient Scottish capital at Scone. A price had been attached: in return for Scots support, Charles had, perforce, to agree to establish the Presbyterian system of church government in England. The Army that the Scots had raised as their part of the bargain had been routed at the Battle of Worcester in 1651, and Charles had been compelled to flee to the Continent to await better times, which duly arrived when he was restored to the throne amid the acclamation of his people in 1660.

The king's tribulations at the hands of the tiresome and argumentative Scots had left him with a strong dislike of Presbyterianism in all its manifestations. On his restoration, he determined to set up the Episcopal system in his kingdom, Scotland included. The heartland of Presbyterianism lay in the south and south-west of that country, where the National Covenant, binding its signatories to support the Presbyterian cause in its most austere form, had been widely circulated in the years just before the outbreak of the English Civil War. Their descendants were no less fervent in what became known as the Covenanting movement, and the attempts of the King and his henchmen aroused fierce and determined resistance. The Covenanters rose in armed rebellion in 1666 and 1679, but were defeated at Rullion Green in the Pentland Hills south of Edinburgh on the first occasion, and at Bothwell Bridge south of Glasgow on the second. The brutality of the ensuing repression had the opposite of the desired effect among the contumacious and stubborn Covenanters, who continued to keep the flame of resistance alive.

Fighting against the Covenanters at Bothwell Bridge were two regiments, one of dragoons and one of foot, which were to form part of the British Army for the next three hundred years. Both were raised in 1678, with the task of policing the smouldering shires of south-west Scotland. The first consisted of three companies of dragoons, mounted infantry who rode to battle but fought on foot, augmented by a further three in 1681, when all six were formed into a regiment with Lieutenant-General Sir Thomas Dalziel of the Binns in West Lothian as colonel. The dreaded General Tam, 'Bluidy D'yell' to the Covenanters, was a fearsome veteran of the Continental wars who had served the Czar of Russia for ten years and who had suppressed the rising of 1666 with a ferocity notable even in that cruel age. His dragoons wore stone-grey coats; the colour was to become permanently associated with his regiment in 1693, when, as the Royal Regiment of Scots Dragoons, they were mounted in grey horses, hence the 'Scots Greys'.

The regiment of foot which fought against the Covenanters at Bothwell Bridge had been raised by the Earl of Mar. They wore red cassock coats and grey breeches, hence 'The Earl of Mar's Greybreeks'. In 1685, the regiment was equipped with the fusil, an early example of the flintlock musket soon to replace the matchlock entirely as the weapon of the infantry. The role of the fusiliers was to escort the train of artillery, where gunpowder was carried in bulk, and where the lighted slow match on the matchlock would have been a constant invitation to disaster. The fusiliers had also to be ready to sling their fusils over their shoulders and bear a hand with the drag ropes when the guns and waggons got stuck in the mud and mire of the atrocious roads of the time, so they were issued with a stocking cap, like the grenadiers, introduced into the British Army in 1677, who also had to sling their muskets before throwing their hand-grenades. With the fusil came the name which the Earl of Mar's Greybreeks were to retain for almost three hundred years – the Scots Fusiliers.

King Charles II died in 1685 and he was succeeded by his brother James, whose avowed intention was to restore the Roman Catholic religion, which led to an unsuccessful rebellion in the west of England in the very year that James came to the throne. The cruelty with which the unfortunate rebels were pursued aroused revulsion among the rest of the population, and when the rebellion was used as a pretext by James to create an army of some 30,000, which he concentrated at Hounslow near London, discontent and suspicion grew apace. The birth of a son raised fears that James would be succeeded, not by his Protestant daughter and her husband, William of Orange, Stadtholder of the Netherlands, but by a Catholic son, and this proved the catalyst which united the different anti-Catholic factions and led to the invitation to William of Orange to take over the throne in what became known as the Glorious Revolution of 1688. Taking with him detachments from all his allies as well as the Scottish regiments in Dutch pay – James had recalled the English battalions some time before – William duly took advantage of 'The Protestant Wind' and landed at Torbay in November 1688.[2]

By the time William landed, all the troops in Scotland had been ordered south to join the concentration of forces preparing to counter the threat of invasion. William had hoped for mass desertions from King James's Army, but in the event these were insignificant and were due more to domestic regimental factors than to any desire to change sides. It was otherwise with the officers, where there were significant desertions among the more senior ranks, and this had an adverse effect on the morale of the soldiers which was exacerbated when William set about ridding the Army of its Jacobite and Catholic officers in the ensuing months, replacing them with men on whom he could rely, but who were strangers to the soldiers.

In Scotland, the Convention of Estates, acting as the Scots parliament, did not declare formally for William until early April 1689. In the meantime, it had become clear that one of William's aims in coming to Britain in the first place had been to secure the British Army for his projected operations in Flanders against the French. This further dismayed the soldiers, many now serving under strange officers, and all thoroughly and understandably unsettled by the political upheavals of the past few months. In mid-March 1689, the two battalions of the Royal Regiment – the Royal Scots – were warned to stand by for a move to Flanders. At Ipswich, the port of embarkation, a significant proportion of the two battalions mutinied, declared for the exiled King James and set off for home, where the Jacobite faction was preparing to revolt. The mutineers were rounded up by William's Dutch cavalry and, by the standards of the time, were treated very leniently indeed.[3] The loyalty of the regiment of Scots Dragoons and the Scots Fusiliers had no doubt been subject to the same stress as that of the Royal Regiment, but both obeyed their new commanders and set off for 'The Lowlands of Holland', as did the Edinburgh and the Cameronian regiments, both raised in the Williamite cause, and therefore not beset by any doubts.[4]

The War of the League of Augsburg, in which William's British regiments first learned and then mastered their trade, lasted from 1689 until 1697, with the six Scots regiments and the Scotch–Dutch brigade prominent in all the ensuing engagements, many of them very hard fought indeed. It was these battles, and not those of the Great War, which first gave rise to the claim that the Flanders poppies had been watered with British blood.[5]

James II had fled without abdicating, a point which was to cause grave difficulties for the succession to the throne, a continuing and damaging conflict of loyalties among those who cared for such things, and much bloodshed in Scotland over the next sixty years. In the meantime, the Convention of Estates had to be supported and law and order maintained. Edinburgh Castle was being held for King James by the Duke of Gordon, and to prevent supplies and reinforcements from reaching it, a blockade had to be set up and manned. David Leslie, Earl of Leven, a veteran soldier, was authorised to raise a regiment to defend Edinburgh and man the blockade. Within two hours eight hundred men had enlisted, and the capital was secure. Leven's regiment was to be incorporated into the British Army as the Edinburgh Regiment of Foot, eventually numbered the 25th, and was, after several vicissitudes, finally named the King's Own Scottish Borderers in 1887.

The Edinburgh Regiment's first taste of action came later in 1689, when it was included in the force sent by William to suppress the first Jacobite insurrection led by the former John Graham of Claverhouse, lately created Viscount Dundee in the dying days of King James's reign. On 27th July 1689, the two armies met at Killiecrankie, some few miles north of Pitlochry in central Perthshire. William's Army included the 'Scotch Dutch', the Scots Brigade in the service of Holland, but even they, experienced as they were, had no answer to the headlong charge, broadsword in hand, which was the sole battle tactic of the Highland clansmen who formed the majority of the rebel force. The newly formed Edinburgh Regiment fought well, however, and as Dundee was killed in the later stages of the battle, the Highland Army, true to the clansmen's form, lost interest and dispersed, and although the rising spluttered spasmodically on, it eventually fizzled ingloriously out in 1690.

With the revolution of 1688 the dour, dogged and determined Covenanters of south-west Scotland came into their long-awaited kingdom. They sent a delegation to treat with the Convention of Estates in Edinburgh and, to underline their point, sent with it an escort of some five hundred followers of Richard Cameron, one of the martyrs of their cause. Those 'Cameronians' were soon sent home, but in the next year, 1689, the Convention decided to enlist a regiment from this source to fight against the Jacobite rebels under Dundee, who, as Graham of Claverhouse, had raised and commanded a regiment of the dreaded dragoons during the 'Killing Time', as the Covenanters called the period when their sect had been so rigorously repressed. To the Covenanters, Dundee was still 'Bluidy Claver'se', so when the word went out against him, twelve hundred men came forth to enlist in the regiment forming to resist his attempt to restore the hated Stuarts, who were, in the eyes of the Covenanters, the arch-enemies of the reformed religion, at any rate as they understood and pracised it.

The role of the new regiment, raised not without the argument, bickering and dissension with which the Presbyterian Church was ever to be associated, was seen as the 'preservation of the Protestant religion, opposition to Popery, prelacy and arbitrary power in all its branches, and the defence of the nation'. The officers were to be 'men whom in conscience they could submit to'![6] However, the ensuing campaign was to show that the Cameronians could fight, as well as drone out the psalms and wrestle mightily in prayer. After the defeat of King William's Army at Killiecrankie, the Cameronians held the little town of Dunkeld on the River Tay against repeated assaults by their hereditary foes, the hated and despised Highlanders, emerging undefeated from the ruins of the town as the Highland Army drifted away into the mist.[7]

Thus emerged the Cameronian Regiment, raised on a religious foundation of extreme Calvinism, the comfortless doctrine of the Presbyterian Kirk. There are grounds for believing that this ultra-religious phase did not last very long when confronted with the requirements of military discipline, and it appears that the more religiously obsessed of the soldiers were soon discharged. Later in its history, the Cameronian Regiment revived the more outward manifestations of the conditions under which it had been activated in acknowledgement of its unique origin. The Covenanters had met to pray and to hear the Word as interpreted by their ministers on the bare and windswept hillsides of south-west Scotland in defiance of the law. These were the Conventicles, at which sentries were posted to warn the congregation of the approach of the hated dragoons and at which the male worshippers attended armed, so as to be able to cover the flight of the preacher and his congregation.

So it became the custom for the Cameronians to march to church in some style, although the march itself was conducted without music, neither the military band, the bugles, nor the pipes sounding on the line of march. If required, however, the military band accompanied the praise during the service. On the march to church, the battalion was led by the chaplain in his robes; by his side marched the junior subaltern carrying the regimental bible; and, in their waistbelts, the soldiers carried the bibles with which all Protestant recruits were issued on enlistment. At the church, sentries were formally posted to cover, in theory, the approaches, and the service began only after the area had been reported clear.

If the whole procedure connected with the business of going to church tended latterly towards the theatrical, in a manner which the original Cameronians would surely have deprecated, the effect on the officers and soldiers taking part, and, indeed, on all those involved – wives, families, former Cameronians, well-wishers, and so on – was striking, effective and, to any Scot brought up in the Kirk, highly evocative of the brave days of the past.

So, from the turmoil and strife of the Glorious Revolution of 1688, there emerged these six regiments which were all to earn honour and glory in the service of the Crown over the next two centuries. Their loyalty was never in question, and they eschewed the dramatics which marred the early years of the Highland regiments of the ensuing century. While it might be more accurate to describe them as British rather than Scottish until the great reorganisation of 1881, this in no way detracts from their contribution to the reputation which the British infantry of the line was to acquire on the field of battle, 'that steady British infantry', as one source was later to describe the regiments of the line.

Only slight details of dress differentiated them from the other regiments of the line. Their drums and fifes, however, steadfastly beat the Scotch Duty until it was abolished in 1816, although there is evidence that the Royal Regiment might have allowed this distinction to lapse towards the end of the eighteenth century. An entry in the accounts of the regimental agent – who ran the financial affairs of the regiment on behalf of the colonel – shows that Drum Major Wilde of the 3rd Foot Guards was paid two guineas in 1806 for instructing two drum majors of the Royals in the Scotch Duty. The 3rd were, of course, the Scots Regiment of Foot Guards, and it is interesting to have confirmation that at this period they, too, beat the Scotch Duty even though the Royals might have allowed it to lapse.

Notes

1. *The Scots Army 1661/1688*, Charles Dalton (Eyre and Spottiswoode, 1909). The present regiment claims descent from an earlier regiment of Scots Guards formed in 1641 but dispersed with the remainder of the Scots Army after the defeat at Worcester ten years later.
2. The expression comes from the song 'Lilliburlero', which was popular in 1688 during the events which led up to the flight of James II and the accession of William of Orange to the throne. There are several versions of the song, written in a pseudo-Irish brogue and mocking the Irish language. In one version, a verse begins:
   Ho! By me shoul, 'tis a Protestant wind!
   Lilliburlero, bullen a la.
   'Lilliburlero' became the theme tune of the BBC World Service.
3. *The British Army of William III*, John Childs (Manchester University Press, 1987).
4. Nor shall I ha'e anither love
   Until the day I dee;
   For the Lowlands of Holland
   Ha'e twined my love and me.
   'twined' = parted
5. *Battle Honours of the British and Commonwealth Armies*, Anthony Baker (Iain Allan Ltd., 1986).
6. Even King William had to accept that his Cameronian Regiment was more likely to obey its chaplain than its officers. The chaplain was the Reverend Alexander Shields, and one source described the soldiers as 'madd men not to be Governed even by mastr Shields ther orachle'. *Glencoe and the End of the Highland War*, Paul Hopkins (John Donald, 1986).
7. In the aftermath of the rising of 1666, some 6,000 Highlanders had been brought down to the Covenanting country in the south-west and had been

billeted at 'free quarters' on the inhabitants, which meant that they were housed and rationed at the householder's expense. They also robbed, looted and plundered as they wished, becoming infamous as 'The Highland Host', execrated in the folk memory of Galloway and south-west Scotland.

The prejudice against Highlanders lingered. There are said to have been instances in the Great War where territorial and service battalions of the Cameronians (Scottish Rifles) objected to serving in the same brigade as Highland troops. And on taking over command of the 1st Battalion The Cameronians in 1917, Brigadier James Jack attributed the unsatisfactory morale of his old battalion partly to the fact that his predecessor had ordered the service dress-jackets of the riflemen to be rounded off in the Highland style. *General Jack's Diary 1914/18*, ed. John Terraine (Eyre and Spottiswoode, 1964).

8. In *Culloden*, his account of the aftermath of the 1745 Jacobite Rebellion, John Prebble recounts how in August 1746, a serjeant of the Scots Guards was shot for proclaiming his preference for the Stuarts and for regretting the part that he had played in the suppression of the rebellion. This so enraged the Duke of Cumberland, who had commanded the victorious Government Army at the Battle of Culloden four months previously, that he demanded that the Scots be renamed the 'English Guards' and that their drums should play only English tunes, an indication, perhaps, that in 1746 the Scots Guards were beating the Scotch Duty, although the Regiment had been stationed in London for thirty years by then.

APPENDIX

REGIMENTAL CALLS OF THE SIX OLD REGIMENTS

Royal Scots Greys

Scots Guards

Royal Scots

Royal Scots Fusiliers

King's Own Scottish Borderers

The Cameronians (Scottish Rifles)

21st Royal North British Fusiliers, Sevastopol, Crimea, 1855

By 1855 the appalling conditions suffered by the soldiers during the first winter on the Crimean Peninsula were a thing of the past. The photograph shows the Band of the 21st playing in their hutted camp. The long, double-breasted tunics replaced the coatee in April 1855. The band and drums tunic was white, the rank and file, red; only sergeants wore scarlet. Well displayed is the 1854 pattern band sword, carried on a waist belt with slings, curved and with a half-basket hilt showing the Royal cypher. The band of the 21st carried the curved sword until 1884. (National War Museum of Scotland)

CHAPTER IV
THE HIGHLAND REGIMENTS

~

The regiments that come first to mind when Scottish soldiers are mentioned are, understandably, but perhaps unfairly, the Highland regiments which wear the kilt. They came late to the field; this is how it happened.

Scotland had been ruled as two nations for centuries when, on the death of Queen Elizabeth of England in 1603, James VI and I, son of the tragic Mary, Queen of Scots by her second husband, Lord Darnley – mysteriously murdered in 1567 – succeeded to the throne of England, thus effectively uniting the two countries as somewhat unwilling partners, given the long history of strife between them. But climate, topography and history had combined to create two separate cultures in Scotland: the Gaelic which had evolved over centuries in the mountainous Highlands and the remote islands of the west, in which loyalty to the clan and its chief was paramount; and the Doric, in which the feudal system, which had been dominant in England, formed the basis of the social hierarchy.

These two cultures had nurtured two separate and distinct languages. In the Highlands, the only language spoken and understood was Gaelic, which bore no relation whatsoever to the dialects of English through which the people of the Lowlands conversed. The tradition of the Highlands was warlike and military, as each clan had to battle for survival amid a complicated and ever-changing pattern of often ephemeral loyalties and interests as the great magnates of the Highlands competed for supremacy. The tradition of the Lowlands, although every bit as bloody and turbulent, was mainly agricultural and, in the coastal towns, commercial.

The clan regarded itself as an extended family in which all claimed descent from a common ancestor. The lines of loyalty within the clan were distinct and clear cut, and led eventually to the chief. When the clan took the field as a formed body in the chief's interest, which the clansmen regarded as synonymous with their own, the social demarcations within the clan were readily transformed into a military hierarchy, with the chief as commander and his kinsmen and relatives performing the functions of junior officers.

This military background, all-pervading as it was, with its emphasis on courage, fortitude, and endurance, together with a high degree of skill in the use of weapons, made the Highlander an instinctive soldier, who only needed to be trained and disciplined to became an asset to any military organisation. It was quite easy to secure employment as a mercenary soldier or a soldier of fortune; and Highlanders were prominent among the many Scots who took service in Europe and even further afield in Russia. 'Rats, lice and Scotchmen' were said to abound the world over.[1] Their creed was simple: 'So that we serve him honestlie, 'tis no matter which prince we serve.'[2] This predilection for mercenary service meant that among the clans there were always men who had been formally trained as soldiers in the Continental wars, so that when the clans set off on some raiding expedition into the Lowlands, or to plunder the lands of their current enemies, they were not the bands of marauding savages which Lowland tradition portrayed, but operated under their own somewhat idiosyncratic system of discipline, and with a considerable measure of tactical skill. This meant that the business of keeping the clans in order was a difficult one, which baffled generations of Scottish governments, and was not to be finally solved until after the rising of 1745.

Frequently, the experiment had been tried of raising bodies of Highlanders in government pay to police the Highlands, most of which had foundered among the obstacles to the maintenance of a coherent policy created by the ever-changing alliances and rivalries between the clans themselves, as well as by the capacity for intrigue and rapacity of the chiefs and their henchmen who commanded the Independent Companies, as these police units were known. Indeed, two companies of Highlanders raised in 1678 had to be disbanded in 1681, to be replaced by two new companies of the Earl of Mar's Greybreeks, to which fell the thankless task of trying to collect taxes and other dues from the Highlanders. These Highland companies had been officered by notables of Clan Campbell, no doubt delighted at being given the chance to extract money from their enemies legally, and always alert to forward the cause of *Clann Dhiarmadh nan Tuirc* – the Children of Diarmaid of the Boar.[3]

Nevertheless, Highland Independent Companies continued to be raised from time to time, more in hope than in anything else, only to be disbanded when it became impossible to determine where their true loyalties, if any, lay. It was not until the road-building programme under General Wade was in progress that it was finally decided, at Wade's suggestion, to enlist six companies again, under their own officers and subject to military law. Four companies were raised in 1725 and two in 1729. They served in the Highlands until 1739, when they were formed into a regiment of ten companies each of one hundred men, later numbered the 43rd, better known as the Black Watch.

By that time, there had been several attempts to restore the Stuarts to the throne, the most recent in 1719, in protest at the importation of King George I from Hanover, the 'wee, wee, German Lairdie' of Jacobite song. All had been unsuccessful, but all had been supported, to a greater or lesser extent, by the Jacobite clans. However, as time progressed, support for the Stuart cause had waned in the Highlands, as elsewhere. When the last desperate throw of the Stuart dice took place after Prince Charles Edward Stuart, the 'Bonnie Prince Charlie' of Jacobite romance, had raised his standard at Glenfinnan in the West Highlands in August of 1745, it was only with many misgivings, all too soon to be justified, that the chiefs of the Jacobite clans, and not all of them at that, called out their often reluctant clansmen to fight for what was already a lost cause.

The rebellion came to a bloody end on 16th April 1746 on the battlefield of Culloden, east of Inverness, with the utter defeat of the Jacobite Army, such as it was by that time, at the hands of the veteran troops of the Hanoverian Government, among them the Royals, the Scots Fusiliers and Sempill's, the later 25th. The subsequent repression was brutal and effective, but, savage though it was, it went by and large uncondemned in the wealthier and more settled Lowlands, where the Highlander was still perceived as an uncouth barbarian, living in squalor and ignorance among his bogs and mountains.

The ultimate result of 'The '45', – 'Bliadhna Thearlaich', or 'Charlie's Year' to the Highlanders – was the destruction of the old Highland way of life and the clan system, while the Disarming Act of 1747 forbade the wearing of the tartan and the Highland dress and its accoutrements in any form, except by soldiers formally enlisted into the regular forces of the Crown. At that time there were in existence two Highland regiments, both wearing the Highland dress in the shape of the kilt. The 'old' or original Highland regiment, the Black Watch, was by 1747 serving in Flanders, along with Loudon's Highlanders, whose early days had been bedevilled by the commotion caused by the outbreak of the '45 rebellion, when three newly raised companies had been captured at the Battle of Prestonpans outside Edinburgh in September 1745.

The War of the Austrian Succession for which Loudon's Highlanders had been raised ended in 1748, and Loudon's had been disbanded, although the 43rd, the Black Watch, was continued in the service. In 1751, the regiment was renumbered as the 42nd, becoming, in 1758, the Royal Highland Foot. The British Government, however, had come to realise that in the Highlands they possessed an almost inexhaustible source of manpower admirably suited to, and well disposed towards, active military service, particularly in units recruited from and composed of fellow Highlanders. It was further realised that one of the attractions of such service was the chance to bear arms while dressed in the garb of their ancestors.

So it happened that in the Seven Years War of 1756–1763, and in the War of American Independence from 1776 to 1783, as well as the wars caused by the expansion of British interests in India, Highland units of battalion strength were activated and fought in Canada, America, and India. Here it is possible to deal only with those Highland regiments which survived the cutbacks and reductions which followed the conclusion of each bout of hostilities. Which did so was very much a matter of chance. It was the practice to disband all regiments whose precedence number was higher than the magic figure of seventy, but the end of the American War of Independence, which, of course, Britain lost, saw war still in progress in India. As a result, all those numbered above seventy in the American and European theatres were 'broke', or disbanded, while those in India, including several Highland units, were simply renumbered and continued to serve. The 42nd, the Black Watch, being the 'oldest', i.e. the most senior, Highland regiment was immune to all those changes of fortune and continued to serve on, earning distinction wherever it fought as *Freiceadan Dubh nan Cath; toiseach tighinn, agus direadh falbh* – 'The Black Watch of the Battles, first in the field, and last to leave'.

The Earl of Cromartie, whose family name was MacKenzie, had been 'out', as the saying was, in the rebellion of 1745, and had, as a result, forfeited all his estates in the North and West Highlands. His son, whose courtesy title was Lord MacLeod, had been 'out' with his father, but had been pardoned on account of his youth. He had then joined the Swedish service, to come home twenty-seven years later as a Swedish lieutenant-general. It was suggested to him that the way back to favour might be to provide a regiment to fight in the war against France in India, and this he did in 1777, largely through his residual influence among those of his name, the Mackenzies. In 1786, his regiment, which had been serving in India since 1779, was renumbered the 71st, and in due course Lord MacLeod was restored to the Earldom of Cromartie, but had to pay £19,000 to relieve the debt on the ancestral lands before they were returned to him. In 1808, his regiment became the 71st Glasgow Highland Foot.

The Earl of Seaforth, whose family name was also MacKenzie, had been 'out' in the rebellion of 1715, and although he had been pardoned in 1726, his earldom and lands remained forfeit to the Crown. They were repurchased by his great-grandson, who was created Earl of Seaforth in 1771. In gratitude, he offered to raise a regiment in 1778, and Seaforth's Highlanders reached India in April 1782, after a ten-month voyage during which the Earl and two hundred and fifty of the soldiers he had enlisted from his lands in Ross-shire and the Isle of Lewis, had died. The regiment, renumbered the 72nd in 1786, served in India from 1782 to 1798 and in South Africa from 1805 until 1822.

The 42nd, the Black Watch, had raised a second battalion in 1780. It was also sent to India, and in 1786 became a separate regiment as the 73rd. The 74th and 75th Highlanders were raised in Scotland specifically for hire to the East India Company, which at that time governed India – albeit under close scrutiny by the home government. By 1805, however, the situation in India was stable enough to permit these regiments to be recalled, although, as was the custom in those days, soldiers were allowed to transfer to other regiments staying, or just arrived, in India. A surprising number did so, 'five shillings a day, and a black servant', as a recruiting poster for the 73rd,

'The fighting, bloodstained Old Mangalores', proclaimed, proving an attraction too great to be resisted when the alternative was a squalid and overcrowded barrack in a dismal manufacturing town in England.

The 78th Highlanders – the first new regiment to be raised after war against France was declared in 1793 – was also formed under the Mackenzie aegis. It, too, served in India, and under Sir Arthur Wellesley, the 78th, together with the 74th, bore the brunt of the Battle of Assaye in 1803, which checked for a time the depredations of the Mahrattas and their allies, great freebooters and reivers from the south-west of the Indian Peninsula. The 74th and 78th were each presented with a third Colour by the East India Company, which was carried on domestic ceremonial occasions.

In 1793, the 79th Highlanders were raised by Alan Cameron of Erracht, at the expense of his father-in-law, a wealthy sugar planter with extensive interests in Jamaica. The 79th, although virtually destroyed by pestilence in the West Indies, was re-formed at home, and, avoiding the long years in India, served in various theatres of war in Egypt and the Continent, becoming one of Wellington's veteran regiments in the Peninsular War of 1808–1813. The 91st Highlanders was a Campbell regiment, raised by the Duke of Argyll from his clan territory at the request of King George III. Prominent on their 'appointments' was the boar's head of Clan Diarmaid. The 91st saw much service in South Africa.

The 92nd was the fruit of the endeavours of the Duke of Gordon and his family, the men coming from the Duke's vast Inverness-shire estates. Recruiting is said to have owed much to the efforts of his Duchess, who offered potential recruits a kiss along with their guinea bounty. The forty-five-year-old Duchess was described as 'well run' and had been separated from the Duke since 1792. She had been a great beauty in her youth, famed for high spirits and unconventional behaviour. Her son, the Marquis of Huntly, was then a captain in the 3rd Guards, but had been appointed to command the 92nd.[4]

The last regiment to be activated under the old Highland system was the 93rd, the Duchess of Sutherland and her henchmen having exerted the influence necessary to persuade her tenants to protect their own interests by sending their sons to enlist in her regiment. It would be unfair, all the same, to single out the Duchess, hated though she later became as a result of the notably harsh and heartless Sutherland clearances, from the other landowners who used this form of conscription to complete the regiments in which they and their sons were involved.

A further regiment which should be noted here is one which, though raised in the Highlands by a Highland landowner, was never classed as a Highland regiment and never wore the kilt. This was the 90th Perthshire Volunteers, raised in 1794 at his own expense by Thomas Graham of Balgowan in Perthshire, and known as the 'Perthshire Greybreeks'. At the time, Graham was forty-six. His young and beautiful wife had died while the couple were on the Grand Tour of Europe. On Graham's sad journey home through France, her coffin had been forcibly opened by the French customs on the pretext of searching for contraband. The 90th was to be Graham's instrument of revenge. From the outset its soldiers were trained as light infantry skirmishers and acted as advance guard to the force operating against the French in Egypt in 1801, although not designated as light infantry until 1815. Graham himself turned out to be a natural soldier and was one of the Duke of Wellington's few trusted subordinates during the Peninsular War. He died as General Lord Lynedoch

Throughout the later decades of the eighteenth century and the first two of the nineteenth, the wars raged off and on. The demands for men were insatiable, and, inevitably, the supply of Highlanders, willing or reluctant, began to dry up at source, in the same way as the supply of Sikhs willing to enlist to serve the Sirkar[5] did in India in World War II. In 1809, it was decided to remove certain regiments from the Highland establishment and to turn them into regiments of the line of no specific connections, territorial, clan or family. This entailed the loss of the Highland dress, the authorities maintaining that the kilt was 'objectionable to the people of South Britain', although the Highland regiments had been glad to welcome Englishmen in the days when threatened with drafting into other regiments because the number of casualties, usually from disease, had weakened them to the extent that they were no longer viable.

Those affected were the 72nd, 73rd, 74th, 75th and 91st. The

94th Scots Brigade, the reconstituted 'Scotch Dutch', was also included, possibly by a clerical error, as there is no evidence stronger than conjecture that the 94th had been raised as a Highland rather than a Scottish regiment in 1793, and when in the Dutch service, the kilt had formed no part of its uniform.[6] Thus there began a sustained battle to have the Highland status and dress restored which was to rage until 1881, although not all the regiments affected took part. The 73rd and 75th seem to have been content to let matters rest. However, their Scottish, if not their Highland, origins were acknowledged in 1862, when they formally became the 73rd Perthshire and the 75th Stirlingshire Regiments, and were allowed to wear the Scottish dicing, red, white and green, on their round 'hummel' forage caps, replaced by the glengarry cap, also of Highland origin, in 1868.

The 71st, the Glasgow Light Infantry, were, and remained until 1948, a special case. An outstanding regiment, the 71st had been selected in 1808 for conversion to the light infantry or skirmishing role. The 71st wore the kilt, and it was considered, sensibly enough, that it would be a hindrance in the widely dispersed and physically demanding operations for which light infantry were required and trained. Commanding the 71st at the time was Lieutenant-Colonel Cadogan, an officer of some influence. He was able to obtain the concession that the 71st might retain such of the Highland characteristics as did not conflict with their new role. The 71st duly went into trousers, but in place of the shako of the line regiments, they wore the 'bonnet cocked as a regulation cap', simply pulling their diced Kilmarnock bonnets over the top of their shakos, the Kilmarnock being what is now called a Balmoral bonnet, but larger in the crown. The 71st also kept their pipers, unofficial though they were at this point, still dressed in the kilt, although it appears that in the field they wore trousers like the rank and file.

From 1834, the 71st was allowed to wear Mackenzie tartan trousers, following the precedent set by the 72nd, which had worn Royal Stuart tartan trousers since its restoration to the Highland establishment in 1823. This sparked off a chain reaction among the regiments that had ceased to bear the Highland designation in 1809. The ensuing representations and negotiations tended to obscure the fact that the 71st had never lost its Highland status, unlike the others, and this was to have repercussions which rumbled on until the kilt was restored to the Highland Light Infantry in 1948 and, in the opinion of some, even later.

What has to be remembered when dealing with the origins of the kilted regiments is that they were not formed in order to perpetuate an ancient and outmoded way of life. They were intended to take their place in the line of battle, shoulder to shoulder with other battalions, all trained on the same system, and all reacting to the same commands, whether given by voice, drum, or bugle. The Highland dress was authorised as a factor likely to aid recruiting, and not because of any advantage, real or fancied, the kilt might bestow upon its wearers.

By the same token, the Highland bagpipe was extraneous to the main issue, which was the creation, in the shortest possible time, of an efficient and effective fighting unit as understood in the operational terms of the time. If pipe music helped the attainment of that aim, well and good; if not, it was superfluous until the contrary was proved.

But no matter what the higher military authorities of the time might have thought, the Highland piper had been a prominent member of the social hierarchy of the clan since the fifteenth century, when the piper seems to have ousted the bard and the harper from their position, filling it himself. Over the next three centuries, the Highland bagpipe was to acquire an essentially martial connotation. When the clan took the field as a fighting unit, the piper went with it, and was able, by means of the robust tone and volume of his instrument, both to entertain the clansmen on their march to the battlefield and in their bivouacs and also to encourage them during the prelude to battle by playing the ancient warlike music of the clan, well described by John Prebble as 'rants composed for men who had been dead for centuries'.[7]

With this, the harper could not compete, nor could the bard. Although he, too, went with the clan to battle, his role was to observe the fight and to compose on it a piece of epic Gaelic poetry, lauding to the skies his own chief and clan when they won, pouring scorn and contumely on the treachery of the other when his side lost.

The piper, on the other hand, once the time for music had passed, handed over his instrument to his ghillie, or servant, drew his broadsword and laid on with the best. It is this last tradition which has brought the Highland bagpipe its unique place in the realm of military music. The piper went into battle with his comrades.

The Disarming Act of 1747, which forbade the wearing of the Highland dress and its accoutrements in any form, made no mention of the bagpipe, and music exists which was composed during the period when the Act was in force. Nevertheless, it would have been a bold man who would have put breath into the bag within earshot of the occupying redcoats. But the new regiments, which were being formed and completed to fight the country's battles over half the known globe, were being recruited through a quite blatant appeal to the old loyalty to the clan and its leaders. The piper and his music were inextricably involved with the martial traditions of the clan, of which so much was being made, and it was therefore as logical as it was inevitable that his presence should be looked for whenever the ancient way of life was invoked in support of the new ventures into the old area – war – where the piper had been such a pivotal figure in the past.

So it was natural that each captain commanding a company of a hundred men, the basic administrative unit, regarding himself as the heir and successor of the almost legendary martial figures in the Highland past, should wish to have at his disposal all the pomp and pageantry of tradition. And thus the piper was to be found in the ranks of the companies which formed the newly raised battalions, none considering itself complete until each captain had his piper at his elbow. Records exist showing the inducements which were extended to persuade pipers to enlist, usually in the form of increased bounties, the money offered to each recruit on enlistment. Family influence was also invoked. In the old days, each chiefly family had maintained its piper, the post frequently being hereditary. The hereditary pipers to the MacDonalds of Sleat, great men in their time, had been the piping family of MacArthur. One of the last of the MacArthurs enlisted in a regiment being raised by the brother-in-law of the then Laird of Sleat, only to die in the West Indies, no doubt of the 'Yellow Jack', the fever which for two centuries more than decimated the British regiments stationed there to defend the Sugar Islands against the French.

Even before the first purely Highland regiments came to be

activated, there is evidence that men who played the Highland bagpipe were to be found in the ranks of those regiments recruited in Scotland. Four appear in an otherwise undistinguished painting of *The Destruction of the Mole at Tangier*, which took place in 1684. Tangier had been part of the dowry brought by Princess Catherine of Braganza on her marriage to King Charles II in 1660, but had proved too difficult and expensive to garrison and defend despite its strategic location on the Straits of Gibraltar. In the painting, the garrison has been turned out to throw the stones forming the mole into the sea. Present was the Royal Regiment; and there also appear four men playing what seem to be three-droned Highland bagpipes, dressed in what might be the Highland garb, although the knee-length cassock coats worn by soldiers of the period make it difficult to be sure.

This painting is of primary importance, illustrating, as it appears to do, the existence of pipers with a Scottish regiment as early as 1684; the three-droned bagpipe almost a century before its general introduction in the Highlands; and Highland pipes playing in concert a century and a half before the pipe band made its appearance. However, there lurks a sneaking suspicion that the pipers might have been a later addition to the picture. They are not drawn to scale, whereas the other soldiers are in rudimentary perspective; and this might explain why there has been, so far, some reluctance to accept *The Destruction of the Mole at Tangier* as authoritative evidence on the points raised above. But, if genuine, this is the first-known depiction of military pipers and also the first to suggest that pipers played in concert.

The factor which frequently arises to bedevil research into the presence or absence of pipers is that the term 'piper' is used when 'fifer' is meant. In the Dutch language, the word means fifer and, wrongly translated, the letters which authorised the raising of Scots mercenaries to fight in Holland in 1572 have been quoted to support claims that, even in the sixteenth century, Highland pipers were considered to be an indispensable part of any Scots fighting unit. As drummers are also mentioned, it might be that the fifers were intended to form with the drummers the 'spil' which was part of the mercenary infantry company at this time.

But, in one case, the evidence is quite unequivocal, and proves that it was not only in Highland units that Highland pipers were to be found. In 1769, the 25th Regiment, now the King's Own Scottish Borderers, was stationed on the island of Minorca in the Mediterranean. One of a series of pictures commissioned by Lord George Lennox, commanding the 25th at the time, features his officers grouped around the central figure, a woman, who is no doubt the commanding officer's lady. To one side stand a piper and a fifer. The fifer wears a white bearskin mitre cap and the reversed colours of the 25th at that period, yellow coat, the facing colour of the 25th, faced red. The piper also wears the yellow coat, cut shorter to accommodate the fullness of the belted plaid, which is in what appears to be the Government or 42nd tartan. His blue Scots bonnet has tufts of black bearskin, making it an embryonic feathered bonnet, and his hose are diced red and white, the traditional 'battle colour' of the Highlands. His bagpipe is made from a light-coloured wood. At this time, bagpipe makers had no access to the African blackwood now favoured, rosewood and boxwood both being popular then. It has three drones, the bass clearly visible, although at the time two-droned pipes were not uncommon.

And there he stands, proving for all time that the 25th Regiment regarded itself as of Scottish origin and tradition, and that, even though the regiment, as Sempill's, had helped to shatter the charge of the clansmen a mere twenty-five years before, the music of the Highland pipe was to be heard as well as that of fife and drum, played by a soldier dressed in the Highland garb. The 25th Regiment continued to prize its Scottish inheritance and nourish its roots, as did the 1st or Royal Regiment, the 1st Battalion of which was authorised to hold a piper on its strength throughout the eighteenth century, a unique privilege extended to no other regiment, Highland or Lowland.

Notes

1. 'Rats, Lice, and Scotchmen', Helen C. McCorry, Journal of the Society for Army Historical Research, Vol LXXIV, Number 297.
2. Narrative of Sir James Turner, quoted in Soldiers of Fortune in Camp and Court, Alexander Innes Shand (Constable, 1907).
3. Diarmaid, the legendary progenitor of Clan Campbell, is said to have killed a supernatural boar which was terrorising the countryside. Like Achilles, the only vulnerable part of Diarmaid's body was his heel. He

stepped on one of the boar's bristles, it went into his heel and Diarmaid died.

4. At this time, officers of the foot guards held rank in the Army two places above their regimental rank in the guards. A captain in the guards, therefore, ranked as a lieutenant-colonel in the line, so that the Marquis's appointment to command the 92nd did not in fact bring him promotion in the Army.

5. 'Sirkar' = Government. 'Raj' is a post-Independence catchword.

6. Regiments hired out to foreign powers were not obliged to serve against their home country. When Holland entered the coalition that formed in support of the American rebels in 1782, the Scots Brigade had been ordered to discard the British red coat and crimson sash in favour of the Dutch blue coat and orange sash and to stop beating the 'Scotch Duty'. The Scots Brigade thereupon opted to disband and come home. Over the years, many of the officers had married into Dutch families and acquired property in Holland, and many of the men had been recruited from the Continent. Therefore, the officers were faced with a difficult choice. On hearing of this, King George III memorably declared: 'Those who remained [in Holland] would not forfeit his regard; those who returned would be assured of his protection.' *The Scots Brigade in the Service of the United Netherlands 1572–1782*, Ed. James Ferguson, Scottish History Society, 1899.

On the outbreak of the war with France in 1793, the 'Scotch Dutch' brigade was reformed as the Scots Brigade, which served with distinction in India under Sir Arthur Wellesley, later Duke of Wellington. In 1803 it was allotted the precedence number 94. The 94th Scots Brigade was disbanded in 1818. Raised again in 1823 as the 94th Foot, it became the 2nd Battalion Connaught Rangers in 1881 and was disbanded in 1922 on the formation of the Irish Free State.

7. *Culloden*, John Prebble (Secker & Warburg, 1961).

APPENDIX
REGIMENTAL CALLS OF THE HIGHLAND REGIMENTS

The Black Watch (Royal Highland Regiment)

Seaforth Highlanders (Ross-shire Buffs, The Duke of Albany's)

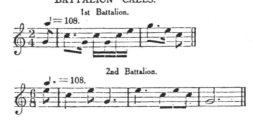

Highland Light Infantry

The Gordon Highlanders

The Queen's Own Cameron Highlanders

The Argyll and Sutherland Highlanders (Princess Louise's)

CHAPTER V
The Music and the Tartan
~

It is now time to turn to a more detailed discussion of the characteristics that set the Scottish regiments apart from those of English, Irish and Welsh origin. These are the music and the tartan, shared by both Lowland and Highland regiments; and the kilt, worn by all ranks in the Highland regiments and by the pipers, and, in one case, the drummers, also, of the Scots Guards and the Lowland. The kilt is also worn by pipers of the Royal Armoured Corps, the Irish Guards and the Royal Irish Regiment.

By music is meant that of the Highland bagpipe. It is divided into three categories.

Ceol Beag

This is the 'Small Music', a literal translation from the Gaelic. It consists of that type of pipe music most frequently heard, and which is played by pipe bands. Into this category fall marches, strathspeys and reels. The march derives from the long association between the Highland bagpipe and the Scottish regiments, while the strathspey and the reel come from dance rhythms in the folk-dance culture of Scotland, Highland and Lowland.

Ceol Meadhonach

The 'Middle Music', again from the Gaelic. It comprises song airs, more difficult to express than the Small Music; and hornpipes and jigs – dance rhythms more difficult to play than the strathspey or reel, although there are exceptions.

Ceol Mor

The 'Great Music'. This is the classical music of the bagpipe. The pieces in this category come under the generic name of *piobaireachd*, pronounced 'peebroch', although the term means simply 'piping'. *Piobaireachd* is not particularly difficult to play, but it is difficult to interpret and equally difficult to appreciate

1st Battalion 25th (King's Own Borderers) Foot, Paisley 1866
Pipe Major John MacKay and his five pipers of the 1/25th, splendidly dressed and equipped with
broadswords and dirks at their officers' expense. Their belts shine from years of spit and polish.
Barely visible above the buckle of their shoulder belts is the regimental crest, the royal crest of
England.
(RHQ King's Own Scottish Borderers)

92nd (Gordon Highlanders) Foot, Jullundur, Punjab, India 1872
Instead of the scarf plaid, Pipe Major Gregor Fraser and the pipers wear a fly plaid in the 92nd
tartan with a yellow overstripe. The plaids have been cut so as to look like the feile mor, the original
belted plaid. In this year the slashed cuff worn by the Highland regiments was replaced by the gauntlet
pattern, and both types can be seen here. The pipe major and two of his pipers 'play on the right
shoulder', or 'walk on the wrong side of their pipes'! (SUSM)

without study, as it has its own musical idioms and conventions.

The bagpipe is not peculiar to the Scottish Highlands. It is an instrument of great antiquity. The principle on which the instrument operates is simple: a bag, blown by mouth or bellows, supplies a continuous current of air to a pierced wooden pipe on which the melody is played, and a drone, or drones, is added to provide a fixed harmony. Although the bagpipe is found in varying forms all over Europe, it is in Scotland that it has reached its most advanced form, both as an instrument in its own right, and not merely as an adjunct to social occasions, and in its music, of which it possesses two highly developed forms, both intricate, and technically difficult for the performer. The first of these is an extension of the Small Music, in which the basic concept of the march, the strathspey and the reel, has been embellished to such a high degree of intricacy and difficulty that the original concept of marching and dancing has become secondary to the execution of the music. Pipers call this 'competition music'; it is the programme music of the solo performer and, to some extent, that of the pipe band as well.

The second of those highly developed forms is the Great Music, or *piobaireachd*, the pieces in which might be described as a theme and variations composed solely for, and played solely on, the Highland bagpipe. Nothing remotely resembling either of those two forms has been devised for any other type of bagpipe, as neither can it be satisfactorily reproduced on any other instrument.

The Highland bagpipe itself consists of a bag made of sheep or other animal skin, although now impermeable synthetic fabrics are being used. The bag must be airtight, and on this factor the tone of the instrument depends, as the volume of air must be constant. Air is blown into the bag through the blowstick, which is fitted with a mouthpiece and a valve. The air is led to the chanter, on which the piper plays the melody by fingering the eight holes which are pierced in it. There are two sound holes at the bottom of the chanter which increase its volume. There are three drones, one bass and two tenor. These are tuned to the tonic of the chanter, which produces an octave of eight notes, with a ninth note one full tone below the tonic, that is, the lowest note of the octave proper.

Although the drones appear to produce a fixed harmony to

the melody played on the chanter, in fact they produce a series of chords, which are heard to full effect only in the slower types of music, the slow airs and, above all, in the opening theme and earlier variations of the Great Music. The scale produced from the chanter differs from those of other European instruments, in that the intervals between the notes differ at certain points in the scale, the fourth note, the sub-dominant, sounding very sharp, and the seventh, the leading-note, very flat, so that the chanter will always sound out of tune to the conventional ear. But it is, quite simply, different; and while the flat seventh of the chanter might offend some, its effect can be electrifying, particularly in the laments in which this note features frequently, suggesting the 'keening' of the women which used to be heard at Highland funerals.

So far, so good! But the Highland bagpipe is a highly temperamental instrument. It is the only one in which four reeds are blown simultaneously, one double reed of the oboe type in the chanter and three tubular reeds, each stopped at one end, in the drones. All the reeds are highly susceptible to moisture and damp. As the reeds are mouth-blown, as distinct from bellows-blown, this problem is ever present, and unless the reeds are carefully selected and a supply of spares always handy, the instrument can simply cease to sound well, or, indeed, at all.

The bag has to be perfectly airtight. In a sheepskin bag, this used to be done by rubbing a solution of treacle or syrup into it, but now special preparations are available. It used to be alleged that either whisky or rum were the best preparations for preventing the bag from leaking, and in the Victorian era in India, when the Gurkha Battalions of the Indian Army were forming pipe bands, some comedian among their Scottish instructors passed this 'tip' on to his Gurkha students, who, implicitly trusting their teacher, solemnly assured their officers that rum, incidentally the Gurkhas' favourite tipple, was essential if their instruments were to continue to function. To this day, Gurkha pipers are still issued with a rum ration to keep their pipe bags airtight.

To sound well, the chanter has to be cleanly and accurately fingered, and here, too, cold and wet can make things difficult for the piper, as the instrument mercilessly exposes slack or clumsy fingering. Constant practice is essential if the requisite finger agility is to be maintained, as it is by fingering alone that the piper can separate two or more notes of the same pitch, or stress a particular note, such as the note falling on the beat when playing for marching and dancing. As the chanter reed cannot be 'tongued', the sound is continuous and the volume is constant. All this has to be done by means of a system of intricate note groups, called 'doublings' – double grace notes – executed very quickly and accurately, and in adverse conditions much of this intricate fingering has to go by the board, resulting in an inferior performance marred by squeaks, groans, and screeches as the piper tries to get his frozen fingers round the tune.

It is against this background of constant difficulty that the stories of the exploits of pipers on active service have to be considered. Too high a temperature produces its own range of complications, and when we read of the part played by the pipers in action in, say, the Indian Mutiny, our admiration for them must correspondingly increase. Similarly, a modern piper can only wonder how the pipers of the Great War kept their instruments in serviceable order in the mud and cold of the trenches before playing their comrades 'over the top'.

The second of the shared characteristics of the Scottish regiments is the tartan, worn by the Highland regiments in both kilt and trousers, and by the Lowland as trousers. Not trews, these are cut close to the leg with the seam on the inside only. Trews resemble the 'overalls', the tight-fitting tartan trousers strapped under the instep of the half Wellington boots, worn by officers of Lowland regiments in Mess Dress. Overalls are sometimes called strapped trews.

Tartan is defined as: 'A woollen fabric with stripes of various colours crossing at right angles, esp. as worn by Scottish Highlanders.' As tartan is understood today, the warp and the weft are identical, although, as early examples prove, this was not always the case. And, by the same token, tartan is not now confined to the Scottish Highlands. Designs abound; and one of the ways in which a modern industrial or other project seeks to promote a Scottish image is by having its own tartan designed and worn by its employees. Tartans are designed in other countries too. The regiments of the Pakistan Army which maintain pipe bands have devised their own, and these have become so closely identified with Pakistan itself that officers of the Pakistan Army have been known to express polite surprise when told that Scottish regiments wear tartan too!

Argument will ever rage about the origins of tartan itself and the authenticity of the so-called 'clan' tartans. Suffice it to say here that the balance of evidence is against the tradition that a Highlander's name and clan could be deduced from a glance at his tartan and, much more conclusively, against the idea that the clans wore tartan as a form of military uniform, which the Highland regiments continued. The clansman's party, faction or side, was shown by the cockade in his bonnet, or by a sprig of fir, heather or juniper, or by the slogan he screamed as he charged, broadsword in hand. This lasted until well after the general introduction of distinctive national uniforms into the standing armies of Europe. By the time of the '45 rebellion the clans still took the field dressed as they were in their daily life, although each clan regiment had its own distinctive banner, which was as important to the clansman as their Colours were to the troops opposing him. The banners of Clan Cameron, Clan Stewart and Clan Chattan – the last a confederation of minor clans headed by Clan Mackintosh – were smuggled from the field of Culloden and hidden for generations by devoted clansmen. Ten clan banners captured at the battle, along with two pikes from which the banners had been ripped, were burned publicly at the Mercat Cross in Edinburgh by the town hangman.

When the Independent Companies – which were later to provide the nucleus round which the Black Watch was formed – were raised by Royal Warrant in 1725, the officers appointed to command them were directed to provide their men with the Highland dress, with the proviso that the plaids of each company were to be 'as near as they can' the same sort and colour. It has been claimed that each officer dressed his company in his own clan tartan, but later evidence seems to suggest that the different companies were distinguished by a coloured overstripe on a common base, and that by the time the companies concentrated to form the original Highland regiment in 1739, this overstripe was uniformly red. Furthermore, from time to time, this red overstripe seems to have been reintroduced, presumably at the whim of the colonel, who might have felt that in view of the different overstripes being introduced by much junior regiments of ephemeral existence, it was in order for the senior to liven up its dark tartan with one as well.

It has always been more or less accepted that the appellation, the 'Black' Watch, '*An Freiceadan Dubh*', arose from the dark colour of the tartan worn by its soldiers. Another theory suggests that the term derives from the black or unauthorised *mal* or rent, paid to the chiefs of the various clans through which the droves of cattle on the way to markets in the south passed in order to safeguard them from the risk of being 'lifted' by his clansmen – in theory, a practice suppressed, but by some accounts carried on by the Independent Companies. As 'blackmail', the expression is now established in the language. Given that coloured overstripes seem to have been a feature of what we now accept as the Black Watch, Government or Universal tartan from the start, it might appear that this latter theory is the more likely; but while it would be a bold man who would assert it unconditionally, given the conditions in the Highlands at the time, it does seem entirely possible. On the other hand, however, it might be equally significant that in its basic form, the Black Watch, Government, or Universal tartan, has been adopted as a clan tartan by the Campbells and Munros, while the Grants wear it as a 'hunting' tartan, all on the ground that three of the original six Independent Companies were commanded the Campbells of Lochnell, Carrick and Skipness, while one of the remainder was led by Grant of Ballindalloch, another by Munro of Culcairn and the sixth by Simon Fraser, Lord Lovat.

This digression has been necessary because the standard Black Watch tartan forms the base on which all but one of the military tartans traditionally associated with the Highland regiments have been created, simply by the introduction of different coloured overstripes. Several clan tartans have also been created in the same way, usually by the adoption by the clan of the tartan of its associated regiment.

For reasons of regimental pride and morale, some of the regiments raised in the middle and later decades of the eighteenth century decided to 'difference' their tartans by adding stripes of various colours to the background of the Black Watch tartan in precisely the same way in which it is suggested that the regiment itself did from time to time. The colour of the stripes was either that of the red of the uniform coat, or of the facings which appeared on the collar, cuffs and lapels, and which were, as far as possible, different in shade, if not in colour, from one regiment to another. The only tartan which appears to have been designed specifically for a regiment was that of the 79th Cameron Highlanders, but this, too, may have been an adaptation of a sett associated with Lochaber, the district round Fort William, where the original 79th was raised, and where the founder of the 79th, Alan Cameron, was brought up.

However, the demand for 'clan' affiliations has been insistent, based apparently on the mistaken belief that the original Highland regiments were formed by clansmen who leapt gladly from the heather in response to the Fiery Cross, the old signal for the clan to muster, sent round by their chief. Thus the tartan of the 79th Highlanders is now marketed as the 'Cameron of Erracht', that having been the home of Alan Cameron, and is now assumed to be a Clan Cameron tartan. Lamonts and Forbeses share the tartan devised for the 74th Highlanders in 1846 by adding a white overstripe, the 74th's facing colour, to the 42nd tartan. Gordons wear the 92nd Regiment's tartan, in which an overstripe in the 92nd's yellow facing colour is similarly inserted. MacKenzies wear the tartan of the 78th Ross-shire Buffs, the 42nd with red and white overstripes, and Murrays, not a clan in the strict sense of the term, that of the ephemeral 77th Atholl Highlanders, disbanded in 1783, which shows three red overstripes on the 42nd tartan base.

Until the great reorganisation of the infantry in 1881, it was the tartan and not the kilt that was the outward and visible sign, not of the Scottish, but of the Highland soldier exclusively. Until 1881, the six 'old' Scottish regiments wore the uniform of their counterparts in the cavalry, the foot guards and the infantry of the line. The 1881 reorganisation created new regiments, each of two regular battalions, supported by a Militia component and a Volunteer element, of which more later. Regiments numbered up to 25 had raised second battalions in 1858, when war with France had seemed imminent, and were unaffected. Those above 25 were amalgamated to form these new ones mentioned above. Officially, the old numbers went into oblivion; unofficially, they continued to be used both in conversation and in correspondence.

The Royal Scots, the Royal Scots Fusiliers and the King's

Own Borderers remained intact, the last named having, at length, its Scottish provenance acknowledged, largely through its own sheer pertinacity, although its name remained unchanged until 1887, when the word 'Scottish' was added; and the King's Own Scottish Borderers the Regiment has remained ever since.

The new 'territorial' regiments were each allotted a separate area in which they were to have a permanent home or Depot, from which each would draw its recruits, not only for the two regular battalions, but also for the Militia and Volunteer units, these being linked formally to the new regular regiment, whose uniform the Militia was ordered and the Volunteers requested to take into wear, all being named as Militia or Volunteer Battalions of the territorial regiment.

The Scottish regiments were affected as follows: The 26th Cameronian Regiment and the 90th Perthshire Light Infantry formed the 1st and 2nd Battalions of The Cameronians (Scottish Rifles) based at Hamilton. The 42nd Royal Highlanders linked with the 73rd Perthshire Regiment as the 1st and 2nd Battalions of the Black Watch, so named from 1881, and centred on Perth.

The 71st Highland Light Infantry and the 74th Highlanders became the 1st and 2nd Battalions of The Highland Light Infantry. The new regiment was asked whether they would prefer to wear the kilt, rather than the tartan trousers which both then wore. The 1st Battalion said Yes, the 2nd said No. The 2nd won! The 72nd and 78th Highlanders, sharing a MacKenzie origin, became the 1st and 2nd Battalions of the Seaforth Highlanders. The Highland Light Infantry Depot was initially at Hamilton, sharing the barracks with the Cameronians (Scottish Rifles) but was eventually located in Glasgow; the Seaforth went to Fort George outside Inverness.[1]

The 75th Stirlingshire and the 92nd Gordon Highlanders became the 1st and 2nd Battalions of the Gordon Highlanders. The 91st and 93rd Highlanders formed the 1st and 2nd Battalions of the Argyll and Sutherland Highlanders. The Gordons were based at Aberdeen, the Argylls, as they inevitably became known, at Stirling.

Left over was the 79th Queen's Own Cameron Highlanders, which, after much discussion, was permitted to continue a lone existence until 1897, when a 2nd Battalion was raised on an augmentation of the Army to meet some long-forgotten threat, thus enabling the Government to accede, without loss of face, to the regularly expressed wishes of the venerable Queen Victoria, ever at heart the soldier's daughter, who had designated the 79th as 'The Queen's Own'; as well as to the sustained pressure from the Highlands, and the the Highland societies world wide.

The effect of the 1881 reorganisation was to increase the number of kilted battalions from five to nine. This was a popular move with the 72nd, which had lost the kilt in 1809, but had been created a 'non-kilted Highland Corps' in 1823, wearing tartan trousers. The 73rd came home, literally, to the Black Watch, as they had been raised as a second battalion of the regiment a century before. The 75th described its demise as the Stirlingshire Regiment and its metamorphosis into the 1st Gordons as a 'glorious resurrection'. And the 91st, another 'non-kilted Highland corps' in tartan trousers, regained, like the 72nd, the kilt it had lost in 1809.

However, the 74th, which had been allowed 'to resume Highland status and tartan trews' in 1846, showed no great enthusiasm at becoming the 2nd Highland Light Infantry. Until all second battalions were disbanded at the end of World War II, the battalions stubbornly referred to themselves and to each other, as the 71st and the 74th. The latter, as the 2nd Highland Light Infantry, succeeded in blocking the introduction of the so-called Light Infantry drill into the regiment in the 1920s.[2] The Seaforth Highlanders posted men from the East of their recruiting area to the 1st Battalion, which they still called the 72nd, while to the 2nd, invariably referred to as the 78th, went the 'Coast Westers' and the men from the Hebrides. In the Cameronians, only the 1st Battalion used that name; all the others were 'Scottish Rifles'. In the Argyll and Sutherland Highlanders, the 1st Battalion stoutly remained the 91st and the 2nd the 93rd, until it, too, disappeared with all the other second battalions in 1948.[3]

Also, in 1881, was the introduction of what a contemporary commentator in the Royal Scots called 'the strange Scottish dress' into the four Lowland regiments which had hitherto been dressed as infantry of the line, albeit with diced bands to the Glengarry forage cap then worn by all the infantry. The head dress of the infantry was now the blue-cloth, Home-Service-pattern helmet, derived from the German *Pickelhaube*, the 'spike bonnet', except for fusilier regiments, which wore a racoon skin busby. These were retained in the Scottish dress, and were worn with the Highland pattern doublet with its Inverness skirts and tartan trousers in the Government or Black Watch tartan. The Cameronians, as the Scottish Rifles, went into the same uniform, except that helmet and doublet were in dark rifle green and buttons and belts were black, in the rifle tradition.

The Royal Scots Fusiliers protested bitterly at the introduction of the new uniform; the Royal Scots, as ever, 'obeyed the last order'; the King's Own Borderers leapt at the chance to display their Scottish identity. Reaction in the Cameronians seems to have been mixed: regret at the loss of the traditional scarlet, in which the 1st Battalion had earned glory over two centuries, tempered perhaps with satisfaction at the regiment's elevation into what had always been considered the élite of the Army, the rifle regiments of which there were only two, the Rifle Brigade and the King's Royal Rifle Corps, although the 1881 reforms created the Royal Irish Rifles from the 83rd (County of Dublin) and the 86th (Royal County Down) Foot. The two newly designated rifle regiments had to lay up their colours. These were not carried by rifle corps, which had originally fought dispersed as skirmishers. So the 1st and 2nd Battalions of the Cameronians gave up their hitherto cherished Queen's and regimental colours, along with their scarlet coats, although neither they nor the Royal Irish Rifles were ever to fight in the true rifle role.

In the new Highland regiments, the uniform of the kilted components had been adopted, except in the case of the Highland Light Infantry, where, of course, the offer of the kilt had been rejected. However, as part of a scheme designed to simplify infantry uniforms, all non-royal Scottish regiments were ordered to wear yellow facings, yellow being the field of the Scottish Royal Arms. Of course, the royal regiments kept their royal-blue facings. Non-royal English regiments changed to white, and non-royal Irish, of which there was only one, the Connaught Rangers, to green. So the Highland Light Infantry and the Ross-shire Buffs gave up their buff facings, but agitated to such effect that their old facings were restored by the end of the century.[4]

The introduction of the Scottish dress into the Lowland regiments meant that the tartan, whether in kilt or trousers, was no longer the distinguishing mark of the Highland soldier, and this was to have repercussions in the Highland Light Infantry, which was now the only Highland regiment not wearing the kilt. Inevitably, over the years this distinction became blurred, especially after the Lowland regiments, in laudable attempts to assert their separate identities, succeeded in changing their tartans from the universal and somewhat uninspiring Government pattern, to the mid-Victorian tartans associated with the families of the notables who had raised them two hundred years before. The King's Own Scottish Borderers went into the Leslie tartan of the Earls of Leven, while the Cameronians chose the Douglas tartan of their first colonel, the Earl of Angus. Not to be outdone, the Royal Scots changed to the Hunting Stuart, a more or less neutral pattern connected with the Royal family, while the Fusiliers stayed in the Government tartan, although there is a tradition that a blue line was added to create a Fusilier tartan, which must have been almost indistinguishable among the dark green, dark blue and black of the Government tartan.

The process of extending the Scottish influence also led to the adoption by the officers of the Lowland regiments of the basket-hilted broadsword slung from the waistbelt, initially, and later from a Highland-pattern shoulder belt with belt plate and slings. The embroidered waist belt was also introduced, but not the dirk. The final departure from the dress of the line regiments came in 1903, when the Kilmarnock bonnet replaced the Home Pattern helmet as the head-dress of the Royal Scots and King's Own Scottish Borderers. The Royal Scots Fusiliers retained the fusilier cap. None of these changes affected the Cameronians (Scottish Rifles), which had reverted to a rifle-green shako.

What this led to was a steady erosion of the Highland identity of the Highland Light Infantry. In 1808, the 71st had been designated the 'Glasgow Highland Foot' and in 1809 the 'Glasgow Highland Light Infantry', only for 'Glasgow' to be dropped in 1810. Since 1881, its subsidiary title had been 'The City of Glasgow Regiment', and this – together with their tartan trousers – led them to be classified with the Lowland regiments, which were similarly dressed, rather than the Highland, where the Highland Light Infantry rightfully belonged, and though the regiment continued to protest loudly. The kilt, however, was, in practice, a double-edged factor, in that it attracted recruits from the industrial Lowlands and England, from where, despite protestations to the contrary, recruits were more than welcome when Scottish sources dried up temporarily, as they did from time to time for one reason or another.

In the Highlands proper, thinly populated as they were, the kilt could be a negative factor in recruiting. Vast areas were devoted to sporting interests, either owned by wealthy men from the south, or rented out to them. Whereas it had been the Cheviot sheep which had led to the clearances of the eighteenth and nineteenth centuries, the grouse and the stag kept the hills bare and the glens empty, except for the employees of the estate and the few surviving crofters permitted to remain on the land. The kilt came to be regarded as a mark of social pretension from its popularity with the lairds and their shooting, stalking and fishing tenants; and as a badge of servitude, being worn almost as a uniform by the stalkers and ghillies who, dressed in the estate tweed and tartan, enforced the game-preservation laws and carried on the war against poachers, very often their fellow native Highlanders, who had for generations asserted their right to an occasional beast from the hill behind their crofts and fish from the river running past their front doors, especially when times were hard.

Notes

1. It was a convention in the Seaforth Highlanders that the definite article 'The' never preceded the name of the Regiment, i.e. the correct form was '1st Battalion Seaforth Highlanders'. The reason given was that the Regiment hoped one day to be allowed to revert to its original name 'Seaforth's Highlanders', the 1st Battalion having been raised by the Earl of Seaforth.

It was also correct to refer to the Seaforth Highlanders as 'The Seaforth'; for an officer to refer to 'the Seaforths' was a grave solecism. The soldiers, however, never referred to their Regiment in any other way.

2. *Light Infantry Drill*: In its original form, Light Infantry drill was a battle drill based on the tactics, formations and evolutions employed by a screen of skirmishers, this being the true role of the Light Infantry and Rifle Regiments. When this system of tactics was taken into use by the rest of the infantry in the 1860s, Light Infantry and Rifle regiments sought other ways of maintaining an outward display of their separate identity. Thus there evolved a different system of parade-ground drill, in which rifles were carried at the 'Trail', ready, in theory, for instant use, instead of at

the 'Shoulder' or the 'Slope'. Words of command were reduced to a minimum, and all drill movements began from the 'Stand at Ease' position.

The marching speed was 140 paces to the minute, and the rifle exercises were performed equally briskly. The instrument of command and routine was the bugle; these regiments had no drummers. The sounding of the bugle reached heights of virtuosity unique to these regiments, and the majority of the marches, slow and quick, for Band and Bugles, originated with them.

The Cameronians drilled as a rifle regiment; the Highland Light Infantry drilled as normal or 'heavy' infantry, although they encouraged the mystique of the bugle. But in the late 1930s, The Cameronians and the Scottish Rifles were still unable to agree on certain details of drill. Conversation with Lieutenant-Colonel S. Storm, The Cameronians (Scottish Rifles).

3. The last occasion on which the old precedence numbers were officially used was in the internal organisation of the Chindit force which operated in Upper Burma between March and August 1944. Each infantry battalion in the force was divided into two independent 'columns'. These were numbered, one taking the precedence number of the 1st Battalion of the regiment, the other that of the 2nd. Thus the columns formed from the 1st Battalion The Cameronians (Scottish Rifles) were numbered 26 and 90; those formed by the 2nd Battalion Black Watch 42 and 73.

4. Although the Highland uniforms did not change, apart from the facings of the non-royal regiments, new badges were designed incorporating features of both the components. The Cameronians added the light infantry bugle horn of the 90th to the mullet of the Douglases, while the Highland Light Infantry's new badge featured the French horn of the 71st – a distinction shared only with the King's Own Yorkshire Light Infantry – with the Assaye elephant of the 74th. The badges of the Seaforth and Gordon Highlanders incorporated the stag's head. The stag had long been venerated as a symbol of strength and virility, epitomised by the position of the dancer's arms and hands in these Highland dances performed only by men.

The colonel-in-chief of the Argyll and Sutherland Highlanders was HRH Princess Louise, Duchess of Argyll, talented and artistic daughter of Queen Victoria. She designed all the badges for her regiment, incorporating the boar of Clan Campbell and the cat of Sutherland, both regarded in the Highlands as symbols of superhuman power since pagan times. Princess Louise linked the two badges with a label of three points from her own armorial bearings, the mark of her cadency as a junior member of the royal family. Saint Andrew, patron saint of Scotland, featured in the badges of the Royal Scots, the Black Watch and the Cameron Highlanders; hence the probably apocryphal story of the response of a Highland recruit to the question, 'Who is the man in our cap badge?': 'Jesus Christ in his bare feet!'

The 93rd Highlanders, Pipe Major James Wilson, c. 1853
In 1853, pipers were still being dressed according to their officers' fancy – only the tartan in this
portrait confroms to the 93rd's uniform. The hose date from a previous regime, under which the pipers
had been clad from head to foot in the red and black 'Rob Roy' check. To this day, pipers of the
Argyll and Sutherland Highlanders wear hosetops in red and black.
(RHQ Argyll and Sutherland Highlanders)

CHAPTER VI
THE KILT

~

'Cam' ye by Athol, lad with' the fillabeg,
Doun by the Tummel or banks o' the Garry?
Saw ye the lads with' their bonnets and belted plaids,
Leaving their mountains to follow Prince Charlie'

James Hogg

The kilt is the ancient and distinctive dress of the male Scottish Highlander. It was worn in two forms: the *breacan feile*, or belted plaid; and the *feilidh beag* (anglicised 'fillabeg'), the little kilt, which is the garment worn today and which has come to be regarded as the national dress not merely of the Highlanders but of Scotland itself.

The belted plaid is a little kilt and plaid combined. It is rarely seen nowadays. It consists of some six to eight 'ells' (an ell was 3ft 9ins) of double-width tartan cloth (about 4ft 6ins), which was pleated and fastened round the waist by a belt. The lower part, reaching to the knees, formed the kilt, while the upper, the plaid, was fixed to the left shoulder by a brooch or pin, leaving the right arm free to wield the broadsword. The belted plaid was worn when travelling and on raids. In wet weather the upper part could be folded to cover the torso and arms; at night, by unbuckling the belt, it became a blanket or wrap. The cloth being woollen, it was warm, and as it swelled when wet, it thus kept out the wind. The old Highlanders, when spending a night in the open, would soak the plaid in the nearest burn, wring it out and sleep wrapped up in the damp plaid. Reliable evidence is scarce, but it is believed that the early Highland regiments wore the belted plaid until 1796.

The little kilt is simply the lower part of the belted plaid, pleated and sewn, each end being left unpleated to overlap the front of the body and secured by pins, a belt, or a strap and buckle. The little kilt became the form worn by the Highland regiments from 1796. In that year the uniform coat was ordered to be worn buttoned across the chest instead of being left open to display the facing

Highland Light Infantry (City of Glasgow Regiment), Military Band, Edinburgh, 1948

After many applications the kilt was finally restored to the regiment in 1948. The Mackenzie tartan kilt was in the wide sett worn by the pipers; the hose were in the traditional red and white; and the sporran was black with three white tassels, the pattern worn by the 6th Battalion of the Territorial Army, which had always worn the kilt. The 9th Battalion, the Glasgow Highlanders wore the kilt, but in the Black Watch tartan. (National War Museum of Scotland) colour on the lapels and the white or buff waistcoat. The coat of the Highland soldier had always been cut shorter in the old Highland-style to accommodate the bulk of the belted plaid, but the 1796 regulation meant that the belted paid could not be worn without severely restricting the wearer's ability to move freely. The original little kilt was made with the pleats uncut, which added to the support and protection it gave to the lower trunk of the wearer and it made the kilt easier to tailor; it also allowed four periods of wear to be had from one length of tartan: by turning it upside down for the second period; inside out for the third; and upside down again for the fourth. Each Highland soldier was issued with six yards of tartan annually in April, which were made up into the kilt in the regiment, the old kilt being used to make tartan trousers or waistcoats.

After the belted plaid had been discarded, the upper part was represented on full dress parades by the 'fly' plaid, a triangular piece of tartan with an attached cloth belt of the same material. The belt was fastened round the waist under the coat. The apex of the triangle had a loop, which was attached to the button of the left shoulder strap in the case of the rank and file. Officers and serjeants wore, at their own expense, a fly plaid which was more generously cut and had a longer apex, which was pulled under the left shoulder strap, to hang down in front almost to the waist belt. These plaids were fringed and worn with an elaborate brooch of regimental pattern, also privately purchased, at the left shoulder.

Highlanders had also worn trews when on horseback or visiting round the crofts. These, too, were of tartan, cut 'on the cross' to fit close to the leg, with a seam on the inside leg only. With trews, a form of plaid could be worn, simply a length of tartan cloth folded across the body or thrown round the shoulders as required. This survives in the 'big', 'cross' or 'scarf' plaid worn by pipers of Scottish regiments and bandsmen of the two divisional bands. Drum majors of the Highland regiments wear the scarf plaid, as does the drum major of the King's Own Scottish Borderers. Drummers of kilted regiments and the Royal Highland Fusiliers (whose drummers wear the kilt) wear the fly plaid, as do drummers of the King's Own Scottish Borderers.

Kilt-making is a skilled business. The length of tartan

required depends on the physique of the wearer, but about seven yards usually suffices. The upper apron of the kilt finishes on the right and is usually secured round the waist with two straps and buckles. Kilts supplied to the Highland regiments used to be secured with pins about four inches long. Old soldiers claimed that with the pins the kilt fitted more snugly and 'sat' better. Civilian kilts are usually pleated 'to the sett' showing the pattern from behind; military kilts are pleated 'to the line', with a stripe running down each pleat. In the Seaforth Highlanders, the white line of the Mackenzie tartan showed, hence the 'silver streakit Seaforths' of the soldiers' song.[1] The Gordon tartan worn by The Highlanders shows the yellow line running down each pleat.

Military kilts are box pleated, which readily lose their definition. The Black Watch kilt had rolled pleats and could not be ironed like the others. The Black Watch and the Argyll and Sutherland Highlanders share the same tartan, the Black Watch pleated to the black line of the pattern, while the Argylls' kilt is pleated to the green, giving a less sombre appearance. In some cases, rosettes of varying colours are worn by officers and pipers, often with kilt pins. The Cameron Highlanders, however, regarded rosettes, kiltpins and other ornaments as so much frippery, preferring to wear the kilt in its simplest and, to the regiment, its most impressive form.

The kilt was the dress of the highland regiments in peace and war until the outbreak of World War 2 in 1939. It had been worn throughout the Great War but, although in the trenches it was covered by a khaki apron, it frequently had to be replaced. Getting the right kilt to the different battalions required a detailed knowledge of regimental idiosyncrasies. Pipers of the Royal Scots wore the Hunting Stuart kilt, as did the 9th (Highlanders) battalion from Edinburgh, the famous 'Dandy Ninth'. The other battalions wore khaki trousers and long puttees,[2] as did the Highland Light Infantry, except for the pipers who wore the Mackenzie in a wide sett. But the 6th (City of Glasgow) battalion wore the kilt, in the same sett as the pipers. The 9th Highland Light Infantry, the Glasgow Highlanders, wore the Black Watch kilt and their pipers the Royal Stuart. The Seaforth Highlanders wore the same Mackenzie tartan, but in a narrower sett than the Highland Light Infantry, except for the 5th (Caithness and Sutherland) battalion, which wore the same tartan as the Argyll and Sutherland Highlanders. The London Scottish wore kilts of 'Hodden Grey' a light heather-mixture, while the Liverpool Scottish wore what to them was the Forbes tartan, but which to veterans of the 74th was still *their* tartan.

The Forbes, Lamont and the 74th tartan are indistinguishable to the layman. When the 74th was restored to the Highland establishment in 1846, the adjutant general, the ultimate authority on dress, directed that the tartan should not be the old Government pattern worn from 1787 –1809 as this was already worn by the 42nd and 93rd, so the 74th were directed to 'difference' their tartan by adding a white stripe, white being their facing colour. As has been mentioned, the Highland Light Infantry tended to be sensitive about suggestions that their Highland origin was spurious. Forty years after the 74th had become the 2nd Battalion Highland Light Infantry, some older officers claimed that the 74th had originally been raised in the Forbes country in Aberdeenshire, hence the Forbes tartan. Counter-claims were made by others that it was a Campbell regiment raised in the Lamont country, the Cowal district of Argyll. However, it is highly probable that neither the adjutant general, nor the staff officer who advised him, nor the clerk who wrote the 1846 letter had ever heard of the Lamont or the Forbes tartan, but were following the accepted precedent of differencing the Government tartan by adding an overstripe of the regimental facing colour,

In the early months of the Great War, an attempt was made to resolve the tartan problem by issuing a kilt-type garment of khaki material 'pleated and attached to a waistband like a girl's skirt'! Uproar ensued as the Highland regiments agitated for the return of their traditional tartans. Possibly because of the adverse effect in recruiting – in England especially men were queuing up, clamouring to join any kilted battalion – the authorities rapidly dropped the idea, and once the clothing industry had been organised to meet the demands of war, kilts of the proper tartans were procured and issued. The 7th Battalion Seaforth Highlanders, however, continued to wear the khaki kilt.There is also evidence which indicates that two of the Service battalions of the Black Watch wore the khaki kilt at different times.[3]

The first Highland units to be deployed in France in World War II were dressed in the kilt, but soon the whole question of its suitability for modern war was raised. The threat of poison gas and the blistering agents was then a very real one and the kilt gave little protection against either. Veterans of the Great War, and many at that date survived, had unhappy memories of the disadvantages of the kilt in the wet and mud of the trenches and of the lice and vermin that had flourished happily in its pleats. The kilt still had its protagonists on the grounds of pride, morale and tradition, but these factors counted for little in the circumstances of the time. Pipers, drummers and bandsmen continued to be issued with the kilt, and regimental sources usually managed to find the associated glengarry caps, belts and sporrans.

The kilt was issued again within a few weeks of the end of the war, and in this, and in the prompt return to their regiments of the King's and Regimental Colours, could be discerned the hand of King George VI, always alert to further the interests of his Army. Although the kilt is still part of the Highland soldier's uniform, under modern service conditions the occasions for wearing it are few and far between. Since the introduction of the high combat boot, it can now only be worn with white spats and coloured hosetops. These are footless stockings, now worn over ordinary socks and once called 'mogans', taken into wear during the Peninsular War of 1809–1814, when spats also appeared. These were devised to stop stones getting into the low shoes then issued. On parade, the kilted regiments wore diced hose and buckled shoes until the late 1850s, when spats and hosetops replaced them. The traditional colours for diced hose were red and white, the battle colour – *cath dath* – of the Highlanders. In 1840 the 79th Cameron Highlanders began a trend when they changed to red and green, which complemented the colours of the regimental tartan. The 42nd Black Watch and the 92nd Gordon Highlanders went into red and black. The 78th Ross-shire Buffs and the 93rd Sutherland Highlanders remained in red and white. After World War II, the Gordon Highlanders reverted to red and white for all ranks, including the pipers. When the Queen's Own Highlanders was formed, the red-and-white hosetops of the Seaforth Highlanders were retained, although the pipers still wore red and green. The Highlanders, formed in 1994, wear red and white, apart from the pipes and drums which kept the red and green and, of course, the 79th tartan.

THE KILT

As a general rule, diced hose were only worn with 'white feet' (spats), plain Lovat green hosetops being worn with ammunition boots and puttees. In tropical dress with shorts, the Lowland regiments wore a khaki hosetop, the turnover being in the regimental tartan. Highland regiments wore red garter flashes under the turnover, a relic of the knots which secured the garters in former days, but of which only the ends survive. The Gordons had a more elaborate pattern, still worn by The Highlanders. Pipers often wore a distinctive garter flash woven in the colours of their tartan.

The correct wearing of the kilt in the Highland regiments became something approaching an art form, so high was the regard in which the ancient dress was held. A careful soldier first put on his 'leg dress', taking care that his hosetops were the identical height on both legs. He then donned his spats, using a 'spat hook', otherwise an old-fashioned button hook, to keep his fingers clean. The next step was to ensure that the seam of the spat coincided with the centre of the dice on the hose and that the correct number of dice appeared above the spat, each regiment having its own rules.[4] The garter flashes then had to be aligned with the proper dice.[5] After all that, the kilt had to be strapped firmly round the waist and the height of the bottom edge adjusted to the correct regimental length, with the kilt itself central on the body. Last came the sporran, with the 'cantle', or sporran head, correctly aligned on a horizontal line of the tartan. His tunic could then be put on, with a final check that the centre line of the buttons coincided with the centre line of the kilt. The final touch was to reach up under his kilt and to pull his shirttails down.

This all took time; and a frequent criticism of the Highland regiments was the time it took them to turn out in case of an alarm when on service in the field. In the days when the others had to wind long puttees round their legs this might not have been critical, but in earlier days there was some justification, although the soldiers prided themselves on the speed with which they could turn out when the occasion demanded. In the days when a quarter or barrack guard was mounted in 'Kilt Order', one extra man was detailed as 'waiting man'. The best-dressed soldier 'got the stick' and became commanding officer's orderly for the day, excused sentry duty and getting a night in bed.

Certain regiments used to run voluntary competitions for the correct wearing of the Highland dress. The Seaforth Highlanders held one every Saturday, judged by the commanding officer at the conclusion of his weekly inspection.

Finally, nothing at all was worn under the kilt by soldiers, although civilians may do as they please. Occasionally the regimental Highland dancing team might be ordered into tartan underpants when performing on a raised stage before a mixed audience but usually the dancers simply pinned their shirttails together between their legs if anyone thought it mattered. Tales of the lengths to which authority went to ensure that nothing was being worn under the kilt are apocryphal. Mirrors on guardroom floors, on the end of pace sticks and so on are nonsense, and no soldier ever thought twice about going up to the top deck of a bus or tramcar.

The kilt seems to have inspired comparatively few pipe tunes. There is a reel 'The Kilt is My Delight'. There are a couple of marches '*Gillean nan fheile*' – 'Lads with the Kilt' in 6/8 time, which was played as the 'Gathering' by the Cameron Highlanders and as the 'Fall In' by the Queen's Own Highlanders. The other is, perhaps, the more attractive; it is a 2/4 march called '*An t'Aparan Boideach*' – 'The Pretty Apron', a traditional air from South Uist in the Outer Hebrides. The apron is that of the kilt. 'Cam Ye By Athol' is not strictly a pipe tune, although it goes well on the pipes in both slow and quick time. The words are by James Hogg (1770–1835) and Neil Gow the Younger (1795–1823), of the famous Scottish musical family, composed the tune.

Notes

1. 'Ye can talk aboot yer Gordons, yer Scotch Gairds an' a',
   Yer silver streakit Seaforths and yer gallant Forty-twa,
   But gie tae me the tertan o' the lads that are sae fine,
   The Argyll and Sutherland Highlanders, the Thin Red Line!'
2. 'Puttees' came from a Hindi word meaning bandages. Puttees were rolls of cloth some four inches wide, wound round the leg from the ankle up to the knee. They were introduced by the 'Piffers', the Punjab Frontier Force, formed for service on the northwest frontier of India and widely held to be the crack troops of the Indian Army. Puttees were adopted by British troops during the 2nd Afghan War of 1878–1880, during which the 72nd Highlanders wore tartan trousers and tartan puttees. Puttees give excellent support to the ankles when moving over rough terrain. The

puttees latterly issued to Scottish troops wrapped round the ankles only.
3. 'Khaki Kilts – An Expansion' by Tom Moles, *Dispatch* The Journal of the Scottish Military Historical Society 155, Spring 2001.
4. For instance, the Cameron Highlanders showed two and a half dice, whereas the Argyll and Sutherland Highlanders showed three.
5. The Cameron Highlanders aligned their garter flashes on the outer dice, the Argyll and Sutherland Highlanders on the centre.

1st Battalion The Royal Highland Fusiliers, Glasgow, 1959
The pipes and drums and military band and bugles leading a guard of honour as it marches through Glasgow shortly after the regiment was formed in 1959. The uniforms of the drum major and pipers reflect the Royal Scots Fusiliers influence, the pipers wearing the Dress Erskine tartan. The drummers wear the kilt and fly plaid, as did those of the Highland Light Infantry, in the same tartan. The dress of the military band closely resembles that of the Highland Light Infantry before the restoration of the kilt in 1948. The tartan is Mackenzie. Sadly, it has not been possible under modern conditions for an Infantry Battalion to maintain such a strong musical presence. (RHQ Royal Highland Fusiliers)

The Highland Brigade Gathering, Cawnpore, United Province, India, 1931
Whenever operational and other commitments permitted, the battalions of the Highland Brigade stationed in India periodically organised an inter-regimental athletic contest. It was run on the lines of a Highland Games and included piping and dancing events. Depicted are the competitors who participated in the piping events, representing the 2nd Black Watch, 2nd Highland Light Infantry, 2nd Seaforth, 1st Gordons and 1st Cameron Highlanders. On the left of the front row is Corporal Jimmy Johnson DCM MM, 1st Cameron Highlanders, who was first in all the piping events. The 2nd Highland Light Infantry was the overall winner.
(Queen's Own Highlanders Amalgamation Trustees)

72nd or The Duke of Albany's Own Highlanders Military Band, Dublin, 1868
The 72nd was the first 'non-kilted Highland corps' and was the only one to wear the feathered bonnet, in which the band wore red hackles. The trousers and scarf plaid are in Royal Stuart tartan in the Prince Charles Edward sett. The band doublet was white faced red and the band shoulder shells finished in red wool tufts. The comparatively recently introduced range of valved bass instruments is prominently displayed. The bandmaster serjeant stands proudly in the centre, foot resting casually on a chair. (RHQ Queen's Own Highlanders)

78

CHAPTER VII
THE MILITARY BAND (1)

~

The drum, fife and bagpipe were all very well in their place, but each carried connotations of the parade-ground and military duty, which all soldiers, at one time or another, wish to forget. The officers of the eighteenth century sought more sophisticated entertainment, and music, in the civilian circles in which they preferred to move when not on duty, played a major part in almost every social occasion. It was, therefore, a logical step for the officers to provide themselves with music of a similar sort to solace their leisure hours. Thus there came into existence the 'Band of Musick', the predecessor of the present-day military band.

The officers, as might be expected, had to finance the project themselves, usually by paying a monthly subscription into a Band Fund, from which instruments were bought and men to play them hired. It goes without saying that it was unlikely that trained musicians were to be found in the ranks, unless they had fallen on hard times or were covering their tracks for some reason or other. Therefore, it was necessary to hire musicians at the going rate if an effective band was to be formed and maintained. Naturally, such a band was understood to be at the disposal of the officers, who were paying for it, and it was not regarded as part of the battalion or regiment.

None the less, a band was an important social asset for the officers. When the Inverness Militia was being formed in 1803, the adjutant wrote to his commanding officer:

'I fell in with Major Rose a few days ago. He said he would join us in a subscription for the band instruments. I am satisfied there is not an officer who would not give his mite. Suppose I put you down for ten guineas and see what the rest will do? I pawn myself to have a band to give any man pleasure by the time you come north, and I'll engage that there is not a regiment in North Britain would do it at three times the cost.'[1]

As they were intended to provide music for indoor social occasions, the earliest bands were not suitable for playing on parade, consisting as they did of eight to ten musicians playing

79th Foot or Cameron Highlanders, Rawalpindi, Punjab, India, 1867

The 79th is drawn up in 'Review Order, Left in front', possibly awaiting the arrival of a senior inspecting officer. The Snider rifles are at the 'Long Shoulder' with bayonets fixed and swords are drawn. Formed up in 'Beating Order' on the left of the battalion are the band, pipes and drums. This is one of the earliest photographs to show a pipe band formed up as such, pipes in front, drums behind. In both the band and the drums, the side drums are the shallow pattern, with the drum carriages worn round the neck. (*Queen's Own Highlanders Amalgamation Trustees*) clarinets, horns, oboes and bassoons – some, no doubt, being capable of playing stringed instruments as well. A group of this nature could tackle chamber or indoor music quite successfully, but for parade purposes some percussion to mark the beat distinctly was essential. If the band was required and agreeable to play on parade, some of the drums would have had to be detailed to accompany it. The early bands of the footguards were so employed, along with the drums and fifes, playing the 'Duties', the New Guard, from Horse Guards Parade, where the guard-mounting parade took place, to St James's, where the Old Guard was relieved with due ceremonial, the band discoursing appropriate music all the while. The changeover complete, the band led the Old Guard back to Horse Guards, where it was formally dismounted.

During the eighteenth-century wars, however, the decisive battles were fought on the mainland of Europe, where the British Army usually took part in conjunction with German allies and often within earshot of their common foe, the French. Both Germans and French had bands of enlisted musicians, whose role it was 'to excite cheerfulness and alacrity' in the soldiers by enlivening with their music the main events of the day: the Reveille, the Troop, the Retreat and the Tattoo. At a later period, the great Napoleon is said to have agreed with a remark attributed to the Abbé Raynal: 'If Frederick the Great owed some of his victories to the speed of his marches, surely he owed others to his military bands.'[2]

King Louis XIV of France had put the military music of the French Army on to a sound and well-organised footing by having his court musicians compose and arrange the trumpet calls, ceremonial music and marches. The French also had a school for training bandsmen and trumpeters, thus ensuring that all the calls and beatings were sounded and played to a standard set by the school and not by individual bandmasters and drum majors, as tended to happen in the British Army, where every battalion was a law unto itself. Where it took their fancy, the French had also borrowed Prussian innovations in instrumentation.[2]

The British, not unnaturally, sought to compete with those foreign armies musically as well as tactically, but the British musician was never the man to be put upon, and as he was usually hired by the month, when things were not to his liking he simply walked off. Thus, there was no alternative to enlisting the musicians as soldiers subject to military law, but it was not until 1803 that authority was given for one soldier from each of the ten companies in the battalion to be employed as a musician and for him to play in the band. One non-commissioned officer was allowed to be employed as 'Master of the Band', but when active service was in prospect, all had, in theory at least, to take up musket and bayonet and return to the ranks. The band then ceased to exist.

Service in a line or 'marching' regiment had little appeal for the professional British musician, unlike service in a band of the footguards, stationed permanently in London, where duty was over by midday and the musician could supplement his income by accepting engagements to play at other events in the afternoon and evening.[3] This system was accepted; it flourished until the middle of the twentieth century, when the excellence of the young musicians being trained by the colleges of music and the change in popular musical taste from the dance band of reeds, brass and percussion, to that of amplified guitars, made it difficult for the serving military musician to secure casual, paying engagements.

The number of musicians willing to enlist was always below requirements, especially when a fresh outbreak of hostilities led to an increase in the marching regiments during the recurrent wars of the eighteenth century. Although some of those regiments were disbanded once peace returned, the demands of the expanding empire led to the retention of others, with a corresponding requirement, not only for recruits to keep them up to strength, but for musicians as well. Even in far-off India, then months away by sea and, perhaps, especially there, the need for the relaxation and entertainment, which familiar music only could provide, was very real. Sometimes, indeed, it was available; and as Sir Arthur Wellesley, then at the outset of a career which was to see him become Duke of Wellington ten years later, wrote to Mrs Gordon, wife of his paymaster, in May 1804 from his Headquarters at Chittendore in South India: 'The floor of my tent is in a fine state for dancing, and the fiddlers of the [19th Light] Dragoons and the 78th [Highlanders], and the bagpipes of the 74th [Highlanders], play delightfully.'[4]

～

The 78th had then been overseas for eight years and the 74th in India for seventeen. Both had distinguished themselves, along with the 19th, at the great battle at Assaye in 1803, suffering severely. Wellington's remarks suggest that both the fiddlers and the pipers provided more than acceptable dance music, and it says much for all three regiments that they had managed to maintain their own sources of domestic music among all the vicissitudes of the First Mahratta War.

When the Elector of Hanover became King George I of Great Britain in 1715, he retained his hereditary position as ruler of Hanover which, in the opinion of many, remained his spiritual home. Consequently, Britain had a foothold among the German states, many of which from time to time sent – or hired out – contingents of their troops to support and augment the British Army in its many campaigns on the mainland of Europe and in America. Germany was then the heartland of military music, and so Britain had access to a ready supply of military musicians trained in the latest developments. Not only were the Germans highly competent instrumentalists, they were also more amenable to discipline than their British counterparts and were less likely to desert. In many cases, and for many years, the entire band was composed of Germans. As late as 1818, an inspection report on the Royal Scots Greys states: 'This regiment, although they have an excellent band, never bring them out mounted to the field. Most are Germans, good horsemen, and all are trained and fit for the ranks and do not exceed the number allowed by the Regulations, but many of the trumpeters also play with the band.'[5]

The number of musicians authorised in the cavalry at this time was one per troop, with an NCO as master of the band. There being six to eight troops in the regiment, each with its trumpeter, their inclusion in the band would have doubled its size, and if, as might well have been the case, the trumpet major and the master of the band had played also, the total might have well approached the strength authorised in the 1980s, which was twenty-one. The fact that the band of the Scots Greys did not turn out mounted would seem to indicate that horses of a suitable temperament were not available, as it was noted that all the bandsmen could ride well. The availability of suitable horses remained the factor that decided whether a cavalry regiment could turn out a mounted band.

With the German bandsmen came German ideas of what constituted military music, that is, music appropriate to military occasions as opposed to social functions. Here we should remember that the sound or tone of the band remained the same, no matter what the occasion or function might be, and that the tempo at which the more popular ballroom dances of the period were performed was very similar to that at which the soldiers marched on the drill square. It is also the case that the earliest bands could not play on the line of march until the roads became fit for formed bodies of troops to march on in step and in time. The role of the bands, as far as military occasions were concerned, was to provide music to accompany the evolutions and manoeuvres on the parade-ground, and for this purpose the pieces played did not have to last for very long, perhaps only for the time it took for a battalion to pass the saluting base at the Ordinary Step of seventy-two to the minute. For this reason, most of the marches of the eighteenth century consist of two quite simple sections of eight or sixteen bars in common time, each section repeated. There was an increasing demand for marches of this type, and over a period these came to be associated with specific regiments, particularly those stationed permanently in the capital cities and larger towns of the princely German states, where the guard or life regiments lived in barracks adjacent to or near the royal palace or residence. One of the sights of the city, and a source of pride to the citizens, might be the daily guard-mounting and changing ceremonies, carried out with music; and one of the special occasions was the beating of Retreat or Tattoo by the bands, drums and fifes, either on the parade-ground where the guards mounted, or in the main square of the city itself. In the garrison towns of the unified Germany of the later decades of the nineteenth century, such occasions included the *Grosses Wecken*, when, at Reveille, the massed bands, drums and fifes of the garrison would play through the streets of the town on New Year's Day, the Kaiser's birthday and similar occasions, led by the adjutant mounted on his charger.

The master of the band, as well as prominent local composers, might produce these short marches for the regiment, which could find itself with several marches, to the despair and confusion of future military historians. Some, indeed, had three or four, all called 'The March of the Umpteenth Regiment'.[6] And not only in the eighteenth century did composers write for the military band. In the early nineteenth, Beethoven composed the 'Yorckschermarsch', to commemorate Count Yorck von Wartenburg, who took his Prussian contingent over to the Russians in 1812, the first step in the eventual downfall of Napoleon. In 1882, the great operatic composer Richard Wagner composed three fanfares for the trumpeters of the cavalry regiment of the Bavarian Army stationed at Bayreuth, which was to become the centre of the Wagnerian cult. The regiment was the 6th Chevaulegers 'Prince Albrecht of Prussia', Chevaulegers – light horse – being the Bavarian equivalent of the hussars of other armies. The 6th treasured the three fanfares, although the trumpet major was heard to mutter 'That idiot Wagner! Nobody could blow this stuff!'

With the bands, small though they were, appearing more and more frequently on parade, it became necessary to introduce an augmented percussion section to mark the beat. Not all soldiers, and certainly not all officers, have an ear for music, and unless the marching rhythm was marked clearly and distinctly and loudly enough for all to hear, some soldier somewhere in the ranks was going to lose the step and throw the whole of his platoon or company into confusion. At first, the drummers, massed, were detailed to accompany the band, effectively drowning its music and, probably, thoroughly enjoying doing so. In Prussia, the financial advisers, clearly soul mates of the present generation of their British counterparts, demanded the abolition of the regimental bands, on the ground that no one could hear them anyway. Frederick the Great's answer was to increase the size of the bands!

At the same time, however, another influence was sweeping Europe in the ever-changing evolution of the military band. The south-east frontier of the Holy Roman Empire marched – in the Scottish sense[7] – with that of the Ottoman, and for centuries, wars of varying intensities had flickered on and off. Over the years, the Austrian armies had become well accustomed to the often intimidating sound of the Turkish martial music, which they associated particularly with the Corps of Janissaries, the household troops of the Turkish Court recruited from captured Christian boys brought up in the Moslem faith. Perhaps the most impressive element in this warlike sound was the novel and striking percussion effect. Turkish military musical combinations included bass, tenor and snare drums, as well as triangles and cymbals of varying pitch and volume. This effect acquired the name 'Janissary Music'.

It appears that complete Janissary bands were presented to the King of Poland – who was also Elector of Saxony – and, later, to Frederick the Great of Prussia. As the original members died, they were replaced by local musicians, and the Turkish reed and brass instruments were discarded in favour of oboes, horns, trumpets and bassoons. The Turkish percussion section was retained intact, and there is evidence that it was a standard element in Prussian military bands by about 1777. This was a logical step in the military context. The augmented percussion, with the accent firmly on the beat, made the music easier to march to but without drowning the sound of the other instruments, as the drums had done The Turkish or Janissary influence soon spread all over Europe.

British military bands were not behindhand in acquiring the elements of the Turkish or Janissary percussion. Another Continental fashion taken up with enthusiasm by the British in the eighteenth century, was the enlistment of black youths to play these exotic Turkish percussion instruments, rather than fresh-faced lads from the plough tail or the slums, which were even then beginning to proliferate in the wake of the industrial revolution.

It was easy for British battalions to find blacks willing to enlist for the band. Not only had some of the battalions spent time in the West Indies, but when slavery was declared illegal in Britain, many of the black servants kept by the wealthier people – more or less as fashion accessories – had been turned out into the street so that their employers might avoid having to pay them wages. But it need not be thought that the blacks were inevitably regarded and treated as inferior beings; three soldiers of the 25th Regiment, stationed in the West Indies at the time, were awarded nine hundred lashes each by court martial, six hundred of which were inflicted, for 'attempting to outrage the person of Susan, a black slave'.

These blacks were dressed in what were fondly supposed to be Turkish costumes, and were encouraged to caper about in appropriately uninhibited style so as to draw attention to themselves and the band. It has been suggested that a relic of this period is seen in the wearing of tiger and leopard skins by bass and tenor drummers and the way in which these drummers customarily flourish their drumsticks. They also made excellent musicians, particularly on brass and percussion instruments, and were popular in the cavalry, where their skill with the trumpet made them much sought after. But at least one turned out to be a proper soldier. Drummer Charles Bogle was a 'man of colour', a fact sedulously concealed by the Victorian chroniclers of his regiment. He died at the Siege of Burgos in 1812, fighting most gallantly, wielding his drummer's broadsword in single combat with a French soldier, who died equally gallantly. Their bodies were recovered, the Frenchman run through with Charlie's sword, his bayonet through Charlie's body.

Notes

[1] *Historical Records of the Cameron Highlanders* (Blackwood & Sons, 1909).

[2] Henri Lachouque, *The Anatomy of Glory*, tr Anne S.K. Brown (Lund Humphries, 1961).

[3] In the years before sufficient barrack accommodation was available, soldiers were billeted on the civilian population. This was highly unpopular, and so the battalion would be ordered to change its quarters fairly often, so as to share the burden out. The battalion marched from one quarter to the next, hence a 'marching' regiment, as opposed to the foot guards, always stationed in London.

[4] *Wellington – The Years of the Sword*, Elizabeth Longford (The Literary Guild, 1969).

[5] *A Hundred Years of Military Music*, Lt-Col P.L. Binns (The Blackmore Press, 1959).

[6] The 'Records of the Royal Scots' include separate quick marches for the 1st and 2nd Battalions, two 'quicksteps' for the 2nd Battalion and the quick march 'Scots Royals'; and two slow marches: 'A March of the 1st Battalion Royal Scots' and 'The Royal Scots March'.

[7] In Scotland, the boundary between two estates or farms is called the 'march'; hence 'the march' or 'the march burn'. The expression means simply the boundary. The properties are said to 'march with' one another.

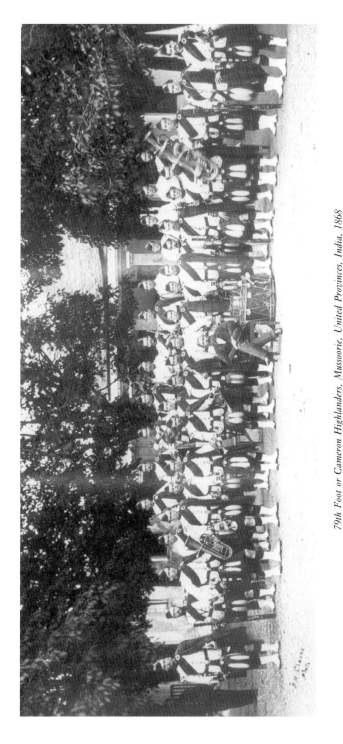

79th Foot or Cameron Highlanders, Mussoorie, United Provinces, India, 1868

The seated figure in civilian clothes is Herr Ernest Fromm, the German bandmaster. In 1844, he was engaged by the officers in succession to Herr Schotte, who resigned on being appointed bandmaster of the Grenadier Guards. During the Crimean War, Herr Fromm remained with the depot at Aberdeen where he 'augmented and perfected the 79th Band'. In August 1857, he embarked with the 79th for India and, on arrival, he and the band remained with the depot at Chinsura, Bengal, until the final suppression of the Indian Mutiny in 1858. Herr Fromm served with the regiment in India until its return to the UK fourteen years later. Bandmaster James MacDonald, a graduate of the Royal Military School of Music at Kneller Hall, succeeded him in 1872. Despite his twenty-eight years with the 79th, nothing else is known about Fromm, and regimental records describe him simply as a 'German civilian'. (Queen's Own Highlanders Amalgamation Trustees)

88

~

The 79th Band 1868	Comparison of Instrumentation	
Instrument	*Regulation*	*79th*
Flutes/Piccolos	3	2
Oboe	—	—
Eb Clarinet	1	1
Bb Clarinet	6	8
Bassoon	—	4
Horns	2	2
Cornets	2	4
Alto Horn Bb	1	2 (Baritone)
Trumpet	1	2
Tenor Trombone	2	2
Bass Trombone	2	2
Euphonium	1	1
Eb Bass	1	1
Bb Bass	1	1
Total Musicians/Bandsmen	*23**	*31*

*The regulation strength of the band was: 1 bandmaster-serjeant, 1 band serjeant, 1 band corporal, and 19 bandsmen, a total of 21 playing members, although there are instruments for 23, surely an invitation to exceed the authorised strength, as most regiments did.

In the 79th photograph, one bandsman is noted as 'tenor drum', which at this period was played like a side drum but with felt-headed sticks. The drum itself does not appear in the photograph.

CHAPTER VIII
THE MILITARY BAND (2)

~

The general acceleration of movement on the battlefield was reflected in a corresponding increase in the speed at which the soldier was expected to cover the ground, both in training and on the parade ground, where the old formal Ordinary Step of seventy-two paces to the minute was relegated to what were called 'occasions of parade'. The rate of marching was stepped up to the Quickstep speed of one hundred and eight to the minute, while Double Time became one hundred and forty; and if that to us appears to verge on the sluggish, we must remember that in the first decade of the nineteenth century the soldier went into battle, and everywhere else as well, carrying all his wordly goods on his back – a crippling burden for a tired or ailing man, but one which was to be part of the soldier's lot for many a long year yet.

Science, too, takes a hand here; and the development of the metalled road surface invented by that worthy Scot, John MacAdam, not only revolutionised the postal service by making it possible for mail coaches to run predictably to a timetable, but also enabled larger bodies of troops to move from one place to another at the Quickstep.[1] This worked out at three miles in the hour, exclusive of halts for rest, and this improved road surface also made it possible for the marching troops to maintain their formation without straggling, and to march in step, always less tiring than when every man sets his own pace and time. As a result, marching to music became possible and, indeed, normal, so that in 1803 we find instructions being issued to cover the hitches which might occur on a long road march. It appears that by this time it had been accepted that the drums and fifes – the corps of drums – and the military band constituted two separate musical entities, each playing in turn on the line of march.

The 1803 Regulation directed that the band – still called the Musick – was to be frequently practised with the corps of drums – abbreviated usually to 'The Drums' – so that when they took over from each other on the march, the correct time or tempo

~

would be maintained. This was a thoroughly practical requirement, as nothing is more tiring and distracting to a laden soldier than constant and nagging changes of speed and step. This remained a difficulty as long as soldiers marched to music, and was recognised as such, to the extent that until 1939, the pipes and drums and the military band of the 1st Battalion The Argyll and Sutherland Highlanders carried out march practice every Saturday morning while the rest of the battalion was being subjected to the rigours of the commanding officer's weekly inspection. It is worth noting, too, that the 1803 order directed that the drum major was to take charge of the practice and not the master of the band. Here might be the origin of the convention whereby the drum major takes command when the band and the drums, or the band and the pipes and drums, parade together, even though the bandmaster, as a warrant-officer, is the senior. This convention is also observed in the foot guards where all the directors of music are commissioned officers, the senior often a lieutenant-colonel, who nevertheless falls in with his band when on parade, conforming to the drum major's orders.

From 1808, the British Army, with its Portuguese and Hanoverian allies, was engaged in operations against the French in Portugal and Spain. In all the plethora of written and printed orders, directions and instructions which emanated from the headquarters of the Army in the field, there is no mention whatever of music, whether played by bands, drums, fifes, bugles or bagpipes. The anecdotal evidence of the presence of all these with their regiments seems conclusive enough at first sight, but, as so often is the case, credulity is strained when we read of bands playing patriotic music while all around them battle rages. It is, for instance, difficult to accept that having played their comrades into action at Talavera in 1809, the band of the 48th Regiment then joined in the hand-to-hand combat which ensued. Talavera was a hard and bloodily contested affair, and the bandsmen are likely to have been fully occupied picking up the wounded of the 48th, their role, even then, in battle.

Similarly, would the Master of the Band of the 88th Connaught Rangers have been so insensitive as to have his band play the doleful Irish love song, 'Savourneen Dileas' – 'Faithful Darling' – just before the assault on the fortress town of Badajos in March 1812? The 88th was celebrated for high spirits and lively conduct, but a song of that nature, which doubtless all the Connaughtmen knew, is hardly likely to have done much for morale, relating as it does how the soldier returns home from the wars, only to find that sorrow at his absence had brought his sweetheart to 'her cold grave', the prospect of which faced all the soldiers in the assault that night.[2]

While there can be no doubt that the bands, the drums, the buglers and the pipers were all present with their battalions in the Peninsula, and that they did play at formal parades and at social functions, it has to be remembered that at best they were very small; that the roads in the Peninsula were, and some still are, execrable; that it is probable that, in battle at least, they left their instruments with the baggage and acted as very necessary stretcher-bearers; and that on the march, they were silent until the occasion arose at which music might have been appropriate.

All tales of war, then as now, skim over one aspect on which all soldiers who have experienced protracted infantry combat would agree: the best are taken first. The earliest casualties fall heaviest among those who can least be spared. 'Always the tallest poppies,' is the German saying, and it is true. What this implies is that war will wreak its havoc as much among the bandsmen, the drummers and the pipers, as among the born leaders and the most experienced men. The more these come to be relied on, the more likely is it that the cruel sport of war will see to it that they suffer out of all proportion to their numbers, so that, for instance, when the cry goes out for the pipes and drums during a period of rest and retraining, the roll call reveals that the best of them have disappeared through death, wounds, or sickness; and that the survivors have all been promoted out of the pipe band.

As with the musicians, so with their instruments. These are rarely constructed to stand up to the hard wear inseparable from the daily business of life in the field in all weathers, which is the inevitable lot of the infantry soldier. Drum heads must have split, spares been lost, fifes, like bagpipe chanters, must have broken, and the band instruments must have become damaged and unplayable if taken into the field at all. The bugle, too, was at this period coiled or wreathed only once, and so must have been battered into uselessness as time went on. So when the band, the drums, or the pipes were called for, the chances of them falling in on parade as an effective musical unit were probably slight.[3]

On the final conclusion of the wars against France in 1815, Paris was occupied by the Allies, the occupying force comprising contingents from the Prussians, Austrian, Russian and British Armies. Inevitably, comparisons were made, and the British bands of ten or so musicians could not compare with those of their allies. By 1816, the Prussians were parading with bands twenty-six strong, and although these were the bands of regiments of three battalions each, and therefore no stronger proportionately than the British, their impact was, of course, much greater. When the occupation ended in 1818, the Prussian bands were established at thirty-two, their instrumentation much like the British, with a percussion section of a bass drum, two side drums, cymbals and a triangle. This was in addition to the *Spielleute*, the drummers and fifers, of whom there were two of each to every company in the regiment, providing the music for the daily routine in barracks and playing as a corps on the march, the fifers also sounding the 'signalhorn', the Prussian bugle, when required.

But in the British Army the mills, as ever, ground exceeding slow, and it was not until 1823 that it was conceded that a band was essential to the credit of a regiment, and the number of men allowed to be employed as bandsmen was increased to fourteen. That was as far as it went. The only instruments provided by the War Department were the drum, the fife and the bugle in the infantry, and the trumpet in the cavalry. These were classified as 'Instruments of Command'. All band instruments had to be bought out of the Band Fund, to which the officers subscribed one day's pay on first appointment, and twelve days' pay a year thereafter. But this, however, was not enough to equip an effective band, because after 1815 the range of essential instruments increased dramatically.

In 1817, the Prussian Army issued its first list of approved marches, to which the regimental bands were to be restricted on all official occasions, parades and reviews. The moving spirit behind this step was King Frederick William III, whose great interest, in the Prussian tradition, lay with his Army and, especially, the outward show and ceremony connected with peacetime soldiering. When the Prussian Army had to be reformed and reorganised after the defeat of 1806 by the French, the King had been allowed to design the uniforms while his generals got on with the real business of reorganisation.

The Army March Collection was organised in three sections. The first comprised marches in the old ceremonial time of seventy-two to the minute. The second contained the new quicksteps at the Prussian tempo of one hundred and fourteen. The third, issued in 1824, was the cavalry section – the infantry was the senior arm in Prussia – and included marches at seventy-two for playing at the walk, tunes in the double time of one hundred and forty or so for ranking past at the trot and in rollicking 6/8 for the gallop past. When ranking past, the band played at the halt opposite the saluting base, and before the regiment reached it the mounted drummer executed the *Galoppvolte*, in which he rode a figure-of-eight pattern at the canter in front of the band, beating time all the while. The evolution demanded a strong and well-trained drumhorse and a confident drummer, as the horse had to be controlled by knee pressure alone.

This was a bold and, on the whole, successful attempt to bring some order into what was, even then, a fairly diffuse subject, and had already been introduced in Russia, where many German military musicians were employed as bandmasters to the Russian Army. As time passed, other marches were added to the lists, until at length there were one hundred and eight slow marches in Section 1, two hundred and sixty-seven in quick time in Section 2 and one hundred and forty-three in the Cavalry Section. A further unnecessary list was promulgated in 1933, but it was from the original lists that regiments chose their marches, one from Section 1 to be played as an inspection tune or *Präsentiermarsch*, with one from Section 2 for the march past at the *Parademarsch*, the famous 'goose step'. Cavalry and horse artillery regiments chose four tunes from Section 3; one stately slow march as the inspection tune, another as the walk past; while for the trot and the gallop past, perhaps one of the many light classical pieces arranged for the cavalry band, which in Prussia comprised brass instruments alone. Although the *Sturm Abteilungen*, the Storm Detachments, the Brownshirts of the Nazi Party, were organised on paramilitary lines with their own bands, they were not permitted to play the regimental marches of the old Imperial Army.

The collection includes two marches which illustrate the evolution in military musical styles. In the early nineteenth century, Paris was occupied twice. Once in 1814, after Napoleon, Emperor of the French, had abdicated; and once, a year later, after the Hundred Days War, the campaign which followed his escape from Elba, where he had been confined after his abdication. Two marches commemorate those two occupations. 'The March of Entry into Paris 1814' is in the old ceremonial time of seventy-two to the minute; 'The March of Entry into Paris 1815' is a quick march at one hundred and fourteen.[4]

Although musical affairs are rarely amenable to the General Staff approach, the Prussian March Collection was a step in the right direction. The drawback was that the earlier marches were scored for an instrumentation which the military or marching band could not at that stage match. As a result, in their original arrangements, the marches, both slow and quick, are perhaps more evocative of the salon and the ballroom rather than the parade ground.[5] But instruments were steadily becoming more sophisticated. The brass instruments, the horn and the trumpet in their different forms, were restricted to the notes of their harmonic series, as the bugle and the cavalry trumpet are to this day. They were therefore unable to produce a scale, unlike the reed and string instruments which some of the bandsmen could no doubt also play. Attempts had been made over the years to modify the brass instruments by the use of crooks inserted into the instrument which altered the length of the tube, enabling a further harmonic series to be played. The range of the horn could also be extended by stopping the bell with the hand. Neither was satisfactory. Crooks were inconvenient and useless in a marching band; stopping muffled the tone of the horn and led to poor tone quality.

Experiments had also been carried out in which holes had been made in the trumpet and bugle, covered either by the player's fingers, as in the fife, the flute and the bagpipe chanter, or by keys operated by the musician, but to little avail, with the possible exception of the key bugle, patented in England in 1810. This was an extension of an idea tried out some years before, when keys had been fitted to a trumpet. The Duke of Kent, soldier brother of the soldier Duke of York, Commander-in-Chief of the Army, encouraged the incorporation of the key bugle into British military bands, the instrument acquiring the name of 'kenthorn' as a result.

It was also called the 'fuglehorn'. When a squad of soldiers was being drilled, the smartest used to be placed in front so that the others might follow and imitate his actions. He was the 'fugleman'; and as the bandsman playing the kenthorn marched as the right hand man of the front rank, where the fugleman would march in a drill squad, the instrument came to acquire the name. The key bugle certainly reached the bands in the Peninsula, and might have been used to sound routine calls like 'The Roast Beef of old England', which, played on the fife and drum, summoned the soldiers to dinner, as it was later to call the officers. Perhaps the key bugles might have been combined to form a rudimentary brass section in the band, as its range enabled tunes to be played, as well as calls to be sounded. The Kenthorn is the earliest example of a brass instrument capable of playing a complete scale, and its descendant still flourishes in the brass band, where it is called the 'flugelhorn', the *Flügelmann* being the German equivalent of the British fugleman, which might itself be a corruption of the German term.[6]

The key bugle had indicated the way ahead, however, and by the 1820s the invention of the valve had released all the brass instruments from the restrictions of their harmonic range. The valve had been invented in 1813 by one Blühmel, who played the oboe himself, but who was nevertheless to revolutionise the whole range of brass instruments through his invention. The valve operated on the same principle as the crook, in that it enabled the length of the tube, and hence the air passage, to be adjusted. Being fitted near the upper end of the instrument, the valve could easily be operated with one hand, a spring device returning the valve to the open position when released. It was quickly realised that the principle could be applied to all the brass instruments, although it was to be some time before all the faults, inherent in any new system, were to be eliminated. The higher register instruments, the trumpet and the horn, were the first to be modified, but the bass had to wait until the appearance of the tuba and its associated range of instruments in 1835.

These were the result of a fruitful period of co-operation

between J.G. Moritz, a Berlin instrument maker, and one Wilhelm Wieprecht, one of the most influential figures in the history of military music. The son of a *Trompeter*, a bandsman in the Prussian cavalry, Wieprecht was a trombonist in the orchestra of the Berlin opera house, and had first become interested in military music while listening to the band at the daily guard-mounting parade. Initially, he tried his hand at composing marches for the cavalry band, the somewhat misleadingly named *Trompeterkorps*.[7] This brought him to the attention of the officer commanding the Guard Dragoon Regiment in Berlin, who gave Wieprecht a free hand to reorganise and improve the Guard Dragoons' band. From the Guard Dragoons, Wieprecht graduated to the band of the *Regiment der Gardes du Corps*, the Prussian equivalent of the British Life Guards. In due course, his fame spread, and he was appointed – still a civilian – as director of music of the Guard Army Corps, which comprised cavalry, infantry and artillery regiments, some ten bands in all.

The new range of instruments which Wieprecht and Moritz perfected are with us to this day. Admirably suited to the military band, they are reliable, portable and within the competence of the soldier musician to master. They imparted a brilliance and sonority to the military band, which transformed its hitherto essentially indoor or chamber effect and enabled a vastly greater range of music to be played. Wieprecht was in the forefront of the movement, and might justly be claimed to be the father of the military band as we know it. A talented arranger, he made many classical and orchestral compositions available to the band and also pioneered the massed military band spectacular in Berlin in 1838 when he conducted one thousand one hundred and ninety-seven bandsmen, drummers, fifers and trumpeters from thirty-two bands. He also conducted a performance of the *Grosser Zapfenstreich*, the Prussian Tattoo ceremony, before Queen Victoria and her consort Prince Albert outside Cologne in 1845, an experience which might well have caused Her Majesty to wonder when she was going to see and hear a similar performance from her own bands. But a performance of this scope and magnitude could only be successful given a common doctrine, a coherent policy and a shared outlook, all of which were some way in the future for the British Army.[8]

An improved and more ambitious quality of parade music also began to be composed. The old, short, two-sectioned marches in slow time went by the board and the earlier quick marches were prolonged by the addition of the 'Trio'.[9] Longer marches arranged from popular operatic themes were now within the capacity of the band, as were selections from the operas themselves, and these, along with popular dance music – waltzes, polkas, and so on – and operatic overtures came to be expected by the audiences in the parks and municipal gardens where military bands were increasingly engaged to play and where a wider range of programme music was demanded than had hitherto been the case.[10]

All those new instruments opened up a brilliant vista of possibilities for the band, but they had, in the Prussian as well as the British Army, all to be bought and paid for, the whole cost falling on the officers, who were naturally not anxious to pay more than they had to in view of all the other calls on their purses. Once the instruments had been acquired, it was only common sense to procure the best possible return on the investment by hiring out the band to play at concerts and similar functions at which music was expected. The clinching factor, in the case of the military band, being that it could play out of doors without any of the problems which playing in the open air of an evening posed for string players, for instance.

The colourful uniforms of the military bands – it was the golden age of military millinery and tailoring – were another attraction, and as the bandsmen were also trained to play standing and from cards rather than sheet music, they could set up and play almost anywhere. Performances by the garrison bands became a popular source of entertainment for the general public, who were prepared to pay to be diverted for a while and to come back for more. But programmes of this scale and scope had to rehearsed and scores had to be mastered and practised, and a sergeant from the ranks, no matter how talented, was unlikely to be able to train and conduct a band of the necessary quality, capable of sustaining a weekly concert programme, each consisting of different pieces, without disaster in some form or another. What was clearly necessary was a trained, competent, and full-time musician rather than a part-time soldier. Britain had its share of such musicians; but the military way of life held

~

no attractions for them, nor was the Band Fund likely to be able to afford the salaries they could demand. So where were such men, capable musicians prepared to accept the challenge of transforming forty soldiers into competent instrumentalists at the modest salary offered, to be found?

After the long wars with France were over, travel to the Continent became possible once more, and almost every visitor could return with tales of the excellence of the Continental European bands. The daily guard mounting was a feature of life in all the garrison towns of Europe, from France to Russia, and the bands not only marched the guards to and from their duties, but also gave a short concert as the duties were being handed and taken over, much as they do in London today, one of the few places where this once general ceremony can still be seen. The best bands were said to be German, so it made sense for the officers who were having to pay for the upkeep of the band – and much more besides – to engage a German bandmaster to train and conduct the band, preferably one who had done his compulsory military service as a 'hoboist', or bandsman, in a German Army band, where the standards of musicianship and parade-ground deportment were equally high. This would make the best use of all those new and expensive instruments and would also enable the officers – or rather the Band Fund – to recoup some of their outlay by giving concerts of a standard sufficiently high to attract a paying audience and consistent enough to persuade them that they wanted to hear the band again. Even in the principal cities and towns, where concerts were frequent, the bands of the regiments in garrison were an important element in the recreational life of the population. In Edinburgh, for instance, the band of the regiment stationed in the castle would play on the castle esplanade of a summer evening, attracting many of the strollers round the sights of the city.[11] Unjust as it might seem, the reputation of a regiment in its own garrison might depend as much on the excellence of its band and the variety and frequency of its performances, as on the behaviour of its officers in local society and the off-duty conduct of its soldiers, of whom, however, not too much was expected.

Enter then, the German bandmaster, a civilian engaged and paid by the officers from the Band Fund, very often given the job on the recommendation of one of the firms dealing with the manufacture and supply of military band instruments. In return, the bandmaster might undertake to persuade the officers to deal solely with that firm and, as an added inducement, he might receive a percentage on any orders placed with it. So it could happen that on arrival, the new bandmaster might condemn all the band instruments out of hand, ordering a new set from the firm to which he owed his appointment, it being highly unlikely that any officer on the Band Committee, which administered the band, would be in a position to disagree.

One of the disadvantages of the civilian bandmaster, no matter how much he owed to the regiment, and especially if he was a foreigner, was that when swords were sharpened in anticipation of battle, or when long years in some fever-stricken outpost of Empire loomed, he was able to take himself off to more congenial and lucrative employment with some regiment just returned from abroad, whose band needed restructuring, reorganising, and re-equipping if it was going to be able to compete for paid engagements against other regimental bands. This happened; but there are other well-documented cases where the foreign bandmaster stayed with the regiment to which he had been first appointed, accepting whatever came in the way of foreign postings. Some stayed for thirty years, longer than most officers; and in such cases the regiment would take the bandmaster, his wife and children to its collective heart, he acquiring that special status which long service alone could bring, treated as an officer in all but name, and – like Wilhelm Wieprecht – conducting the band of the regiment in frock coat and cravat to the very end.

Notes

1. 'We were hurried off one fine morning (in 1813) in charge of a splendid detachment of five hundred men to join Lord Wellington in Spain. MacAdam had just begun to do for England what Marshal Wade had done for Scotland seventy years before; and we were able to march twenty miles a day with ease until we reached Portsmouth.' *The Reminiscences of Captain Gronow,* Christopher Hilbert (Ed.) (Kyle, 1991).
2. *Songs and Music of the Redcoats,* Lewis Winstock (Leo Cooper, 1970).
3. Shortly after the Battle of Waterloo a Court of Inquiry was convened in the 92nd Highanders to establish the circumstances under which, among other matters, some of the bandsmen had lost their instruments.
4. On 14th July 1920, France's National Day, the Tricolour outside the French Embassy was removed by some disgruntled Berliners smarting at the injustice of the recently imposed *Diktat* of Versailles. Accordingly, the

71st (Highland) Light Infantry, Military Band, Malta, 1873
In 1873, the band was issued with scarlet doublets instead of white – note that the 71st tied the scarf plaid at the shoulder without a brooch. Also note the civilian bandmaster – a dying breed by this time – the breadth of the bass drum, the bandsman's ornate sleeve badge and the drum carriage of the side drummer, which is worn around the neck. The band boys sit in fromt with their pets, while several of the older bandsmen wear campaign medals from the Crimea and the Indian Mutiny.
(RHQ Royal Highland Fusiliers)

74th (Highland) Foot, Military Band, 1873
Although the rank and file of the 74th wore the shako with diced band, the band wore feathered bonnets with a red hackle – a head-dress adopted by the bands of the Highland Light Infantry when the 71st and 74th amalgamated in 1881. The band appears to include an alto and tenor sxophone, although twenty years were to pass before the instrument was to be accepted in British military bands. Note, too, the string double bass, an almost essential member of the bass section when playing as a concert band. The drum major, pipe major and five pipers stand in the background. Since 1854, Highland regiments had been allowed to maintain six pipers at public expense. (National War Museum of Scotland)

101

German Government was ordered to parade a Guard of Honour and Band to pay the appropriate compliments as the replacement Tricolour was hoisted.

Watched grimly by the Berliners, and with satisfaction by the staff of the French Embassy, the parade was carried out with true Prussian precision by an immaculate guard and band of the Reichswehr. But, as the guard marched off at the parade step, the band played 'The March of Entry into Paris'. *Armeemärsche*, J. Toeche-Mittler (Kurt Vowinckel Verlag, 1971).

5. The early marches were arranged by Georg Abraham Schneider, director of music at the Royal Opera House in Berlin. Schneider was a chamber musician, and this is reflected in the instrumentation and tone colour of the marches he arranged.

6. Other sources claim that the term derives from the horn sounded by the *Flügelmeister* – the 'wing master' – during the hunt in Germany, perhaps to control the line of beaters driving the game towards the guns. *The New Oxford Companion to Music* (Oxford University Press, 1983).

7. Wieprecht's first compositions are scored for a valved brass ensemble based on the Eb cornet, Bb cornet, Eb trumpet, tenor horn, euphonium and bass trombone, the earliest record of an all-brass band.

3. In June 1851, during the Great Exhibition, the first Grand Military Concert took place at the Crystal Palace in Hyde Park in London, performed by the massed bands of the 1st and 2nd Regiments of Life Guards; the Royal Horse Guards (The Blues); the Royal Artillery; the Grenadier Guards; the Coldstream Guards; and Scots Fusilier Guards.

9. The 'trio' was the centre section of a minuet, or a march constructed as a minuet, which so many eighteenth-century marches resembled in form and tempo. Such sections were originally scored for two oboes and a bassoon, hence the name. The term is now applied to the third section of a march.

10. *Marche Militaire No 1* by Franz Schubert (1797–1828) is an example of this approach. The first of three, originally published as piano duets, it was composed about 1822, when the impact of the improved road communications was at its height. Popular as a piece for orchestra or military band, it was played to great effect by the massed corps of drums at the Aldershot Tattoo in 1932.

11. In the dying days of peace in the late summer of 1939, the band of the 2nd Battalion Royal Scots Fusiliers, wearing scarlet doublets, tartan trousers and diced glengarries, played of a Sunday afternoon at the gate of Redford Barracks for the entertainment of the many strollers round the suburb of Colinton outside Edinburgh.

CHAPTER IX
The Military Band (3)

~

As we have seen, the earliest military or regimental bands had been engaged by the officers primarily for their own entertainment, and were composed of civilian musicians, eight or ten in number, playing oboes, trumpets, horns, clarinets, or bassoons. The entire cost was borne by the officers, who, not unnaturally, regarded the band as their own property, at their sole disposal. Even after a somewhat grudging authority was given in 1803 for one serjeant to act as Master of the Band, and one soldier per company to be employed as a musician, making a band of ten at the most, the whole expense of the instruments and their upkeep fell on the officers.

By any reckoning, the expense was considerable The records of the Royal Scots disclose that in 1802 clothing for the band came to over £400 in the case of the 2nd Battalion, with a further £200 being spent on clothing three years later. In 1807, swords for the musicians cost almost £100. A recurrent item of expenditure in all four battalions of the 1st Royals, as they were then, was the cost of buying and emblazoning, and sometimes of replacing, the twenty brass drums each battalion held. This would appear to indicate that the drums issued from Ordnance sources were wooden and that smart regiments with a reputation to maintain, like the 1st Royals, preferred to buy brass drums from a private source, perhaps for their enhanced tone and appearance. The drum major's staff, and shoulder belts, bugles, fife cases – then made of brass with the regimental device – caps, feathers, all had to be bought and paid for, although some of the expense may have been recoverable from the Government.

The 1st Royals had been unique among the regiments of the line in that they had been allowed to hold a drum major and one piper on the strength of the 1st Battalion, but when, in 1769, the 2nd Battalion applied to be granted the same privilege, King George III refused, saying that the regiment's honour and reputation were secure without the addition of further privileges. It appears, however, that other battalions enlisted pipers. In

1st Battalion, The King's Own Scottish Borderers, Military Band, Lucknow, India, 1914
A typical military band at full strength, from the days when the infantry marched. The bandmaster wears the blue frock coat of his calling with Leslie tartan trousers and diced forage cap. The officers of the Lowland regiments wore this head-dress with the blue patrol jacket in certain orders of dress until 1939. (RHQ King's Own Scottish Borderers)

2nd Scottish Rifles, Military Band, Landi Kotal, Khyber Pass, India, 1929
Taken at the end of the 2nd Scottish Rifles overseas tour, the band wears, hot-weather, 'playing-out' order with white jackets and Douglas tartan trousers. Note the black belts and buttons worn by rifle regiments. The commanding officer and adjutant sit in front, beside the bandmaster and band serjeant. (S.J. Sellwood Collection)

1807 the 4th Battalion of the 1st Royals bought a 'pair' of bagpipes for one Donald MacDonald at the order of Colonel Hay. In 1812, the Colonel of the 1st Royals, the Duke of Kent – he of kenthorn fame – tried to enlist no fewer than forty-four 'complete' pipers, one for each company in the four battalions of the Royals. It is, therefore, all the more surprising that pipers seem to have entirely disappeared from the regiment thereafter until they were authorised, but at regimental expense, in 1881. Not until 1918 were the Lowland regiments placed on the same footing as the Highland, with a pipe major and five pipers in addition to the establishment.

The band might have been a costly affair and a burden on an officer's purse, but, as we have seen, in the Peninsular War it took the field along with its battalion, playing as and when it could. On 15th June, the eve of the Battle of Quatre Bras which preceded that of Waterloo – the 'three days' fight', as Serjeant Wheeler of the 51st Light Infantry accurately described it – the Duchess of Richmond gave a ball, which was to become one of the most celebrated in military, if not in social, history. The ball was held in Brussels, Headquarters of the Duke of Wellington, Commander-in-Chief of the Allied Army, with many of the British troops being billeted in Brussels itself. During the ball, attended by many of the regimental and staff officers stationed locally, a report came that the French were advancing, led by the great Napoleon himself, thus taking the Allies, including Wellington, by surprise. The troops were turned out, a scene of high drama, the atmosphere well captured by the poet Lord Byron, in 'Childe Harold's Pilgrimage':

And wild and high the 'Camerons' Gathering' rose,
The war-note of Lochiel, which Albynn's hills
Have heard, and heard, too, have her Saxon foes:-
How in the noon of night that pibroch thrills,
Savage and shrill! But with the breath which fills
Their mountain-pipe, so fill the mountaineers
With the fierce daring which instils
The stirring memory of a thousand years,
And Evan's, Donald's fame rings in each clansman's ears!

Byron's mother was Catherine Gordon of Gight in

Aberdeenshire, a distant relative of the Duke of Gordon, and he had been christened George Gordon Byron. Much of his childhood had been spent on Deeside, in the heart of the Gordon country, under the shadow of 'Dark Lochnagar', subject of a later poem.

The 92nd had been raised by the Duke of Gordon as the Gordon Highlanders, but was commanded in 1815 by Lieutenant-Colonel John Cameron of Fassiefern in Lochaber, Clan Cameron country, but of which the Duke of Gordon was feudal superior, and from where many of the 92nd had been recruited, some by Cameron of Lochiel, Chief of Clan Cameron, himself. Byron's reference to 'The Camerons' Gathering' might therefore be to the 92nd, and not to the 79th Cameron Highlanders – recruited partly in Lochaber by Alan Cameron of Erracht in defiance of the Duke of Gordon – to whom it has always been ascribed in regimental folklore. Fassiefern was killed in the encounter battle fought the day after the ball at Quatre Bras.

There is a tradition that the pipe tune played to rouse the soldiers of the Highland regiments in the early hours of that fateful morning was not 'The Camerons' Gathering'. Several tunes have been known by that name, one of them called *Chlanna nan con, thigibh a seo 's gheibh sibh feòil* – 'Sons of dogs, come here and get meat' – the slogan or war-cry of Clan Cameron. The tune said to have been played to turn the soldiers out is 'Lord Breadalbane's March', the tune of a song from Strathspey in the Central Highlands. 'People of this Glen, Awake!', the song begins, and goes on to warn that James Grant of Carron on Speyside, a notorious ruffian and reiver, has been seen in the glen with his henchmen. 'People of this Glen' is also said to have been played in the gloaming of the winter's evening before the massacre of Glencoe in February 1692, in a last-minute attempt to warn the people of the treacherous attack that was planned for the next morning. It was played by Hugh MacKenzie, piper to Robert Campbell of Glenlyon, who commanded the soldiers of the Earl of Argyll's Regiment who carried out the massacre. The tune, and its connotations, would have been well known to the Highland soldiers of the Black Watch, the 79th and the 92nd who heard it in the first light of that June morning.

106

Despite the foregoing, it is significant that when the 79th marched off on the road to Quatre Bras and Waterloo, it was not to the sound of the pipes, as might be expected, but to the music of their band. The tune they played was 'Loudon's Bonnie Woods and Braes', more familiar now as a strathspey tune for dancing, but perfectly suitable as a march in common time. Given the situation and the occasion, however, the words seem highly appropriate for the time:

> Loudon's bonnie woods and braes, I maun leave them a',
> lassie;
> Wha can thole when Britain's faes wad gie Britons law,
> lassie?
> Wha wad shun the field of danger? Wha tae fame wad be a
> stranger?
> Now when freedom bids avenge her, wha wad shun her ca',
> lassie?

The years that followed the successful completion of the Waterloo campaign were marked by an increased emphasis on parade-ground display and impact, at least for those troops stationed at home. In 1830, the bands were ordered into white coats, while the drummers, who had hitherto been dressed in 'reversed' colours − their coats were the colour of the regimental facings − were given red, like the rank and file.[1] The trend had been for some time towards different tartans for the band, and scarf plaids and dirks also began to appear, although the weapon of the bandsmen was the broadsword in the Highland and the band sword in the Lowland regiments, which we must remember were at this time dressed as infantry of the line, where the swords issued to the band were curved and were worn from waist belts with slings, unlike the shoulder belts of the Highlanders.

It seems ludicrous that at a period when so much emphasis was placed on dress, and in which so many exotic band uniforms were tolerated, that no attention whatsoever was paid to what the bands played, or how they played it. The instrumentation of the band depended entirely on the preferences or whims of the foreign civilian bandmaster, as did the arrangements in which the band played its repertoire. Nemesis came during the early days of the Crimean War of 1854–1856. The Allied armies, the

French, British and Turkish, were concentrated at Scutari, on the shores of the Bosphorus opposite what is now Istanbul. A parade, attended by all the dignitaries of the armies, was held to celebrate the birthday of Queen Victoria. All went well until the time for the Royal Salute, when the massed bands of the British Army struck up the National Anthem, 'but not with that perfect unanimity which could be desired'. Each band played its own arrangement, in its own key and pitch, and at its own tempo. In terms of military public relations, the parade was a disaster.[2]

After the war, HRH The Duke of Cambridge, grandson of King George III and cousin of Queen Victoria, became Commander-in-Chief of the British Army, a position he was to hold for almost forty years. He had commanded the 1st Division in the Crimea, although whether he had been present at the débâcle at Scutari is not clear. He had heard the excellent bands of the French and, later, the Sardinian contingents, and for whatever reason, he gave his weighty backing to the plan which now matured, that of setting up a school of military music for the Army. The authorised strength of the band had by then risen to one serjeant and twenty bandsmen, which was, in theory, enough to provide a musically effective band on the square or in the bandstand. In practice, as was to be found out yet again a century and a half later, a band of this size is rarely complete, there being always one or two bandsmen absent, with or without leave, or sick, or on one of the innumerable excuses the ever-fertile mind of the soldier can always devise. It was the accepted practice for the band to be augmented by 'acting bandsmen' attached nominally to the different companies of the battalion, but employed permanently with the band, returning to the ranks before an official inspection and rejoining the band thereafter. In some cases, the effective strength of the band was almost doubled as a result.

The Royal Military School of Music began life as the Military Music class in 1857, after the usual wrangle about who was to pay for what. It was accommodated at Kneller Hall at Twickenham, then in the country outside London, always an important point, as the further the soldiers were from the fleshpots, stews and temptations of a big city, the more attention they paid to their work. The money to run the school was subscribed by all the regiments in the Army which maintained bands. The staff consisted of a commandant from the half-pay list, the retired list of the period, re-employed and paid as a captain. There was a superintendent and there were professors teaching the various band instruments. Eighty students attended the first course, and four women were officially attached to the class, presumably to do the students' laundry, three being the wives of students, the fourth the mother of a 'lad', as older 'boys' were known.[3]

The Scottish regiments sent nine students. The 1st Royals sent two 'Lads'; the 25th King's Own Borderers a drummer and a bandsman, indicating that the 25th had a corps of drums at the time, and that the drummer sent to Kneller Hall was probably a flute player. The Black Watch sent a lance-corporal and a boy. From the 79th came a lance-corporal, one of the first to qualify on the course, later, appointed bandmaster of the 3rd Buffs. The 93rd sent a bandsman.[4]

The aim of the course was to instruct bandsmen to a higher degree of proficiency than was possible within the battalion or regiment and to produce NCOs fit to be bandmasters. This included training the bandsmen in their separate instruments, as well as in the production of a functioning band that could meet all the musical needs of the regiment from providing music on the line of march, the most important aspect as far as the regiment itself was concerned. From the point of view of the band president, and of the bandsmen themselves, playing on the march was a chore to be got through, the all-important factor being the ability of the band to attract paid outside engagements and the skill of the bandmaster in securing them, preferably well away from the regiment and as lucrative as possible, to the benefit of both the bandsmen and the band fund, which took a percentage of all paid engagements.

The unspoken aim of the course was to oust, in time, the foreign and civilian bandmasters, replacing them with graduates from Kneller Hall. This was achieved, but it took a long time, the last civilian director of music retiring in 1906, albeit with an honorary commission. The post-Crimea reforms made provision for the appointment of a bandmaster serjeant, presumably trained at Kneller Hall. The band itself consisted of a band serjeant, a band corporal and twenty bandsmen. The bandmaster serjeant ranked as a 1st Class staff serjeant, his precedence with, but after, the serjeant major, the schoolmaster, the quarter-master serjeant, and the serjeant instructor in musketry. The drum major also ranked as a 1st Class staff serjeant, but was held against the establishment of drummers, whereas the pipe major, another of the élite 1st Class staff serjeants, had his own niche in the Highland regiments and the Scots Guards.

The badge of rank of the 1st Class staff serjeants was a four-bar chevron originally worn point down between the elbow and the shoulder, surmounted in the case of the serjeant major by a crown, while the drum major wore an embroidered drum above his. In time, the chevrons were ordered to be worn point up, between the wrist and the elbow, and there they remain to this day, worn as a badge of rank and office by drum and pipe majors both in the Army and in civilian pipe bands. The bandmaster serjeant wore no chevrons, but was distinguished by gold shoulder cords. His band serjeant wore three chevrons, and ranked with the platoon serjeants.

In 1881, the rank of warrant-officer was introduced, to which both the serjeant major and the bandmaster serjeant were promoted. By then all the fancy and fanciful uniforms of earlier periods had disappeared. Since 1873, the band had worn the scarlet tunic or doublet, which became the dress of all the Scottish regiments in 1881, kilted and non-kilted. Some distinctions remained. The bands of the Highland Light Infantry wore scarf plaids and feathered bonnets with their tartan trousers, with a red hackle in the bonnet, as did the band – and the drummers – of the Seaforth Highlanders. The Argyll and Sutherland Highlanders bandsmen also wore a red hackle and a white sporran with two black tassels in place of the 'swinging six' of the rank and file. When the Leslie tartan was introduced into the King's Own Scottish Borderers, the bands were given scarf plaids in the same tartan. The Gordon Highlanders' bandsmen had a red and white hackle in the feathered bonnet, while those of the Camerons kept up the black leather waist belt they had worn in the days of the white band doublet. Thus it was that in many different ways the sense of separate identities was kept alive, setting the regiments apart from each other and the bands from the rest of their battalions, and this was to endure through the two world wars of the next century, right up until the regimental bands themselves disappeared in 1994.

Notes

1. Some regiments had dressed the 'Musick' in white coats from the beginning. The idea of a separate band tartan also dated from the earliest days of the Highland regimental bands, the indications being that the Royal Stuart was the most popular, to the extent that it became known as 'the Musick tartan'.
2. *A Hundred Years of Military Music*, Lt-Col P.L. Binns (The Blackmore Press, 1959).
3. The sons of soldiers on the Married Roll could be enlisted at the age of fourteen for training as pipers, drummers, buglers, bandsmen or tailors. They were attested as 'boys' and on reaching their fifteenth birthday were 'promoted' to 'lad'.
4. Lt-Col P.L. Binns, op. cit.

1st Battalion, The Argyll and Sutherland Highlanders, Pipers, 1912
This photograph shows eighteen pipers and the officers of the pipes committee, which administered the perennially impoverished pipe fund. The pipers wear the green serge jacket, worn overseas in cold weather, with regimental shooulder shells and diamond-shaped buttons. The pipers of the 91st wore the boar's head of Clan Campbell above the buckle of the shoulder belt, those of the 93rd, the 2nd battalion, the wild cat of Sutherland. (RHQ Argyll and Sutherland Highlanders)

1st Battalion, The Argyll and Sutherland Highlanders, Malta, 1912

The 91st, as the 1st preferred to be called, is parading for the general officer commanding on the Palace square at Valetta before embarking for India on the next leg of its overseas tour. The battalion is at the 'Present'; the band playing the regulation 'first part of a slow march'. The battalion, including the drummers and bandsmen, is wearing full marching order with packs and khaki spats; the seventeen pipers are excused packs, but wear their greatcoats en banderole over the right shoulder, making it awkward to reach the chanter when playing. Note the white hackle worn on the left of the Wolseley helmets. (RHQ Argyll and Sutherland Highlanders)

CHAPTER X
THE PIPERS

~

We have noted how the approval and support of the officers was a prerequisite when any deviation from the strictly practical and somewhat tedious business of basic soldiering was involved, or when the objective was simply to make the military life more bearable, both on and off duty. In addition, any efforts to increase the impact of a battalion or regiment either on others similarly placed or on the civilian population had to have the support, moral and especially financial, of the officers. It is now time to take a look at the influence of the Scottish, and particularly the Highland, regiments in this business of going one better than the competition, an art at which the Scottish regiments were in time to excel.

In the hierarchy of the clan, the chief had held the clan land on behalf of the clansmen, a theory which proved to have no validity at all in the years after Culloden in 1746. Thereafter, the chiefs had treated the land as their own personal property, to be disposed of as they saw fit. But in the old days, the chief had sub-let parts of the clan lands to his relations or other men of substance and standing. These were the tacksmen, who in turn rented out part of their tacks to the poorer or more humble members of the clan. When the clan had taken the field as a military unit, these tacksmen had provided the intermediate and junior officers, and when the clan system, moribund though it might have been, was invoked in aid of the recruiting effort during the eighteenth century, it was to the tacksmen that the chiefs turned when looking for men to complete their so-called 'clan' regiments. It was believed, in many cases rightly, that the tacksmen were more in touch with the remnant of the clan still occupying its ancient homeland, than the chief, who now tended to live most of the time in London, the centre of power, patronage, and influence, both political and financial.

The tacksmen's reward was a commission in the new regiment, their rank, in the bad old days when recruits were at a premium, depending on the number of men they could induce to enlist – twenty recruits procured an ensigncy, the lowest officer rank, thirty a commission as lieutenant and forty might bring a captaincy. These commissions were all worth money under the purchase system then in force, which lasted until 1871 and was intended to ensure that the officers of the Army had a financial interest in maintaining the status quo and to discourage them from political meddling. Each step up the promotion ladder also had to be paid for, but an officer could sell his commission at any time, very often for more than the official rate, especially one in a distinguished regiment of the line like the 1st Royals, or a London-based and therefore socially influential regiment of the foot guards or household cavalry, where, however, the style of life which an officer was expected to maintain was extremely expensive. Much the same applied to the cavalry of the line.[1]

In the case of impecunious Highland farmers, for such the tacksmen were, his commission was often his sole financial resource, either through its market value by direct sale, or by the right to half pay for life which its possession conferred on its holder. Its value could be enhanced by succession to a death vacancy in battle; such a step was free, but the family of the unfortunate deceased lost everything. The manifest injustice of the situation had led to the first rudimentary pension scheme for widows which came into effect during the Napoleonic Wars.

These then were the men who led the Highland regiments in the wars against France during the eighteenth century and who helped to set off the explosion of interest in all things Highland which followed the final and decisive Waterloo campaign of 1815. Another factor was the publication of Sir Walter Scott's novel *Waverley*, the first to portray the Highlander as a 'Noble Savage', all of whose sons were valiant and daughters virtuous. The culmination of the process was the State visit of King George IV to Scotland in 1822, at which the festivities, stage managed by Sir Walter, assisted by Major-General David Stewart of Garth, were predominantly Highland in character, if not in authenticity.

David Stewart was a Highlander by birth, a native Gaelic-speaker and an ardent Scottish patriot. In 1822, he had just published his *Sketches of the Highlanders*, a study of his native country and its people, which included short histories of the Highland regiments then existing, Their deeds lost little in the

telling, particularly those of the Black Watch – which he calls
the Old Highland Regiment – and the 2nd Battalion of the 78th
Ross-shire Buffs, in both of which Stewart had served. But
whatever his shortcomings as an objective historian, Stewart did
make one telling point. It was pride in the exploits of the kilted
regiments which rekindled and revitalised Scotland's sense of
identity as a nation in her own right and prevented her from
becoming merely the province of North Britain, as had been the
trend ever since the Act of Union in 1707, the Royal North
British Dragoons – the Scots Greys – and the Royal North
British Fusiliers – the Scots Fusiliers – having been deliberately
so named in 1707 and 1712 respectively.

The kilt was now the passport to instant fame and glory. The
charge of the Scots Greys at Waterloo, with the soldiers of the
92nd Gordon Highlanders clinging to their stirrup leathers,
apocryphal though the story was, caught the public imagination,
and totally overshadowed the quick thinking and tactical
expertise which had shattered the final attack of Napoleon's
Imperial Guard at the end of the day. As a later historian of the
British Army was to write of the highly distinguished 38th Foot
– later the South Staffordshire Regiment – 'If this regiment had
worn the kilt, theirs would be a household name!'

The year 1815 also saw the end of that period in which the
Highland and, to some extent, the Lowland, regiments were
officered by men from what was essentially the same social
background as the soldiers. 'The Scotch were most engaged, so
there is no officer wounded whom one knows,' thus wrote Lady
Georgiana Lennox, daughter of the Duke of Richmond and belle
of her Mama's celebrated ball, which had been positively ruined
by the unexpected advance of the French. She was writing about
the Battle of Quatre Bras, the encounter battle fought two days
before Waterloo, and by 'Scotch' she meant Highlanders, as the
brunt of the fighting had been sustained by the Black Watch, the
79th Cameron, and the 92nd Gordon Highlanders, and, equally
closely involved and suffering equally heavily, the 3rd Battalion
of the 1st Royals, under Major Colin Campbell. All fought with
steadiness and courage and suffered severely, even if their
officers failed to attain Lady Georgiana's social criteria.

After Waterloo, the Army was reduced in size, with the
majority of the officers being placed on half pay, while the

soldiers were discharged. The memoirs of Elizabeth Grant of Rothiemurchus describe the half-pay Highland officers, often from humble backgrounds, who farmed in Strathspey after the war. Their places were taken by men from an entirely different social level, financially better off and, consequently, able to afford the much heavier expenses of peacetime life in the officers mess of a smart regiment. Although frequently devoid of Highland or even Scottish connections, these men came from a sophisticated background, their recreations were those of their own kind, and they were at home in the fashionable society of the Regency. In short, they were men whom Lady Georgiana would have 'known'!

It might have been expected that the influx of men of this stamp would have led to the gradual erosion of the distinctive character of the Highland regiments. On the contrary: they seized every opportunity to emphasise those unique attributes which set the Highland regiments apart, and which were, after all, the aspects which had attracted the new breed of officers in the first place. It was through them, and the influence they were able to exercise through their family connections, that several of the former Highland regiments, which had been removed from the Highland establishment in 1809, were able to recover their Highland status as what were termed 'non-kilted Highland corps', that is, Highland regiments wearing tartan trousers, it being the tartan and not the kilt, which was at this stage the outward and visible distinction of the Highland soldier. With the tartan trousers came all the accoutrements of the Highland dress in its early Victorian form, the scarf plaid and its brooch, the broadsword, the dirk, and diced band round the cap. Contrary to what might have been expected, this new breed of officers was only too happy to be allowed to spend lavishly on the embellishment of the Highland dress, whether the regiment wore the kilt or the tartan trousers.

After the uniform, it was the music which was the most prominent feature of the regiments. The pipers, from time immemorial, had been held against the authorised establishment, the number of men the Government was willing to pay for, so that in theory the battalion was that number of fighting men short. In other words the pipers, clothed at the expense of the officers, who also provided their instruments, represented a reduction in the fighting strength of the battalion. It was this last point that was the dangerous one; nobody cared what the officers did with their own money, but it was another matter when it came to defrauding the public by diverting men from their proper duties, as the administrators saw it.

It used to be suggested that the rules were sometimes circumvented by holding a piper against a drummer's vacancy and doing without the drummer, but the number of drummers was by no means excessive given their duties, especially since the fifers counted as drummers, and it is clear that at this stage the Scottish regiments maintained a corps of drums and fifes. Nor was there ever any attempt to conceal the pipers, hence the threats and fulminations of empurpled inspecting general officers at the sight of the pipers, totally unauthorised, on the half-yearly inspection parade.

Not that the threats of inspecting generals worried the new breed of Highland officer much. They were wealthy enough not to have to look to the Army for their livelihood. Nor were they worried about their future careers, as few served on after they had come into their inheritance or after they had married. They had paid for their commissions and for their promotions, and well knew that they could sell out for a price far in excess of the 'regulation', which limited the amount payable for each step, at any time they wished, commissions in Highland regiments, like those in the cavalry, being particularly sought after by wealthy parents eager to set their sons up in such a fashionable branch of the Army, and one so splendidly attired as well.

The pipers, being unofficial and under nobody's control except the officers, could be treated as show pieces, a process highly congenial to the pipers themselves who, then as now, enjoyed parading before an admiring audience. Accordingly, they could be dressed in whatever variety of the Highland dress took the officers' fancy; and what these costumes lacked in authenticity, they made up in splendour, and this, in turn, instilled in the pipers a pride in, and concern with, their own appearance which more than repaid the expense involved.

All armies have an unofficial 'pecking order' into which their component units range themselves. A place in the order depends on many factors, not simply martial prowess. Style and presentation have much to do with it, and in the not invariably friendly rivalry between regiments of the British Army Highland battalions are thought to have an inbuilt advantage which is not always felt to be justified, a feeling in which the Lowland regiments, regarding the Highland as overdressed 'Johnny come latelies', lacking antiquity, might at one time have been said to share. The principal advantage the Highlanders had was, of course, the kilt, with the pipes a close second, although it was to be some time before the pipers were placed in front of the band of musick and behind the pioneers, a position for which their outlandish dress and music might have been thought to have entitled them from the start. Argument raged for years about who should lead, the band or the pipers. Early prints show the pipers firmly at the rear of the band and usually behind the drums and fifes. The question finally came to a head in 1871. It was referred to Queen Victoria. Her characteristically no-nonsense decision was 'The pipers must always lead.'[2]

Until peace came in 1815, the pipers had played either individually or in small groups. They are on record as having played Retreat in the villages of Spain; at Waterloo, they played from time to time inside the squares formed to receive the French cavalry; and at that battle one played outside the square as the French cavalry advanced. If they had played on the march, it had been more to cheer the soldiers up than to keep them in step, the roads being narrow and rough and the soldiers heavily laden. All this was to change with the arrival of the metalled road, which was to lead to the emergence of the bagpipe-and-drum combination and an avalanche of compositions in march tempo for the bagpipe itself.

If the pipers were to form part of the head of the column, to use the French term, they would have been expected to play, and it would have been pointless to have the pipers playing if they were unable to keep the marching troops in step and time. For this reason, any marching musical combination must have a strong percussion element to pick out and emphasise the beat, the bass drum and, above all, the bass drummer being particularly important. A bass drummer who could maintain a steady beat was worth his weight in gold to the troops marching behind. Of course, two such paragons were required, one in the band, and a second in the drums, if an even pace was to be maintained when the two changed over.

THE PIPERS

In the Highland bagpipe, the volume is constant, and the sound continuous. For anyone not closely familiar with pipe music, or not gifted with a musical ear, it is very difficult to detect the beat, which is why at the so-called Highland balls, a drummer has to accompany the pipers when reels are danced, as those dancers unused to dancing to the pipes alone find it impossible to pick up and follow the beat. The same applies in the matter of marching to the pipes; some form of percussion accompaniment has to be provided if the marching soldiers are to be able to hold the step and keep the time.

The obvious answer was to detail some of the drummers to accompany the pipers by playing an appropriate beating to the tune the pipers played, as they already did for the fifers. Indeed, so obvious was this solution that nobody ever thought of recording when it first became standard practice. Contemporary photographs are of no help here, as they all show the battalion drawn up in formal order, band leading, followed by the drums and fifes, with the pipers, usually only about five or six, behind the fifers. In many of such photographs, it is impossible to tell where one begins and the other finishes, so haphazard is the formation by modern standards.

However, there is other evidence that the pipers and at least some of the drummers played together in the sense that the pipers played a tune, and the drummers a beating. In 1848, a vessel transporting a Highland regiment from Gibraltar to Canada encountered thick fog in the St Lawrence river. The pipers and drummers were ordered up on to the forecastle to warn other ships ahead 'by their discord', as the account puts it. Several unrelated pieces of evidence support the theory that it was about this time that the first pipe bands began to feature in the life of the regiments. In 1848, the 78th Highlanders was stationed at Belgaum in south-west India, recouping their strength after having lost five hundred and thirty-five officers and soldiers and two hundred and two wives and children in a cholera epidemic while stationed at Sukkur in the province of Sind. When the battalion left Belgaum for Bombay, an unidentified piper composed a march in 2/4 time of four measures which he called 'The 78th's Farewell to Belgaum', and obligingly dated 1848. While at Bombay, the 78th provided a detachment to garrison Aden, and there Piper James Mauchline composed a similar march which he named, appropriately, 'The Barren Rocks of Aden', a tune familiar to all Scots. The first two measures went well on the flute, so the march was taken up by many corps of drums, eventually becoming a standby, played frequently by the drums of English regiments which had no idea of its provenance and who would accuse the pipers of stealing their tune.

'The Barren Rocks' has been played and whistled wherever Scots soldiers have been stationed. A former generation used to sing to the air of the first measure:

> See the laddie ower there
> Wi' the tartan kilt and the twa legs bare,
> And a' the ladies they declare
> 'She's a fine braw chiel is her nainsel'.

This is an example of the kind of fun which used to be poked at Gaelic speaking soldiers, always in the minority. The last line mocks the difficulty which native Gaelic speakers had with the English language. 'She's a fine braw chiel' means a handsome sturdy lad; 'her nainsel', her own self, i.e. the speaker.

Some thousands of miles to the west, the 79th Cameron Highlanders left Gibraltar for Canada, also in 1848. Pipe Major John MacDonald composed another four-part march in 2/4 time which he named 'The 79th's Farewell to Gibraltar', perhaps with tongue in cheek, as the transport lay off Gibraltar for some days, delayed by contrary winds. These three marches are, from their form and structure, intended to be played by the marching pipe band. None is difficult in the technical sense and all will stand repetition without becoming tedious. It is from this seminal era that we can trace the evolution of the bagpipe march as a musical form in its own right.

From the time of Waterloo in 1815, continuous efforts had been made to have the pipers recognised as an integral part of the musical resources of the Scottish regiments, as at this period we have evidence of pipers in three out of the four old Lowland regiments – the Scots Fusiliers, the King's Own Borderers and the Cameronians – as well as the Highland regiments, kilted and trousered. It is often claimed that the 'Horse Guards', the War Office of the time, resolutely refused to recognise the need for pipers at all, but correspondence of the period reveals that the authorities had no objection whatsoever, merely insisting that the number of bandsmen and drummers be correspondingly reduced. Ten pipers, one per company, was the number applied for, and it was the insistence that the number of bandsmen be reduced from twenty-one to eighteen and the drummers from seventeen to ten, including the drum major, which stuck in the craw of the Scottish regiments.

But in early 1854, war with Russia loomed. On 11th February, the Horse Guards authorised every battalion in the Army to recruit to complete their numbers to one thousand rank and file, and described how these soldiers were to be divided between the six 'service' companies, which were to go abroad, and the four 'depot' companies, which remained at home, employed on internal security duties – there had been much political unrest – and in training recruits to replace the losses in the service companies. Tucked away in a footnote was the authorisation for each Highland regiment to hold one pipe major, who was to rank as a serjeant, and five pipers in excess of the establishment, all six to go abroad with the service companies, which is why six were allowed and not ten, and is the first indication that it was recognised that the place of the piper was with his comrades in the field, in the ancient tradition of the instrument.

The kilted Highland regiments involved were the 42nd or Black Watch; the 78th Ross-shire Buffs; the 79th Cameron; the 92nd Gordon; and the 93rd Sutherland Highlanders. The non-kilted were the 71st Highland Light Infantry; the 72nd Duke of Albany's Own; and the 74th Highlanders, the last two restored to the Highland establishment in 1823 and 1845 respectively, In 1853, the Scots Fusilier Guards had appointed a Serjeant Ewan Henderson, aged twenty-two, and son of a serjeant in the Gordons, as pipe major of the 1st Battalion, but when the Crimean War ended in 1856, Ewan was ordered to return to duty as a serjeant.[3] By that time the Duke of Cambridge was Colonel of the Fusilier Guards – and as he was also Commander-in-Chief of the Army by that time – he exerted his influence to procure the authority for each battalion of the Scots Fusilier Guards to hold a pipe major and five pipers on establishment. The first pipe major of the 2nd Battalion was Donald MacPherson, who transferred from the Black Watch; and it is, perhaps, a result of this connection that the Scots Guards play as their 'Lights Out' call, the march 'Donald Blue', as do the Black Watch and, indeed, did the Gordons, and that the pipe bag covers of the Scots Guards are in the Black Watch tartan.

The senior Lowland regiments refused to take this lying down, and in 1862 the King's Own Borderers and The Cameronians were permitted three pipers per battalion, it being conceded that permission for the Borderers to have pipers was lost in time, as was their right to wear the Royal Stuart tartan. The Cameronians' case rested on the evidence of the bandmaster – 'a very respectable man' – who recalled that there had been pipers in the battalion when he had joined it thirty years before. The catch was that the pipers were to be clothed and equipped as such entirely at regimental expense and no extra men were allowed. So it was with the Scots Fusiliers, too, which was allowed three pipers per battalion at regimental expense and to be held against the strength of the band, a proviso to which we can be certain no attention whatsoever was paid.

In 1864, the 91st Argyllshire Regiment had joined the non-kilted Highland corps, acquiring Campbell of Cawdor tartan trousers, a pipe major, and five pipers. Scottish titles were restored in 1862 to what then became the 73rd Perthshire and the 75th Stirlingshire Regiments. The 99th Lanarkshire had been so named when raised in 1824. But although these three, like the Scots Fusiliers, the Borderers and The Cameronians, were allowed a diced band to their forage caps as a mark of their national origin, they seem to have been content to leave it at that. The 90th Perthshire Light Infantry seem to have been equally content to let their name alone convey their Scottish roots.

The senior regiment of the British Army, the 1st Royals, despite all the social pressures to the contrary aroused by the intense interest taken in Scotland by Queen Victoria, whose father had been Colonel of the Royals, seem to have quietly but deliberately let their Scots connections slip in the years after Waterloo, when they were colloquially known as the 'Scots Royals'. From 1781 until 1838, the Highland Society of London held annual and, latterly, triennial, competitions for the playing of *piobaireachd*, the classical music of the Highland bagpipe. Donald MacEarchar of the Scots Royals, competing against the finest pipers in Scotland, was in the prize list on the three occasions on which he competed in 1793, 1796 and 1798. In 1798 he was awarded the first prize and so was debarred, under the rules of the competition, from entering again. In 1799, Hugh MacGregor, pipe major to the Scots Royals was placed third; and in 1813 Francis MacNicoll, piper to the Scots Royals, was placed fifth.

Thereafter, no piper of the Royal Scots features in the annals of this or any other major piping competition until 1905. The memoirs of Sir George Bell, who commanded in succession both battalions of the regiment between 1826 and 1856, makes no mention of pipers or piping, although he mentions the band and choir and only obliquely refers to the Scottish roots and connections of the regiment, to which he was extremely proud to belong. He was an Irishman; did he have a hand in the suppression of the pipers? Or was the Scots connection simply unpopular in the regiment? In 1868, the glengarry forage cap, of impeccably Scottish provenance, was introduced into the Army to replace the round hummel bonnet, of equally Scottish origin. The 1st Royals had worn the hummel bonnet with the red band of a Royal Regiment, and the proud numeral '1' above it. In its place, the soldiers were issued with a glengarry cap with a diced border, which they proceeded to kick round the barrack-rooms, claiming it made them look like boys from a children's home![4]

Three years later, their title was changed to the 1st or Royal Scots Regiment. But pipers were not reintroduced until 1881.

The Highland regiments might have owed the approval of their pipers to the indirect influence of Queen Victoria. Regarding herself very much as a soldier's daughter, she took an intense personal interest in her Army. By 1854, her love affair with the Highlands was in full flower and it was never to fade. On earlier visits, she had stayed with some of the more wealthy Highland magnates, all of whom maintained personal pipers. The Queen decided she must have one herself. Her first piper served her from 1843 until he had to retire from ill-health in 1854. Piper Thomas Hardie of the 79th, a fine-looking man and a good piper, was chosen to replace him. A Gaelic-speaker from Skye, he seemed fair game to two of the Cockney footmen, who sought to make him ridiculous by mocking his Skye accent. After vainly warning them, Hardie threw off his jacket and gave both a sound thrashing. Queen Victoria was famously tolerant of her Highland servants, but this was too much! Hardie was returned to the 79th, becoming pipe major in 1860. The next contender was Pipe Major William Ross of the Black Watch, who held the post until his death in 1891. Since the accession of King George V, the pipers to the reigning monarch have been selected from qualified pipe majors of the Scottish regiments, Highland or Lowland and the Scots Guards.

In the meantime, the Highland regiments had gone off to war in the Crimea, each with its pipe major, and five pipers. We shall be hearing more of them there.

Notes

1. *The Military Adventures of Johnny Newcome*, by an Officer (Methuen & Co, 1904).
2. Historical Records of The 42nd Royal Highlanders (Royal Highland Regiment, the Black Watch). In the Scots Guards the order of march is the Regimental Band, Corps of Drums and Pipers, reflecting their regimental seniority. However, when the Regimental Band is not on parade, the Pipers lead, followed by the Corps of Drums.
3. The Scots Guards was named the Scots Fusilier Guards in 1831 for its part in the defence of the farm of Hougoumont during the battle of Waterloo. The titles 'Fusiliers' and 'Light Infantry' were bestowed in recognition of past services, e.g. in 1836 the 5th or Northumberland Foot was renamed the 5th or Northumberland Fusiliers in recognition of its record in the Peninsular War and in 1858, the 32nd (The Cornwall) Foot became the 32nd (Cornwall) Light Infantry for its defence of Lucknow during the Indian Mutiny.

The Scots Guards 'welcomed back their old name' in 1877, the occasion marked by a pipe march composed by the Duke of Atholl. However, it was decided to maintain the old fusilier custom whereby the flank companies were so named, unlike the rest of the line, where they had been known until 1860 as the grenadier and light companies. Hence the companies of the 1st Battalion were called Right Flank, B, C and Left Flank; those of the 2nd were Right Flank, F, G and Left Flank, a point which has puzzled many pipers as they work their way through the excellent collection of regimental pipe music published by the Scots Guards in 1954.
4. *The Thistle*, Journal of the Royal Scots, 1912.

ABOVE: 2nd Scottish Rifles, Pipers, Landi Kotai, Khyber Pass, India, 1929
The pipes of the 2nd Scottish Rifles were decorated with Graham tartan ribbons in honour of their
founder, Sir Thomas Graham of Balgowan, Perthshire. The pipers' sporran of the regiment was grey
with three black tassels. (S.J. Sellwood)

BELOW: 42nd (Royal Highland) Foot (The Black Watch), Bareilly, Rohilkhand, India, c. 1864
An early photograph showing all the current orders of dress, and popularly known as a 'mannequin
parade'. Both the piper and the bandsman are wearing the Royal Stuart tartan. The bandsman's
doublet is white with blue facings and the piper's is green. The drummer's broadsword is carried in a
frog on the the waist belt and his drum is the shallow pattern introduced following the Crimean War.
(RHQ Black Watch)

125

26th Cameronian Regiment, Piper Colin Mackenzie, 1881
Colin appears to have been photographed shortly before the amalgamation of the 26th Cameronians
with the 90th Light Infantry to form The Cameronians (Scottish Rifles) in 1881. He wears full
Highland dress with kilt and scarf plaid in the Douglas tartan, that being the family name of the
Cameronians' first colonel, the Earl of Angus. Colin has rearranged his plaid and drawn his
broadsword for maximum dramatic effect. His black sporran has two white tassels, the pattern which
the battalion retained after amalgamation, although the Government tartan was to oust the Douglas –
only for the original to reappear ten years later. (National War Museum of Scotland)

CHAPTER XI
Dressing the Pipers
~

The period between the defeat of France in 1815 and the outbreak of the Crimean War in 1854 saw frequent and major changes in the dress of the pipers of the Scottish regiments. For the researcher and the student, it is one of maddening inconsistency.

In 1817, Sir Walter Scott published his novel Rob Roy, which romanticised and sought to justify the depredations and outrages committed by the notorious Highland ruffian and bandit Rob Roy MacGregor. By the time of King George IV's state visit to Edinburgh in 1822, when the privilege of escorting the Scottish regalia, the Honours of Scotland, had been given to the clan, the star of Clan Gregor was well in the ascendant, a complete reversal of the situation of the clan from 1603 until 1775, when the very name of MacGregor had been proscribed by law, and by a statute of 1633 it had been declared not a punishable offence to hunt down and kill anyone of that name.

So all the omens were favourable when in 1826 Lieutenant-Colonel Duncan MacGregor assumed command of the 93rd Sutherland Highlanders, which he commanded until 1838. He forthwith dressed the 93rd's pipers in kilt doublet and scarf plaid of the tartan known as Rob Roy, a simple red and black check, and the band in the MacGregor tartan.[1] In 1848, under a different régime, the pipers reverted to the dark Government tartan worn by the rest of the 93rd, but were given a scarlet Highland doublet. The band wore the MacGregor tartan until 1834. The Royal Stuart tartan in the Prince Charles Edward sett was worn until 1862, when the band reverted to the regimental Government tartan. The MacGregor period is commemorated to this day, however, by the red-and-black diced hosetops still worn by the pipers of the Argyll and Sutherland Highlanders, but the fact that a Highland regiment raised in the north should once have had its pipers and bandsmen dressed in a Perthshire tartan continues to bedevil research and bemuse researchers.

Equally puzzling to the student of uniform is the question of the tartan worn by the band and pipers of the Black Watch. Some illustrations show them in the Government tartan, others in the Royal Stuart. There exists a painting of a Black Watch piper by the French artist Edouard Detaille, whose special study was uniform: his piper wears a Government tartan kilt and a Royal Stuart scarf plaid! The solution would seem to be that the bandsmen and pipers were issued with kilt and scarf plaid in both tartans – the Royal Stuart presumably at regimental expense – and that the regimental tartan was worn on less important parades, the Royal Stuart being kept for special occasions. The band appear to have discarded the Royal Stuart tartan in 1873, the year which saw the scarlet doublet replace the time-honoured white which all bandsmen had worn since 1830, the consequent colour clash making the Royal Stuart inappropriate. The pipers wore the Royal Stuart on important occasions until 1881, when both the 1st and 2nd Battalions reverted to the Government tartan until 1890, the year in which Queen Victoria gave formal permission for the Black Watch pipers to wear the Royal Stuart, as they do to this day. By this period, only the Black Watch pipers were wearing the feathered bonnet with the red hackle unique to the regiment. All others wore the glengarry cap, and here a word on the evolution of both types of headgear seems appropriate.

The traditional cap of the Highlanders and, indeed, of all the Scottish peasantry, was a round, flat, blue bonnet, fitted to the head with strings which ran round the inside of the brim and capacious enough to be 'scrugged', or pulled down to cover the ears in bad weather. This was the head-dress of the early Highland regiments, but compared with the tall mitre cap of the grenadier companies and the drummers, the flat blue bonnet looked unmilitary and made the wearer seem smaller than he was. The bonnet was therefore 'cocked', or set up, by inserting a stiffer piece of material to make a pill-box shape. Its height thus increased, the bonnet looked more impressive and the wearer taller. But the art of millinery fascinates the military mind, and it soon became fashionable, and in time obligatory, to attach pieces of bearskin in imitation of the grenadiers. Fur gave way to feathers; and in due course there appeared the modern feathered bonnet, a creation owing nothing to the Highlands, and all to the Highland regiments.

The bonnet continued to be issued in its original form as a flat round hat but with a diced headband, an imitation of the strings which had once fitted the cap to the wearer's head. The soldier bought the feathers and the so-called foxtails which hang down on the right of the bonnet. Every company had its 'bonnet cocker', the soldier who was skilled in the art of setting up the feathered bonnets in the regimental manner. Until the Great War, soldiers in a Highland regiment had a small amount stopped from their weekly pittance for the upkeep of the feathered bonnets.[2]

The feathered bonnet was the full dress head-dress of the kilted regiments, the non-kilted wearing the shako with diced band, except for the 72nd Duke of Albany's Highlanders, which wore the feathered bonnet with Royal Stuart tartan trousers.[3]

A bonnet cocked but without feathers was called a 'hummel' – not 'humble' – bonnet. A stag lacking antlers is a 'hummel' stag; the analogy is immediately apparent. After Waterloo, the hummel bonnet became the forage or undress cap of the whole Army, horse and foot alike. It was widely worn during the Crimean War in preference to the hated 'Albert' shako, hot, heavy, and uncomfortable but, being round, the hummel bonnet was difficult to carry in a knapsack without losing its shape, as contemporary photographs show.

During the visit of King George IV to Edinburgh in 1822, the clansmen in the 'tail', or entourage, of Colonel Alasdair Ranaldson MacDonell of Glengarry had appeared in the hummel bonnet, pressed flat, whether by design or simply because nobody had thought about it, is not now clear; probably the latter! Being flat, it could now be carried conveniently in a haversack or between the straps of the knapsack. It was eventually taken into wear by the 79th Highlanders as a forage cap, for which the soldiers paid. The pattern was higher in the crown than the present day glengarry but, tailored and shaped, it was a very handy, smart and comfortable head-dress, and it is worn today by all the Scottish infantry regiments except the Black Watch, where it is only worn in certain orders of dress by officers and serjeants, the round blue or khaki 'Cap Tam o' Shanter' with the red hackle being the usual head-dress. The glengarry replaced the hummel bonnet as the forage cap of all the infantry in 1868.

The pipers of the 79th took the glengarry into wear as their full dress head-dress, with a wing feather of the golden eagle. At the same time, they were wearing green doublets, the colour of the 79th's facings; the kilt and scarf plaid were in the 79th tartan; and the broadsword and dirk were supported by black leather shoulder and waist belts, with white metal buckles. This was a simple and attractive costume with an authentically Highland look about it. By the end of the Crimean War, the majority of the Scottish regiments were wearing a very similar costume, green doublets with their own regimental tartans, the preferred plume for the glengarry cap being the tail feathers of the black cock, rather than the golden eagle of the 79th, provision of which was to become difficult once the bird was declared a protected species in the next century. The pipers of the 2nd Seaforth, like those of the old 78th, wore no feather at all; neither did those of the Black Watch when parading in the glengarry. But whereas the glengarry worn by the Black Watch and The Highlanders is plain dark blue, that worn at the present time by all other Scottish infantry regiments is diced red, white and blue or green – red and white in the Argylls. However, the pipers' glengarry is always plain dark blue, except, once again in the Argylls, where it is black. The former Cameronians and Highland Light Infantry also wore what they claimed was a black glengarry, which was in fact rifle green.

As has been noted, the shotgun weddings of 1881 were rarely greeted with much enthusiasm by the battalions concerned, those whose precedence numbers had been above the magic figure of 25. There were minor but significant signs that it was going to be some time before the new organisation settled down. Several ways could be found in which the old identity might be perpetuated One was the way the pipers were dressed, as the old idea that the pipers were the officers' business and no one else's was still current; and with justification, as the pipers of the Lowland regiments were all clothed and equipped by the regiments, while in the case of the Highland, all those in excess of the permitted six were similarly clothed and equipped at the regiment's expense, which, in both instances, meant that the officers paid.

The Royal Scots were now firmly in the Scottish camp, and both battalions set about raising pipe bands. Sensibly, they did this by enlisting pipers of note, appointing them pipe major and letting them train pipers within the unit: a sound move, as one good piper, especially a good pipe major, will attract other good players. But whereas the 1st Battalion dressed its pipers in the Government tartan, those of the 2nd wore the Royal Stuart, which they gave up in 1892 in favour of the Hunting Stuart which the whole regiment was to adopt in 1901. The pipers of the Scots Fusiliers also went into the Government tartan, but those of the King's Own Borderers kept their Royal Stuart – permission for which, as we have seen, was conveniently agreed to be 'lost in time' – even after the regiment went into Leslie tartan trousers in 1901. The pipers of the 2nd Battalion, however, continued to wear in their glengarries the old forage cap badge of the 2nd Battalion, while those of the 1st wore the regimental badge.

The pipers of the 1st Battalion The Cameronians (Scottish Rifles) had to give up the Douglas tartan of their founder in 1881, and to don the universal Government tartan. The 2nd Battalion, the former 90th Perthshire Light Infantry, had considered itself a light infantry rather than a Scottish regiment, but they too had perforce to start a pipe band, which was trained for them by the 1st Seaforth, the old 72nd. But so that the pipers of the 2nd Battalion, which preferred to be known as the 2nd Scottish Rifles, would never be mistaken for those of the 1st Cameronians, a sporran was devised for them, grey with three black tassels, that of the 1st being black with two white tassels. Not to be outdone, the pipers of the 1st Battalion, instead of changing to the new regimental cap badge, kept their old one, the plain 'mullet', the five-pointed star of the Douglases – originally a spur rowel – with a scroll lettered simply 'The Cameronians'. And others continued to commemorate the old days by badges on the pipers' shoulder belts, devices on the waist belt buckle and, in the case of the 1st Seaforth, by a pipe ribbon in their old Royal Stuart tartan. The pipers of the 1st Seaforth also kept their white metal mountings on shoulder and waist belts and on their dirks. All these were brass in the case of the 2nd Battalion, as were there plaid brooches and sporran fittings. The 1st Battalion shoulder belt carried the star of the Duke of Albany; the 2nd Battalion the elephant awarded for service in the 1st Mahratta War. The 1st Seaforth piper's sporran was white with two black tassels; that of the 2nd was grey with two black tassels, a pattern adopted by the Queen's Own Highlanders from 1961 to 1994. It was the case in most Highland regiments that the piper's sporran differed from that generally worn, with either a specially designed metal cantle, as in the Black Watch, the 1st Seaforth and the Gordon Highlanders, or of a special pattern as in the Camerons, where the piper's sporran was grey with two white tassels; or the Argylls, where pipers wore a grey sporran with three black tassels, the pipe and drum majors wearing white sporrans also with three black tassels.

Pipers of the 1st Argylls, however, continued to bear on their shoulder belts the boar's head of the old 91st, while those of the 2nd Battalion bore the wild cat of Sutherland and the old 93rd.[4]

In 1994 The Highlanders was formed by the amalgamation of the Gordon Highlanders with the Queen's Own Highlanders. It was decided that the tartan of the Gordons would be adopted for the kilt of the new regiment, but that the Pipes and Drums would continue to wear the 79th tartan worn by the Pipes and Drums of the Queen's Own Highlanders. The sporran of the Gordons, white with two black tassels, was taken into wear by the pipers along with the Gordons' distinctive plaid brooch and belt ornaments. The intention was good; but the former Cameron Highlanders and later the Pipes and Drums of the Queen's Own Highlanders had always worn a dark sporran which complemented the subdued red of the 79th tartan admirably. Those interested in such matters agreed that the effect of the white sporran diminished the impact of the tartan and that it would have been better to keep the Queen's Own Highlanders pipers' sporran, grey with two black tassels.

The permission granted by Queen Victoria for the pipers of the Black Watch to wear the Royal Stuart appears to have been the first occasion on which that tartan was treated as personal to the Sovereign. The 21st Royal North British Fusiliers had unofficially maintained pipers dressed in Royal Stuart tartan, blue doublet and feathered bonnet over a long period, and on becoming the 21st Royal Scots Fusiliers in 1877 both battalions were authorised to hold a pipe major and three pipers on strength 'at no expense to the public'. When the regiment was ordered into the Government tartan in 1881, the pipers

conformed but continued to wear Royal Stuart hose and
hosetops, changing these to the Dress Erskine, the family tartan
of their founder, the Earl of Mar, after the Great War. In 1928,
the 250th anniversary of the raising of the regiment, the pipers
were granted the right to wear the Dress Erskine tartan kilt and
plaid. This is a green overcheck on a red ground which set off
the blue doublets of the pipers and the dark trousers of the
drummers to perfection and, with the associated regimental
accoutrements, which were of striking design, made the Scots
Fusilier pipers the best dressed in the Army. They were also the
last regimental pipers to carry the broadsword in full dress.
Their distinctive cap badge, suitably altered but retaining its
outline, is worn by the pipers, drummers and bandsmen of the
Royal Highland Fusiliers.

In 1933, the Royal Scots celebrated 300 years of service,
perhaps with a grateful backward glance at King William's Rules
of 1694, which had secured their precedence as 1st of Foot.[5]
Their Colonel-in-Chief was The Princess Royal, daughter of
King George V, but the anniversary parade was reviewed by the
King himself, who announced in his speech to the 1st Battalion
that it gave him 'great pleasure to confer upon your pipers the
right to wear my personal tartan, the Royal Stuart'. His
successor, King George VI, used similar terms when he
conferred the same right on the pipers of the Queen's Own
Cameron Highlanders in 1943, their 150th anniversary. This the
Camerons accepted dutifully rather than enthusiastically, in
much the same way in which they had accepted the insertion of
'The Queen's Own' into their title in 1873 by Queen Victoria. It
was felt that to be the only Highland regiment raised by a
private Highland gentleman, Alan Cameron of Erracht, wearing
the tartan he had devised, was distinction enough.

The pipers of the Scots Guards had worn the Royal Stuart
since their introduction into the regiment in 1853. When the
Royal Scots Greys formed an official pipe band in 1946, King
George expressed a wish that their uniform was to conform as
far as possible to that of the Scots Guards. The pipers
consequently went into the blue doublet, feathered bonnet, and
Royal Stuart kilt and scarf plaid as worn by the Scots Guards,
although there were those outside the regiment who felt that a
great opportunity to introduce the Dalziel tartan in

remembrance of old Tam – 'Bluidy D'yell' – and the stone-grey doublet of the Royal Regiment of Scots Dragoons, the original Scots Greys, had been missed.

Notes

1. The 'Rob Roy' tartan seems to have acquired its name, and its association with Clan Gregor, only through having been worn by the actor Tom Powrie when playing the part of the hero in the dramatisation of Scott's novel of that name during the visit of King George IV to Edinburgh in 1822. The King attended a performance. The MacGregor tartan worn by the band of the 93rd is described as that of the Glengyle branch of the clan, to which Rob Roy belonged.

2. Conversation with Captain James Murray. Dress Regulations for each regiment specified the number of foxtails which hung from the right of the feathered bonnet. The diced band differed, too, between regiments. Feathered bonnets were not worn abroad, the tropical helmet being issued in lieu. A Highland battalion warned for overseas service would hand over its feathered bonnets to the one coming home, regardless, apparently, of the dicing pattern or number of foxtails, such rules applying only to the officers.

3. In 1879, the officers of the 72nd, then serving in Afghanistan but under orders for home, voted to subscribe two rupees a month to a Feathered Bonnet Fund to improve the feathered bonnets of the soldiers on the 72nd's return to England.

4. Under the boar's head was the legend XCI; under the wildcat was XCIII. The 2nd Battalion shoulder belt buckle was inscribed 'Sutherland Highlanders', and the belt was tipped with the old 93rd cap badge, the figures '93' surmounted by the Queen's Crown and surrounded by a wreath of thistles.

5. *King William's Rules* 'Last in, first out' was the principle applied in theory whenever the Army was reduced after a war, although influence at court was often the decisive factor. The precedence of a regiment was therefore of primary importance to its colonel, to whom it was a source of income, and to its officers, to whom it was a source of salaried employment. Disputes over seniority were frequent and bitter, and in an effort to prevent such squabbles King William III ruled that the date of a regiment's seniority was to be calculated from the date of its being taken on to the English establishment and paid by funds approved by Parliament, as distinct from the revenues of Scotland or Ireland, which maintained separate forces, primarily for internal security.

According to its raising on the Scots establishment in 1678, the Royal Scots Fusiliers should have ranked fourth in seniority; but it was not taken on to the English establishment until 1689, becoming under King William's Rules twenty-first in seniority, and was so numbered in 1751.

42nd (Royal Highland) Foot (The Black Watch) Band, Simla, India, 1864

This photograph shows the band wearing the regimental or Government tartan with the hummel bonnet, or plain, blue Kilmarnock, and the white drill order jacket, originally a sleeved waistcoat. The piper on the right also wears the regimental tartan with a plain, blue Balmoral bonnet, laid aside in 1868 when the Glengarry cap replaced the hummel bonnet as the forage cap of the Infantry. (RHQ Black Watch)

135

92nd (Gordon Highlanders) Foot, drummer, 1866
Ye're nae a sodger if ye're nae a Gordon!

This young drummer, who glares so pugnaciously at the world across a century and a half, may well be a 'barrack rat', the son of a serving soldier enlisted straight from his family to the drums at fourteen, or even earlier, to earn his meagre keep. His drum is of the shallow pattern and, young as he is, he is armed with a man-sized broadsword carried in an adjustable shoulder belt. (National War Museum of Scotland)

CHAPTER XII
THE DRUMMERS

~

The antiquity of the drum and the importance of the drummer's role on the battlefield have already been discussed. In this chapter the evolution of the distinctive clothing worn by military drummers will be described – traces of which can still be seen in the uniform of the drummers of the foot guards and in those regiments of the line which, at their own very considerable expense, have preferred to dress their drummers in the traditional scarlet, rather than in the uninspiring blue uniform issued from official sources and known as Number One Dress.

It is to the bands of the household cavalry and the drum majors of the foot guards that we have to turn for an example of the dress worn by drummers of the period immediately after the restoration of King Charles II in 1660. The State Dress worn by the musicians and the drum majors derives from the military costume of that time. The red coat faced blue, so lavishly adorned with gold lace and braid that little of the coat itself can be seen, is worn with a blue-velvet, jockey-type cap; but while the musicians of the mounted bands wear white breeches and jacked boots, the drum majors wear the long gaiters, or spatterdashes, which were the parade dress of the foot guards until they were replaced by trousers in 1823, whch were white in summer, blue/grey in winter.

Illustrations of the uniform, or costume, worn by the regimental drummers of the period indicate that they wore very much the same as the men in the ranks, with perhaps a feather in the broad-brimmed, shallow-crowned hat and a bunch of coloured ribbons at elbow and knee. The soldiers wore red coats, grey breeches, stockings and shoes. There was, apparently, a grey coat worn as a working dress, sensibly, as the red one had to last a year and the annual issue of clothing might be long overdue when it eventually arrived. The muster-rolls of the often ephemeral infantry companies raised from time to time in Scotland include the names of the two drummers, which follow those of the corporals; but the drummers got 1s. 6d., while the corporals got 1s. 0d. per day.

In 1689, King William was already deploying his newly acquired

British Army, including the household cavalry and foot guards, in support of his native Holland and against the French in Flanders and the Low Countries – modern Holland, Belgium, and Luxembourg – in the War of the League of Augsburg, which was to last until 1697, and was to win for some of the regiments involved, albeit belatedly (in 1910) the battle honour 'Namur 1695'. This was the period during which drummers began to wear 'reversed colours', meaning that their coats were the colour of the regimental facings, the colour of the lining of the soldiers' coats, which appeared on the cuffs and, later, on the collars and lapels as well, so that if the soldiers' coats had yellow cuffs, the drummers wore yellow coats faced red. Some regiments, such as the later Royal Scots, had already been designated 'Royal', and in those, the soldiers' and the drummers' coats were red faced blue, the colour of the Royal livery.

Although this conspicuous costume probably owed its origin to the days when the drummers had also had a heraldic role in bearing messages, challenges and cartels between the two sides, the tactical implications might have been paramount. In battle, the drummer's place was by the side of his officer, ready to signal – beat – any orders without delay. In this distinctive dress, the drummer would easily be spotted; and wherever the drummer stood, his officer could not be far away. For the same reason, for their role was analogous, the cavalry trumpeter was mounted on a grey horse. The trumpeter's place was beside his regimental, squadron or troop commander; spot the trumpeter and an officer would not be far away. Before a charge, a considerate cavalry officer might tell his trumpeter to ride with the troop instead of behind him, so that the trumpeter might be less exposed.

The infantry drummer was also distinguished by his head-dress, which was the mitre cap, as worn by the grenadiers and fusiliers. It was originally a plain stocking cap, which over the years was made to look more impressive by increasing its height by stiffening the cap internally and embroidering the front with various martial devices and crests.

In the early eighteenth century, it also became regulation for the soldiers to have the buttonholes and cuffs of their coats trimmed with a distinctive regimental lace or braid. Such embellishments could be varied at the whim of the colonel, who, at this stage, was virtually the proprietor of the regiment and whose arms and crest might appear on the colours and drums. The braid on the coats was originally the livery braid worn by the colonel's domestic servants, and when the colonelcy changed hands, so the braid on the soldiers' coats might also be altered. This braid was placed lavishly on the drummers' coats; and as the colour of the regiment's facing often appeared on the colonel's livery as well, the focus of loyalty might appear, outwardly at least, to be the colonel rather than the Crown. This was further emphasised as at this period the regiments were known by their colonel's name, so that at Culloden in 1746, the regiment which we know as the King's Own Scottish Borderers was called Sempill's.

All this finery had to be paid for, an expensive business, as all embroidery had to be done by hand. The money was found by deductions – the detested 'stoppages' – from the soldiers' pay. In theory, a guardsman received 10d. (4½p) a day; an infantryman got 8d. (3½p). This they never saw, far less touched. Every soldier had to buy his uniform and accoutrements, apart from his firearm, which was issued by the Goverment. 2d. (1p) was deducted from his daily rate of pay as the 'off-reckoning', and out of this sum – the 'gross off-reckonings' – had to come sundry stoppages before the balance – the 'net off-reckonings' – were calculated. From the net off-reckonings was paid the cost of the annual issue of clothing – hat, coat, breeches, shoes and shirt – as well as other expenses such as drummers' clothing, drum heads and sometimes the drum major's salary as well.

The balance of the net off-reckonings belonged to the colonel. All other kit came under the heating of 'necessaries', and had to be bought by the soldier out of what remained of his daily pay. Whatever might be left was 'subsistence money', and out of it the soldier had to provide the cost of his board and lodging. Cavalry privates drew 2s. 6d. (12½p) and dragoon privates 1s. 6d. (7½p).[1] They were subject to the same stoppages as the infantrymen, and also had to feed and look after their horses. Incredible as it may seem, soldiers not only survived under this regime, which lasted until the Crimean War, but in some cases married and brought up children as well. Soldiers and their wives were consequently always on the lookout for part time jobs – moonlighting is a very old Army tradition – and for this reason we read in regimental standing orders of the period that 'officers are on no account to give their washing outside the regiment', as this was a perquisite of the married soldiers' wives.[2]

All this was to change under regulations issued between 1743 and 1751, which allotted a precedence number to each regiment by which it was thenceforth to be known until 1881, and designated the badges which regiments might display on their Colours, which were also standardised, and on the drums. The colonel's lace disappeared and was replaced by braid of regimental pattern.

The drummers continued to wear reversed colours until 1831, when they were ordered into the red coatees worn by the rank and file, which were laced across the chest with the regimental braid, the drummers retaining their lavish braiding, which now included chevrons on the arm, point up. The coatee was replaced in 1855 by the tunic, a change which had been under consideration for some time, but which was accelerated by the experience in the early days of the Crimean War. The 1855 issue to the drummers was white, the same as the band, but the next year's issue was red. There was no braid on the rank and file tunic, but the drummers continued to wear the regimental braid in a modified form on the tunic until 1866.

In that year, a universal pattern of drummers' braid was introduced for the infantry of the line. This was white with a crown in red at regular intervals, known officially as 'Crown Lace' and unofficially as 'Crown and Inch'. Drummers of the foot guards continued to wear the Royal Lace, which has a dark-blue fleur-de-lis embroidered at intervals, perhaps the last outward manifestation of the historic claim of the kings of England to the throne of France. Both types can be seen today. The tunic of the foot guards drummers is laced across the chest, on the back and on the arms in the old style; that of the line only along the back and arm seams, the latter without the 'point up' chevrons of the guards. The piping on the line tunic is white flecked with red; that of the guards, white flecked with dark blue. Shoulder shells, often called 'wings', are worn by both guards and the line, both fringed, dark blue and white for the guards, red and white for the line, the braid on the guards drummers' collars being fringed as well.

The mitre cap of the early and mid-eighteenth century was replaced in 1768 by one of black fur – white in the case of some drummers – with a brass frontlet. In 1800, the shako was introduced, ousting the traditional hats of the centre companies

ABOVE: 1st Battalion, The Argyll and Sutherland Highlanders, Drummers, Aldershot, 1896
Twelve drummers, including boys, parade under the drum major in Review Order, perhaps while
waiting for the pipers to tune up before before they all formed up for the march to the square. Note
the correct angle of the feathered bonnets and how well they are set up to display the ample white
hackle, a credit to the drummers' 'bonnet cocker'. Soldiers in Highland regiments were 'stopped' a
small amount from their pay for the upkeep of their dress – including the feathered bonnet which was
groomed rigorously. The facings on the scarlet doublet is yellow, although this is difficult to see in this
old photograph. (RHQ Argyll and Sutherland Highlanders)

BELOW: 7/9th (Highlanders) Battalion, The Royal Scots (The Royal Regiment) (Territorial Army),
Pipes and Drums, Edinburgh, 1935
The 'Dandy Ninth' was the only battalion of the Royal Scots to wear the kilt – in Hunting Stuart
tartan. Here, the pipes and drums lead the battalion to the High Kirk of St Giles for their annual
church parade. The pipers had worn the Royal Stuart tartan since 1933, the 300th anniversary of the
raising of the regiment. Note, also, the length of the drum major's staff.

141

and the light leather helmet of the light, the company which stood on the left of the line on parade and acted as the battalion's skirmishers. The grenadier companies wore their fur caps on great occasions, but the shako on service in the field. It could be that the drummers gave up their bearskin caps in the years after Waterloo, although there are prints showing drummers wearing both.

The post-Crimea reforms established one drum major and twenty drummers for each battalion of infantry, the drum major apparently still counting as one of the drummers. Light infantry and rifles had a bugle major and twenty buglers. Drums, flutes and bugles, the 'instruments of command', were issued free, appearing in the equipment tables under the heading of 'Arms', and listed immediately after 'Swords and Scabbards'. But bagpipes, like band instruments, had to be bought out of the Band Fund.

Provided from Ordnance — at that time the source of all good things authorised by the Government — were ten side drums, ten flutes and ten bugles. The drums came complete with ticken covers, the flutes with cases and the bugles with strings, or cords, so that they could be slung over the shoulder. The strings for Royal regiments were interwoven red, yellow and blue, and for all others, green, hence 'Cords, Royal', and 'Cords, Grassy Green'. Ten leg aprons were issued to protect the drummers' trousers from undue friction while playing.

In theory, each company had on its strength one drummer with a side drum, and one bugler, who also played the flute. But the type of flutes provided make it clear that the drummers were intended on occasions to play and beat as a corps, the scale of issue being six flutes in Bb, two in F and two piccolos, one in Bb and one in F. No bass drum was issued, nor was there a bass drummer to beat it. The bass drum was specified as having to be bought from the Band Fund, and was presumably meant to be played by a bandsman. From the Band Fund, apparently limitless, also came the drum major's accoutrements, his lavishly embroidered shoulder sash, as well as his mace or staff, which might have originated in the wand of office carried by the footmen who preceded the great and mighty through the streets in the eighteenth century.

The side drums were of the narrow or 'cheese' pattern, adopted, no doubt, in imitation of the drums of the French in the Crimea, or perhaps influenced by the Prussian model, which itself had replaced the older, deeper pattern simply because the shallow drums were cheaper. The drum was tensioned by a system of cords and small pulleys, and there are photographs showing this type of drum on parade both with corps of drums and with pipe bands. The drum came with a buff strap for carrying it slung over the shoulder, in the same way as the drag, or dress ropes, properly the back carriage, enabled the deeper drum to be carried when it was not being played.

This shallow drum was much lighter and less unwieldy than the older pattern and for this reason it might have been preferred for use on the line of march. The shallow drum was also popular with the youth organisations and cadet companies which began to proliferate in the later decades of the nineteenth century, and they can also be found in photographs of the bands and corps of drums in the units of the New Armies, the early volunteers of the Great War, borrowed, perhaps, from the bands of Boy Scout troops, or from Boys and Church Lads Brigade companies.

For all that, the shallow drum was never to become fully accepted in the British Army, one reason perhaps being that the narrow shell made it impossible to display the Royal Arms, or the badges and devices of the regiments, or the battle honours which had adorned the old drums and which gave the drums their significance among the treasures of the regiment. This custom still holds good, and the drums of a well-established battalion of the line are nothing less than works of art.

For their personal protection in battle, the drummers of the four senior Scottish regiments, dressed as infantry of the line, were issued with the standard drummer's pattern sword, which in the years between 1815 and 1857 was largely an ornamental weapon. Bandsmen, too, got the same sword as drummers. The 1830 pattern was short and curved, the 1854 longer and more curved – almost like a scimitar – while the 1857 sword was short and straight. This sword lasted with minor modifications until 1905, when the bandsmen, drummers and buglers of the line regiments finally lost their swords, although the musicians of the foot guards continued to carry them on parade until the outbreak of World War II in 1939. The buglers of the 2nd Royal Green Jackets carry the bugler's sword to this day.

Drummers of Highland regiments were provided with what was officially called a claymore, but which was a Highland broadsword with its basket hilt, giving complete protection to the hand, but making it difficult to use the broadsword other than as a cutting weapon. Highland bandsmen also got the broadsword, as did the pipers. All carried it in a shoulder belt, black for the pipers, white for everyone else. As a weapon it was far in advance of the infantry drummer's sword, but in the years after the Crimean War this excellent weapon was to disappear.

We are accustomed to see the side drum carried hooked to a belt, the drum carriage, slung over the drummer's right shoulder. This method of carrying the drum was only arrived at after decades of argument. For centuries, it had been the practice for the drum carriage to be slung round the drummer's neck, like a necklace, making, in the opinion of many, the drum easier to play. With the drum carriage in that position, it was possible for the shoulder belt supporting the broadsword to be worn over the right shoulder, with the hilt pushed well to the rear, so that the broadsword lay across the drummer's back, where it did not interfere with the free movement of his arms as he played.

After the Crimean War, the drum carriage of the shallow drum was worn over the right shoulder, as it is today. Besides being awkward, this placed all the weight on the drummer's right shoulder, so the shoulder belt was discarded, and the broadsword carried in a frog on the waist belt. This, too, was not satisfactory, as the basket hilt tended to interfere with the free movement of the drummer's left arm and the weight of the broadsword must have dragged the waistbelt down.

The final blow came in 1871 when a completely new system of carrying the soldier's personal load was devised. The system adopted was years ahead of its time and, possibly because of its novel appearance, was soon discarded in favour of one which looked smarter on parade, this being the British Army, after all. The old knapsack, carried behind the shoulders, was replaced by a valise slung low behind the hips. This made it impossible for the broadsword to be carried at all, so Highland pipers, drummers and bandsmen lost their trusty broadswords, which were replaced by the dirk, basically a knife with a twelve-inch blade, worn on the right side, although the 'full' or established pipers had a revolver by 1882. Bandsmen, pipers and drummers were issued with a plain dirk with a crown on the pommel. In full dress, however, pipers usually wore a more ornate dirk of regimental pattern, generally with a small knife and fork in the scabbard, purchased from the Pipe Fund. A regimental-pattern sgian dubh – stocking knife – was also provided. In many cases, owing to the expense of replacing regimental items, pipers now wear the Government-issue dirk and sgian dubh.[3]

The drum, pipe and bugle majors were ranked with the 1st Class staff serjeants, which meant that all their clothing was of the highest quality. The drum and bugle majors wore scarlet tunics instead of the red of the rank and file, who were first issued with scarlet tunics in 1873. The Lowland regiments wore round forage caps with a drooping peak, instead of the glengarry of the serjeants. The staff carried by the drum major was about five feet long, made from bamboo, with a round top of gilt metal and gilt collar, and a similar ferrule, with chains or a silk bugle string running criss-cross down its length. The staff was used to give signals to the band or the drums, directing them to halt, wheel, cease playing and so on. It was the custom for the drum major to flourish the staff while the band played on the march, and the drum major was apt to be judged as much by his dexterity with the staff as by the quality of the music produced by the drums, the tone of the flutes, the stick drill of the drummers and the competence of the buglers.

The shoulder belt with whatever regimental motifs and battle honours were embroidered on it had always borne the insignia of the drummer's trade, two miniature drumsticks set into the belt, a reminder of the days when the drum major had also beaten the drum, and one shared with the drum majors of several Continental armies.

The reorganisation of 1881 reduced the number of companies in the battalion from ten to eight and the number of drummers to sixteen. However, the number of boys who could be enlisted for training as drummers, pipers, bandsmen, buglers or tailors was enough to offset this loss, which in any case was largely ignored. Boys had always been eligible for training as musicians, it being an article of faith that the younger the boy started, the more likely he was to become proficient enough to take his place, not only on parade with the drums, pipes, band, or bugles, but, what was more important to the others, also on the roll for orderly piper, drummer or bugler, which meant that the duty did not come round quite as frequently as before.

A diminution of the status of the drum, pipe and bugle majors was also seen in 1881. They were reduced in status from 1st class staff serjeant to serjeant, although they continued to wear their distinctive badges of appointment: four chevrons, point up, surmounted by an embroidered or metal drum, bagpipe or bugle, as they do to this day. At the same time, the ancient titles were abolished, and they became serjeant drummers, serjeant pipers and serjeant buglers, although they tended to be so described only in official documents and correspondence. It is difficult to understand why this was done, as although it could not be claimed that the pipe major had much of a tactical role to play in the field, the same could not be said of the drum and bugle majors. The bugle continued to be the only means of intercommunication on the battlefield for some time to come.

About 1893, the officers of the 1st Battalion Royal Scots decided to commemorate their two hundred and fifty years of unbroken service by purchasing a suitably impressive drum major's staff. It is six feet long, silver, and is heavily decorated with regimental motifs and battle honours. Surmounted by the figure of St Andrew with his cross, it is too massive to be flourished, far less thrown into the air, but makes a dramatic impression on the onlooker when carried at the head of the pipes and drums. The original, now in the Regimental Museum in Edinburgh Castle, cost forty pounds; its replacement four thousand pounds. It is known to the Royal Scots as 'Big Andy'!

Notes

1. Until 1919, everyone holding no other rank or appointment – NCO, bandsman, drummer, piper, bugler or trumpeter – was officially and legally a 'private'. This applied to all arms. In that year, a private in the cavalry became a 'trooper'; in the foot guards, a 'guardsman'; in the rifles, a 'rifleman'; in the fusiliers, a 'fusilier'; and in the Royal Artillery, a 'gunner'. By regimental custom, a private in the King's Regiment became a 'kingsman'; and in the shortlived Royal Irish Rangers, a 'ranger'; private soldiers in The Highlanders are referred to a 'Highlander'.
2. 'Old Belle MacPherson, a soldier's widow, had followed the 92nd all over the world and had learned to make up the Marquis of Huntly's shirts at Gibraltar, box pleating all the frills.' *Memoirs of a Highland Lady*, Elizabeth Grant of Rothiemurchus (Canongate Classics, 1988).
3. The dirk and sgian dubh issued to pipers of the Highland Light Infantry had no blades, the hilts and scabbards being made in one piece. Information kindly provided by Pipe Major David Aitken, BEM, late Highland Light Infantry.

ABOVE: The Royal Scots (The Royal Regiment), Pipe Major Patrick Moorcroft
The Pipe Major wears the long tartan hose and buckled shoes, the dress for playing at the officers mess
and similar occasions. As was the Lowland regiments' custom, his blue doublet is laced with silver
braid – Highland regiments wore gold. His pipe banner was presented by the Merchant Company of
Edinburgh. (RHQ The Royal Scots)

INSET: 1st Battalion, The Royal Scots (The Royal Regiment), Big Andy
The beautiful and impressive head of the staff carried by the drum major on ceremonial occasions. Six
feet long, the staff is silver, decorated with the royal and ancient badges of the regiment. (RHQ The
Royal Scots)

147

ABOVE: 26th Cameronian Regiment, 1877
The 26th is about to march off in column of route, led by the Pioneers, with their felling axes, and
followed by the band, drums and pipers. The soldiers are wearing the scarlet frock, or second tunic,
faced yellow, and the Glengarry forrage cap, diced red, white and yellow. On the left of the band are
five senior NCOs of the regimental staff. Beyond and to the left are the signallers with furled flags.
They always marched at the head of the column in case they were required to transmit a message
during the march. (National War Museum of Scotland)

BELOW: 90th Perthshire Light Infantry, Nowshera, Northwest Frontier, India, 1866
The 90th is formed up on the parade ground of the British Lines – still standing and occupied by the
Pakistan Army – in winter, wearing cold-weather drill order. In front, stand the Pioneers, all bearded
in the tradition of their craft, several wearing medals awarded for the Crimean War and Indian
Mutiny. Behind them stand the band and bugles; the band in white tunics, the bugles in red. As Light
Infantry, the 90th had no drums, but the buglers were expected to learn to play a brass instrument and
to play in the band. The bugle major carries a cornet. Possibly, the bugles formed a separate brass
band, which could relieve the military band on the line of march.
(National War Museum of Scotland)

148

CHAPTER XIII
THE BUGLE (1)

~

How the drum became the instrument through which tactical
command at the lower levels was exercised on the battlefields of
Europe has already been discussed. By the middle of the
eighteenth century, strategy and tactics had become stylised to
the point of formality. In the opinion of one school of thought,
the most successful general was he who attained his aim through
manoeuvre alone, avoiding battle, and thus forcing his opponent
to sue for peace without the loss to either side of expensively
trained soldiers and the consequent difficulty of finding
replacements. This comfortable and comforting theory received
an unwelcome shock in the War of the Austrian Succession from
1742 to 1748. The larger armies, which the nation states were
now obliged to maintain in the field if they were not to be
defeated, required long and slow-moving supply columns, which
lumbered along the appalling roads between the 'magazines',
where supplies were collected and stored, and the forces in the
field. These clumsy supply columns were vulnerable to
interference from small but daring parties of the enemy, able to
live off the land – particularly where the population might be
friendly – while maintaining the ability to move fast and far,
often by night, when operations by the main forces tended to
pause, almost by mutual consent. Against opponents of this type,
the rigidly trained and strictly disciplined regular soldiers of the
period had little to offer.

The need thus arose for specially trained and equipped units
able to counter those incursions by the enemy light troops,
so-called because they were lightly armed and carried less on
their backs than soldiers trained to fight in the line of battle.
Courage and endurance were the prerequisites, together with
quick wits, skill in the use of ground and cover, mastery of the
weapons involved and the ability to subsist on whatever might
come to hand. Men suitable for training in this role were to be
found in Europe among the populations of the frontier provinces
of Austria and the hills and forests of France and Germany. The

2nd Scottish Rifles, Meanee Barracks, Colchester, 1911
The 2nd Scottish Rifles is marching to church, headed by the pipes, drums and bugles, and with the band playing behind. As the battalion is under orders to proceed to Malta on the first leg of its overseas tour, the riflemen are wearing the white tropical Wolseley helmet. The home-service shakos have been issued to the 1st Battalion, recently returned from India. A small regimental cap badge is worn on the front of the helmet. The buglers and riflemen carry the Bible in thier right hands, which all Protestant recruits were issued with on enlistment. (Tony Burgess)

2nd Scottish Rifles, Buglers, Landi Kotal, Khyber Pass, India, 1929
As a rifle regiment, each battalion of the Cameronians (Scottish Rifles) maintained a strong corps of buglers under the bugle major, seen here seated on the right of the front row. Although eleven of the buglers also acted as drummers with the pipe band, they continued to take their turn on the duty buglers' roster and to sound 'Retreat' when the pipes, drums and bugles were on parade.
(S.J. Sellwood Collection)

Grenzers of the frontier provinces, and the gamekeepers and foresters of France and Germany were the sources from which the regiments of *Chasseurs* and *Jäger* were recruited, as their names imply. It is the tradition of the forester, the hunter and the gamekeeper, with all that it implies in terms of fieldcraft, patience and skill, which forms an important element in the ethos of the light troops all over Europe. In Britain, the Highlanders of Scotland, with their predilection for the raid, the ambush, the sudden onslaught and the speedy withdrawal, were similarly a suitable source for the provision of light troops, and although the early Highland regiments were used in this role both in Europe and in Canada and America, they soon, by order, reverted to that of the conventional 'heavy' infantry.

In the forests, thickets and swamps where the Seven Years War of 1756–1763, and the War of American Independence of 1776–1783, were waged in Canada and America, the British were perforce compelled to adopt the tactics of first, their Indian allies and, later, of their former colonists. All were adept at the operations of what military theorists called the 'Little War', that of ambushes, raids and surprise attacks in places far behind the 'front'.

The answer was, of course, to take the enemy on at his own game. Clothing, weapons and equipment had all to be modified – the Highland regiments, sensibly, wore trousers in the field – and specialist units of lightly armed and appropriately equipped troops, selected from the regular battalions serving in the theatre, were improvised and trained in the skills and tactics of forest warfare. These units were augmented by companies of Rangers raised from loyalists among the colonists and, during the War of Independence in America, by *Jäger* and light infantry units hired from friendly German states.

Control in those scattered engagements, fought at close range from behind trees and across streams in unmapped country, was much more difficult to exercise than in the open field of Europe. The drum of the period was heavy, cumbersome and unwieldy, always susceptible to puncture by thorns and branches. A split in the batter head made the drum – and the drummer – ineffective until the punctured drum head, made of cured sheepskin, could be replaced – a complex and time-consuming affair in which the drum had to be dismantled. In addition, a greater range of signals than the drum could readily provide was required to cover the eventualities which might arise during a skirmish in close country, where the soldiers might have to operate on their own, at distances well beyond the range of the human voice, even though the level of noise might be below that of the conventional battlefield. Some of the drum signals conveyed different meanings when beaten 'on the flam' instead of 'on the roll', a distinction not always immediately apparent to the hard-pressed light infantryman in the heat of an skirmish.

When the French and the German states had recruited such soldiers from the men of the forests and the woods, they had allowed them to keep, to some extent at least, their distinctive clothing,[1] and to a greater extent, their music. In the course of the chase and the stalk, they had been accustomed to keep in touch by means of calls and signals sounded on horns of different types and sizes. Expertise in their use had been one of the requirements of their trade, both in sounding and in identifying the appropriate calls. These horns were conical in the bore, which gave a mellow tone readily evocative of the atmosphere of the deep woodland in which the hunt took place. As time went on, the horns became larger and, therefore, louder, and were shaped into forms convenient for carrying over the shoulder, as in the *Cor de Chasse*, still played by the *Chasseurs* of the French Army, and the *Waldhorn* of the *Jäger* Battalions of the Imperial German Army. These horns were not simply a means of intercommunication, important though that was. They were part of the musical accompaniment to the hunt; they sounded fanfares before the hunt began; played hunting songs during the lunch break; and, at the end of the day, when the spoils of the chase were collected and exhibited. They were essentially effective, if restricted, musical instruments, unlike the hunting horn of the English shires.

After the American War ended, a reaction set in, and light infantry went out of fashion until the outbreak of the war against France in 1793. The French revolutionary armies were hastily raised levies, trained perfunctorily on the march and consequently insufficiently disciplined to perform the manoeuvres necessary to move flexibly and quickly in mass formation on the battlefield. Therefore, a French Army attacked, preferably from a flank, with its regiments deployed in close columns, as broad as they were deep, thus breaking the opposing enemy line by sheer weight of numbers. The columns were preceded by 'clouds' of light troops and sharpshooters who unsettled and harassed the enemy, distracting them while the columns approached. Should the column have to retire, the skirmishers swarmed out again, to snipe and harry the advancing enemy in their turn. Should the enemy withdraw, the sharp-shooters and skirmishers hung on to his rear and flanks, annoying and distracting him in every possible way, by picking off the officers and by causing casualties which had either to be picked up and carried, or abandoned, a stark choice for a retreating force.[2]

Once again, the British had to take on their enemy at his own game, forming a 5th Battalion, composed of Germans, of the 60th Royal Americans, one of the specialist units of light troops formed after the Seven Years War in America. The 5/60th was commanded by Baron Francis de Rottenburg, an experienced German *Jäger* officer, who produced a training manual for light troops in 1798. In 1800, the Experimental Corps of Riflemen was formed from drafts of four NCOs and thirty men – one of whom was to be a bugler – from fourteen designated regiments armed, like the 5/60th, with the rifle instead of the smooth-bore musket of the infantry of the line. Several Highland regiments had been called upon to provide drafts, and so a Highland company was formed in the 95th, as the Experimental Corps was later numbered. One officer came from North Argyll, and the set of bagpipes played by the company piper was also in the possession of a West Highland family. The Highland soldiers' first language was almost certainly Gaelic, which the officers would also have spoken or at least understood.[3]

This was only one aspect of a difficulty which was to assume considerable proportions once active operations in Portugal began in 1808. The British skirmish or outpost line by then included British, Portuguese and German riflemen from both the 5/60th and the Light Battalions of the King's German Legion, Hanoverian soldiers who had thrown in their lot with the British when Hanover, then a fief of the British Crown, had been overrun by the French in 1803.

With this polyglot skirmish line, a uniform and universally understood system of command and control was essential. De Rottenburg had included a rudimentary range of horn signals in his manual on the training of the Light Infantry, and this was augmented and developed as a result of experience in the field and on the training area. The instrument itself was also perfected as time went on, and the result was the bugle.

The bugle is officially described as 'made of brass or copper, with brass mounts'. It consists of a conical tube some four feet long, ending in a bell. The regulation bugle is now issued in Bb low pitch but, as it is treated as a transposing instrument, the calls are written in the key of C.[4] The low-pitch bugle can be sounded in concert with the military band; the older, high-pitch bugle had to be fitted with a shank, which made the tube longer, thus lowering the pitch when required to sound along with the band. All five notes of the harmonic series are used in the regulation calls – these are written as middle C, G, C, E and G. Brass bugles have a crisper tone than copper; silver bugles give the best tone, more mellow, and sweeter than either brass or copper. The bugle is wreathed, or coiled, twice for ease of handling and to decrease the chance of accidental damage. In the field of military musical instruments of all kinds, 'Murphy's Law' rules: what can get broken, will be!

The introduction of the bugle was to have an important effect on the music that had hitherto been heard in camp, quarters and, to a certain extent, in the field: the music of fife and drum. Eventually, the bugle would oust the fife completely and, in time, the drum as well, these two being heard only on the line of march and at the beating of Reveille, Retreat and Tattoo. The process began in the light infantry and the Rifle Brigade – as the 95th became after Waterloo in recognition of its outstanding record in the Peninsular War of 1808–1814. This high reputation, shared to some extent with the light infantry, made these the trend- and pace-setters among the infantry of the line.

In the cavalry, the bugle was to replace the trumpet as the instrument of command; it was louder, and its higher pitch cut through the hubbub of battle more effectively. The regulation trumpet is made of brass and consists of a cylindrical tube some six feet long, the last two of which are slightly conical, ending in a bell. The harmonic range is considerably greater than that of the bugle, but only five notes are required to sound the regulation calls. These are written as G, middle C, E, G and C. The call to 'Stables', however, uses D and E, which can tax a young trumpeter's ability. The trumpet is issued in Eb, and again like the bugle, it is treated as a transposing instrument, the calls being written in the key of C. The trumpet is also wreathed twice. The trumpet was used for dismounted duty – the routine calls in barracks, fanfares, and so on – and the bugle in the field, although at one time the field calls sounded on the bugle by the commanding officer's trumpeter were repeated on the trumpet by the squadron trumpeters by way of acknowledgement.

The Duke of York became Commander-in-Chief of the Army in 1795, after a somewhat disastrous campaign in the Low Countries had made it quite clear that even if he was a son of King George III, his military talents lay elsewhere than in the field. But his interest in the Army was real and unfeigned and eclectic as well. It was with his support that the first manual of field and barrack calls for the trumpet and bugle was published. There was, at one time, a fondly held belief that the calls used by the British Army had been composed by Joseph Haydn during a stay in England. Sadly, the truth is more prosaic. The first set of calls was collected and arranged by Joseph Hyde, 'Of the Opera House, and Trumpet Major to the Gentlemen of the London and Westminster Light Horse Volunteers', one of the proliferation of volunteer units that sprang into existence when invasion from France was threatened and which were to be the precursor of the present Territorial Army.

The New and Complete Preceptor for the Trumpet and the Bugle Horn begins with instructions for sounding the trumpet. There then follows the 'Trumpet Duty' for the Cavalry, consisting of barrack and routine calls. Of these, the following still appear in the 1966 edition of *Trumpet and Bugle Sounds for the Army*. The current application follows in brackets.

'Officers'; 'Serjeants'; 'Boot and Saddle'; 'Trumpeters'; 'To Horse' (now 'General Parade'); 'Stables'; 'Watering Order'; 'Orders'; 'Dinners' (now 'Mess'); 'Parade March' (now 'Royal Salute'); 'Reveille'; and 'Watch Setting'. In the old tradition, Hyde divides 'Watch Setting' into four 'Posts', i.e., sentry posts. The call thus symbolised the progress of Grand or Visiting Rounds – the field officer or subaltern on duty and his escort – as they toured the perimeter. His first two 'Posts' constitute 'Watch Setting – First Post' as sounded today. The current 'Watch Setting – Second Post' is the same call with an altered opening phrase.

Hyde goes on to set out the 'Bugle Horn Duty', clearly meant to apply to the Cavalry, as calls are included for 'Trot'; 'Gallop'; 'Charge!'; 'Halt'; 'Retire'; and 'Return Swords'. These also appear in the 1966 manual. The current bugle calls 'Reveille' and 'Rouse' first appear in the 'Bugle Horn Duty for the Cavalry'; and the first section of his 'Setting the Watch' is 'Tattoo – First Post', while his 2nd Post is the present 'Tattoo – Last Post'. Both calls are arranged for two bugles.

The next section of Hyde's *Preceptor* is the 'Bugle Horn Duty for the Light Infantry as used in the Foot Guards'. It includes only a few tactical calls, ending with 'Turn in the Whole and form in a Line on the Left of the Right', which seems a somewhat arcane manoeuvre. But although his tactical 'Retreat' has not survived, his routine 'Retreat' appears in a later pamphlet: *A Practical Guide for the Light Infantry Officer*, published in 1806, and a most attractive call it is too, as is his 'Tattoo for Four Bugle Horns'.

Hyde's next section consists of 'Duetts for Two Bugle Horns' by one F. Fraser. The time signature in the first six Duetts indicates that they are in fact marches in Ordinary Time. The first 'Duett' turns out to be the call now known as 'Retreat', although it was apparently some time before it ousted the call in the 'Bugle Horn Duty'. Then follow seven 'Quick Marches'; four in 2/4 – one with a trio; two in 6/8; and one in 3/8. All are written in two-part harmony.

It is clear that Trumpet Major Hyde, part-timer though he was, is one of the great unsung heroes in the history of British military music. There is evidence, however, to confirm that some of Hyde's calls were in existence before he published the *Preceptor*. The Tattoo call in the United States Army begins with the French call '*Extinction des Feus*', followed by the British 'Tattoo - First Post', the opening phrases of which are unchanged although the later have been curtailed.[5] From 1783 until 1917, the American and British Armies had little contact, but until 1776, and even thereafter, regiments of colonists had fought alongside the British, and it might be assumed that the survival of the British 'Tattoo – First Post' as part of an American Army bugle call is a relic of this period.

The United States cavalry did not use the trumpet, whereas the British used both the bugle and the trumpet. The United

States cavalry call 'Stables' is almost note for note the same as the British when sounded on the bugle, and this, too, would seem to indicate that these calls, and doubtless many others, were being sounded in the British Army long before Hyde had put them on paper.

The number of different calls that can be produced from the five notes of the bugle is seemingly without limit. Not only did each regiment, and in most cases each battalion, have its own distinctive regimental call – which preceded the executive call and defined who was to respond – but also each company within the battalion. Over the course of the nineteenth century, the range and number of the infantry field calls was progressively reduced, but in 1895 there were still calls for 'Advance', 'Extend', 'Retire' and 'Halt'; and the Right, Centre and Left of the line could still be nominated to respond separately or together to an executive call, that is, an order conveyed by bugle. There was also the vast range of field calls for the cavalry which were sounded on the bugle, among them 'Pursue', 'Rally', 'Halt', 'Fours About' and the call mentioned by Winston Churchill in his account of the charge of the 21st Lancers at Omdurman in the Sudan in 1898: 'Right Wheel into Line'.

In the light infantry and rifle regiments, the bugle was the sole source of music apart from the military band, which in the early days in the Peninsula was weak in numbers and instrumentation. Therefore, it fell to the buglers to provide the music which lifted spirits on the march. The 1882 Rifle Brigade manual contains some twenty-nine bugle marches, for the most part simple eight-bar phrases repeated, and in this respect very like the bagpipe march. It would therefore appear that on the march the buglers could be divided into two sections, playing each phrase alternately and thus conserving their embouchures, their 'lip'.

Some of those bugle marches have names. The first is 'The Peshawar March', harking back to years on the north-west frontier of India. 'Over the Hills and Far Away', the march forever associated with the Rifle Brigade's service in Portugal and Spain, is followed by 'Come Back, Come Back, You've No Boots in Your Pack!' There are two 'Spanish' bugle marches, a legacy perhaps of the Peninsular War, and the 'Zouave Bugle March', which might have been picked up in the Crimean War, when the British and the French for once fought as allies; the

Zouave Battalions were composed of Frenchmen, but were dressed in the North African style. The tune of the Zouave march is that of the French Army call '*Pas Redoublé*', or quickstep, and is also that of the French Army marching song '*As-tu vu la casquette du Père Bugeaud?*'[6] It is now the air of a Foreign Legion song with words dating from the 1930s: '*As-tu vu le Fanion du Légionnaire?*'.[7]

A corps of buglers, like the corps of drums and the pipe band, had the advantage of being able to split up into smaller but still musically viable units which can still function adequately. The range of the bugle is, as we have seen, limited, and an undiluted diet of bugle marches can become monotonous and thus lose its impact. The firm of instrument makers, Henry Potter, therefore evolved the 'Valve Chromatic Attachment', a three-keyed device which fitted into the mouthpiece tube of the bugle, enabling a complete chromatic scale to be played. It was quite usual for a battalion to devise its own calls for special occasions, particularly the officers mess calls. These tend to be brief fanfare-type pieces, and in the Seaforth Highlanders the officers mess call was sounded on bugles fitted with the valve chromatic attachment by three drummers, each taking a part, and on Guest Nights by nine.

When the pipes, drums and bugles of the 5th Royal Gurkha Rifles (Frontier Force) beat Retreat, the buglers carried small satchels containing the chromatic attachments and at certain stage in the ceremony these were fitted to the bugles. The buglers then played 'Old Towler', the march past of the King's Shropshire Light Infantry. Nobody knew why!

It should be noted that there were certain customs connected with the bugle mystique which set the light infantry and rifle regiments apart from the infantry of the line, and which were sedulously fostered. A bugle major carried a short parade cane, of walking-stick length, instead of the staff of the drum major. With a silver top and ferrule, the cane itself was ornamented with a twisted rifle-green cord, it was used to give the necessary signals to the band and bugles behind. The cane was never flourished or thrown, but there were ways of showing it off on the march by the manner in which it was swung from front to rear. The buglers, too, flourished their bugles when coming up and down from the playing position, the flourishes varying from regiment to regiment and adding to the impact of the sound as the light caught the silver of the instruments before each blast of the bugles.

The light infantry carried colours, but had no drums; the rifles had neither colours nor drums. In both, the bugles took the place that the drums of the line regiments held among their household gods.

The issued bugles are supplemented by a set of silver bugles, either presented separately or purchased as a set. Embossed and engraved, these were things of beauty in their own right, stored with the Officers Mess silver, reverently polished once a week under the eye of an NCO, who saw each bugle safely returned to its case. And whereas a military dignitary visiting a line battalion would be greeted by the Quarter Guard presenting arms, in the light infantry or rifles he might be welcomed by a Bugle Guard, six, eight, or more, buglers sounding a fanfare on what Serjeant Wheeler of the 51st Light Infantry called the 'soul-stirring bugles'.

Notes

1. Brown or green were the usual colours. In the Peninsular War, the 95th – the Rifle Brigade – wore dark green, and was the first British unit in the Regular Army to be dressed in a uniform appropriate to its role in the field. The coatee of the line was red – not scarlet – and was considered too conspicuous for troops operating as skirmishers, ahead and on the flanks, of the main force. This had long been recognised, and in the American Wars some Ranger units had been dressed in darker colours. The 5/60th and the two light infantry battalions of the King's German Legion also wore green. The Portuguese *caçadores* – riflemen – wore brown. All wore black buttons, belts and accoutrements.

2. The skirmishers – *voltigeurs* – who preceded the French columns in the attack came from the light infantry battalions, which were organised in the same way as the battalions of the line and were controlled by the drum. In 1805, one company in each battalion was designated as sharpshooters – *tirailleurs* – and both *voltigeurs* and *tirailleurs* were issued with the 'cornet', a small circular horn. A situation then arose perhaps more typical of the British than the French Army. It was discovered that the cornet had been issued before any calls had been devised for it, and as it lacked both tone and volume it was soon discarded in favour of the drum. The bugle made famous by the infantry of France – the clairon, once wreathed and built in the key of Bb – was introduced in 1822 to replace the cornet. The clairon was equally unpopular at first, but was finally established by Royal command in 1831, together with calls for drums, bugles, and drums and bugles composed by Melchior. *Swords around a Throne*, John R. Elting (Weidenfeld and Nicholson, 1988). Personal communication M. J-P Maingam 1993.

3. The Highland regiments ordered to provide men – four NCOs and thirty privates each – were the 71st, 72nd, 79th and 92nd. In January 1812, seven men of the Light Division who had deserted to the enemy were executed by firing squad. 'One of the poor wretches was the shoemaker of our Highland company, by name M'Giniss [Macinnes?] whom I had known for many years, and who formerly bore an excellent character.' *Twenty-five years in the Rifle Brigade*, William Surtees (The Military Book Society, 1973).

4. A transposing instrument produces a sound at a fixed interval above or below the note written. The bugle is built in the scale of Bb; when the bugler sounds the note written as 'C', his bugle produces the note Bb, one tone lower. The trumpet is built in the scale of Eb; when the trumpeter sounds the note written as 'C', his trumpet produces the note Eb, one and a half tones higher. The Highland bagpipe is also a transposing instrument; when the piper fingers the note written as 'A', the pipe chanter produces the note Bb – or thereabouts, as the pitch of the chanter is a matter of taste.

5. *Extinction des Feus* was composed for the Army of Napoleon and said to have been his favourite call. 'Tattoo – First Post' is said to be based on an old Neapolitan cavalry call *Il Silencio*. *Army Officers Guide*, Lieutenant-Colonel Lawrence P. Crocker, US Army (Stackpole Books, 1993).

6. Maréchal Thomas Robert Bugeaud de la Piconnerie (1784–1849) fought against the British in the Peninsular War. One of France's greatest colonial soldiers, he conquered and pacified the tribes of Algeria. Attacked one night in camp, he turned out and directed the defence wearing his nightcap, made, apparently, from camel hair. A 'wag' among the soldiers set words to the bugle call *'Pas Redoublé* – 'Quick Step'.

Thereafter, instead of ordering the bugler to sound 'Pas Redoublé', Bugeaud would call for *'La Casquette'*. Personal communications, J.-P. Maingam.

7. *The Foreign Legion*, Douglas Porch (Macmillan, 1991). The fanion was a little banner bearing a regimental device attached to the fixed bayonet of the *porte-fanion*, a selected soldier.

Serjeant Bugler J. Maugham, 2nd Battalion, The Highland Light Infantry, 1910
The feathered bonnet and the long, heavy, infantry mace were peculiar to the 2nd battalion. Note the
Assaye elephant on the crown of the mace and the light infantry cap lines looped across the chest. In
the 2nd Battalion, the shoulder belt was worn on top of the silk sash, as shown here. Maugham wears
an officers' pattern shoulder belt, waist belt and dirk, along with his broadsword.
(RHQ Royal Highland Fusiliers)

Bugle Major Arthur Bendy, 1st Battalion, The Highland Light Infantry, 1930
The traditional titles of the appointments were restored in 1928. Bugle Major Bendy was a noted boxer and athlete. The green cock-feather shako plume was worn only by the bugle major. He carries the short, light infantry bugle major's cane and wears an officer's pattern shoulder belt, broadsword, waist belt and dirk. (RHQ Royal Highland Fusiliers)

CHAPTER XIV
THE BUGLE (2)
~

The light infantry and the rifle brigade battalions emerged from the Peninsular War and Waterloo campaigns with much the same enhanced reputation as did the commando and parachute units from World War II, although there were, no doubt, those in 1815, as in 1945, who felt that invaluable though the contribution of such units had been, the true heroes were the regiments of the line, which had borne the heat and burden of the heaviest fighting and had suffered the highest casualties. Nevertheless, it was realised that the tactics of the light troops were those of the future, and these were widely adopted and practised, even by the 'heavy' infantry.

It was soon clear that more signals were required if the line of skirmishers was to be controlled with the flexibility which a fluid and ever-changing tactical situation demanded. So it was that *The Bugle Horn Major's Companion*, which appeared soon after the end of the war with France, contained a list of bugle calls which was comprehensive in the extreme and could be used by the battalions of the line as well as the light troops for whom it was primarily intended. The shape of the instrument seems to have changed, too, presumably for easier handling. The frontispiece of Trumpet Major Hyde's *Preceptor* features two cavalry trumpets and a bugle horn, which is round, like a horn. *The Bugle Horn Major's Companion* shows two bugles wreathed or coiled once only. They look like trumpets, and seem less likely to become damaged or distorted than the circular horn.[1] But after the Crimean War of 1854–1856, the bugle was coiled for two and a half turns, the shape it remains today.

One of the difficulties of controlling operations, or anything else in the military field, by sounds which everybody can hear is that the wrong people will inevitably react, those to whom the signal is directed claiming that they didn't understand that it applied to them. As mentioned in the previous chapter, this was overcome by sounding a preliminary signal, the regimental, battalion or company call, before the executive call, which

1st Battalion, The Highland Light Infantry, 1937, Drummer
Drums were not introduced into the 1st Battalion until 1908, but even after their appearance, the pipe band was known as the 'pipes and bugles'. Although he wears a bugle badge on his sleeve, the 1st Battalion drummers had originally worn an embroidered drum. The white spats were taken into wear in 1926 as a distinctively 'Highland' item of dress. The dirk was an Ordnance issue to bandsmen and drummers, but pipers were equipped with a more elaborate pattern, privately purchased at regimental expense. (Douglas Anderson Collection)

~

conveyed an order. The *Companion* sets out calls for each company from one to ten and also for each Grand Division.

An infantry battalion forming up to fight in line was divided – 'told off' – into eight equal 'Divisions', two of which made a 'Grand Division'. A battalion of rifles in the skirmish line, or screen, operated by companies, with its men acting individually. The infantry battalion fired in volleys, the rifles fired more or less at will, each man selecting his own target once 'Commence Firing', or 'Skirmishers may engage' had been sounded. The infantry might fire volleys or manoeuvre by grand divisions, by divisions, or by right or left sub-divisions – also called platoons – according to the situation. Whereas until the end of the eighteenth century the necessary orders would have been passed by the drums, it was now possible for the battalion in line to be similarly but far more tightly controlled by the bugle.

The functions of the rifles, supported by the light infantry, included reconnaissance, and the protection of the main body from surprise attack or ambush by moving well ahead, and far out to the flanks, of an advancing force. There are calls to send out and recall the advance guard, the rear guard and the flank guards; to extend from the right, the left or the centre; to change direction; to form line, column or square; to halt; and to lie down. In the opening pages of C.S. Forester's novel *Death to the French*, he describes a skirmish in the Peninsula in exciting terms. A bugle sounds. '"Fire and Retire!" murmurs the officer, "Listening to the high, long-drawn notes."' It would be a pity to spoil what is an excellent story, which captures exactly the 'feel' of the campaign, by pointing out that the notes are, in fact low and staccato!

Information could also be obtained, and passed, by sounding the call for one of the detached parties followed by the 'Interrogative'. There were twelve calls, covering the enemy's strength, formation and direction, which the Advance or Flank Guard bugler could sound in reply, the section ending with 'Charge', and 'Pursue the enemy'!

'The Camp and Barrack Sounds' are also detailed and comprehensive, and the shape and sound of the present-day calls are beginning to emerge. They open with the 'Dressing Bugle', sounded in three-part harmony before a Commanding Officer's Parade. There are separate 'horns' for bread, meat and vegetables, suggesting that centralised cooking was yet to come. There is no 'Tattoo' call; but 'Setting the Watch', 1st and 2nd Posts, are the current 'Tattoo – First Post' and 'Tattoo – Second Post' respectively.

A study of all the plethora of bugle calls, especially all those designed for use in the field, confirms the light infantry and rifle tradition that an entirely different standard of training and discipline was demanded from that expected of the stolid soldiers of the line, who fought shoulder to shoulder, closely supervised. The riflemen, especially, were required to respond individually to a wide range of bugled orders, which had to be recognised and acted on forthwith. Not only had a livelier and more intelligent type of soldier to be recruited, but he had to be trained in such a way as to encourage him to think for himself without fear of reprimand or punishment if he did the wrong thing.

The officers, too, were clearly dedicated soldiers. Courage could, at this period, be taken for granted, but the sheer amount of time and concentration required, first to master and then to teach the new tactics in a way to which the illiterate soldiers of the time could respond needed, and found, exceptional men.[2] This was totally at odds with the beliefs of the time, which held that soldiers were only produced by hours of close-order drill on the barrack square. In fairness, it must be admitted that the manoeuvres and evolutions of the period were complex enough, such as when the battalion was called upon to change front to the rear by means of a right about backwards wheel on the centre of sub-divisions.

A conventional military historian would not perhaps regard *Trumpet and Bugle Sounds for the Army* as a very promising source of material, but nevertheless the different editions published over the years are a reliable guide to the expansion of the Army to meet the needs of a wider Empire, as they also chronicle its contraction. The 1895 edition, for instance, has the regimental trumpet and bugle calls for all the regiments of the British Army in existence at the time, cavalry, artillery and infantry.

That edition also reveals yet another way in which the old pre-1881 battalions quietly maintained their sense of identity through their regimental and battalion calls, always sounded before the executive call whether there was another battalion within earshot or not. Ten of the twenty-four 2nd battalions raised in 1858 by the regiments numbered two to twenty-five had devised calls different from those sounded by their 1st battalion. Out of forty-four regiments created in 1881 from the single battalion regiments numbered higher than twenty-five, thirty-four of the 2nd battalions were sounding their old call, a situation which was to last until all 2nd battalions were disbanded in 1947. Of the Scottish regiments, only in the Royal Scots Fusiliers, the King's Own Scottish Borderers and the Cameron Highlanders did both battalions share the same regimental call.

In the last decade of the nineteenth century, the strength of the Army was increased in line with the growing needs of the Empire. In 1897, those regiments with fruitful recruiting areas were doubled, from two regular battalions to four. In Scotland, the Cameron Highlanders, which had been the only single battalion regiment in the Army since 1881, was allowed to recruit a 2nd battalion. These 3rd and 4th battalions disappeared after the Great War – the 2nd Camerons survived – with many of the Imperial responsibilities in the distant parts of the Empire being devolved to troops recruited and trained locally.

The fate of the 'field calls' also reminds us of the rude shock the British Army received at the hands of the Boers in the South African War of 1899–1902, which led to a thorough reassessment of its organisation and tactical doctrine from the top down. There was a drive to simplify battle procedures, and to encourage the soldiers to think for themselves. By 1903, the field calls had been reduced to two: the 'Charge' and the 'Alarm'. The reformers, however, had got the bit between their teeth, and in their anxiety to make a fresh start abolished all the cavalry camp and quarters calls, substituting those of the infantry, but sounded on the trumpet one octave lower. It is highly unlikely that anyone in the Cavalry paid the slightest attention because by 1927 all the cherished trumpet calls had been restored.

The second bugle call sounded at the Cenotaph in Whitehall on Remembrance Sunday used to be introduced as 'Reveille', but it is in fact the 'Rouse', once known as 'Turn Out' and used for getting the soldiers up at a time other than 'Reveille'. The 'Rouse' was known to an earlier generation of soldiers as 'The

Donkey'. It is a dismal call, especially when heard against a background of rain on tent canvas. The published 'Reveille', often called 'Long Reveille', is a beautiful call and would be more appropriate. Light infantry, rifles and the Royal Marines sound a call in 3/4 time called 'Charlie, Charlie, Get Up and Wash Yourself!'[3]

An interesting and somewhat mysterious call appears in the 1927 edition of *Trumpet and Bugle Sounds*. It is 'The Soudanese Reveille', which was apparently sounded by the Sudanese battalions of the old post-1882 Egyptian Army, largely British-officered. Following a series of mutinies fomented by their Egyptian officers after the Great War these were all disbanded, the renowned 9th Sudanese surviving until 1930. The Sudanese battalions were replaced by the British-officered Sudan Defence Force, which also seems to have sounded 'The Soudanese Reveille'. It was also sounded by the 4th Battalion King's African Rifles, which traced its origin to a body of Sudanese soldiers brought in to pacify what is now Uganda in 1890, 4 KAR knew the call as 'The Turkish Reveille'. Egypt and the Sudan had nominally remained part of the Ottoman Empire, and the Turkish influence remained strong in the Army where the Turkish ranks were retained even after the British reorganisation. It is an excellent example of a regulatory call, one sounded to notify an event rather than to convey an order and comes a close second to the standard 'Reveille' as a piece of music for the bugle.[4]

However rude, uncaring and licentious the image the soldier tried to project, there was, at least until the whole business of soldiering changed over the last three decades, an almost sentimental attitude to certain aspects of the military life. When in camp, 'Last Post' was sounded at 10 p.m., silence would fall over the lines while the call lasted, particularly when a good drummer was on duty and the call was well sounded. After the call, best heard among friends, there was little left to say.

Due to its outstanding record in the field, in 1809 the 71st Highlanders, raised in 1777, had been selected for conversion to the light infantry role, becoming the 71st Highland Light Infantry in 1810, a title it was to keep until amalgamated with the Royal Scots Fusiliers in 1959. The Scots Fusiliers had been raised in 1678, and therefore took precedence. So Scotland lost its light infantry regiment and, with it, its unique distinction of being both highland and light infantry which the Highland Light Infantry had so sedulously maintained since 1810.

The Cameronians (Scottish Rifles) adopted the trappings of the rifle tradition with enthusiasm on its formation in 1881 – the dark rifle-green doublet with its black buttons, the black accoutrements, the short, sharp, rifle step and the cult of the bugle. In 1968, The Cameronians (Scottish Rifles) was disbanded, and the light infantry and rifle tradition, and its associated expertise with the bugle, disappeared from the Scottish order of battle. But while those regiments lasted, their distinctive traditions had been maintained with zest and devotion, leavened, be it said, with tact and good humour and a refreshing lack of the pomposity and arrogance which long tradition, perpetuated only for its own sake, so often entails. Scotland – and the Army – is the poorer for their loss.

Notes

1. The instrument associated with the French chasseurs – light infantry – is the circular cor de chasse, the open horn without valves sounding only its harmonic series of notes. It features in many of of the chasseurs' marches along with the clairon, the bandsmen 'doubling' on both. Although the cor de chasse does not appear to have been used to sound tactical calls in the field, it is so used during the formal hunting of the stag in the forests of France. The march 'Sidi Ibrahim' is the 'Chant des Chasseurs', who march past, like the British light troops, at 140 paces to the minute.
2. Many were Scots. The reintroduction of light troops was carried out under the general supervision of Lieutenant-General Sir John Moore, son of a Glasgow doctor. Thomas Graham of Balgowan, a Perthshire laird, raised the 90th Light Infantry in 1794. The 90th was trained in light infantry tactics by Colonel Kenneth MacKenzie from Broughty Ferry who was later appointed to train Moore's own regiment, the 52nd, converted to light infantry in 1803. Lieutenant-Colonel William Stewart, whose enlightened approach to discipline lies at the heart of the whole rifle corps ethos, was the first lieutenant-colonel of the Experimental Rifle Corps. The importance attached to marksmanship in *Instructions for the Conduct of Infantry* published in 1807 by Lieutenant-Colonel John MacDonald was the first step towards the 'mad minute', the fifteen aimed rounds in sixty seconds that stopped the Germans in their tracks at Mons in August 1914.
3. Until 1923, the Corps of Royal Marines consisted of two branches, the Royal Marine Artillery and the Royal Marine Light Infantry. The bugle call derives from the latter; the Royal Marine Artillery used the trumpet.
4. *Drummers Call*, Newsletter of the Corps of Drums Society, No. 47, 1995.

Appendix
Field Duty and Camp and Barrack Sounds

Fire and Retreat.

Nº 39.

At the signal to commence firing, immediately followed by the signal to retreat, the front rank fires, goes to the right about, marches in double time 24 paces to the rear of the rear rank, fronts and loads. The rear rank hearing the ramrods of the front rank working, makes ready, fires, then faces to the right about, marches in double time 24 paces to the rear of the front rank, fronts and loads. In this manner both ranks retire supporting each other. When the fire in retreating is to cease, the Commanding officer orders the signal for "Cease firing" to be made.

Halt.

Nº 40.

Lie Down.

Nº 41.

Rise up.

Nº 42.

Nº 43. March.

Nº 44. Quick March.

Nº 45. Double Quick.

If the column is marching in ordinary time, and the signal Quick march, or Double Quick is given, it is not to alter its pace until the sound is finished.

The Enemy has Artillery.

Nº 70.

The Enemy's Infantry are advancing.

Nº 71.

The Enemy's Cavalry are advancing.

Nº 72.

The Enemy are inclining to the right.

Nº 73.

The Enemy are inclining to the left.

Nº 74.

The Enemy are in Line.

Nº 75.

The Enemy are in open Column.

Nº 76.

The Enemy are in close Column.

Nº 77.

The Enemy are in small numbers.

Nº 78.

The Enemy are in force.

Nº 79.

The Enemy are halted.

Nº 80.

The Enemy are retiring.

Nº 81.

Pursue the Enemy.

Nº 82.

The Charge.

Nº 83.

END OF THE FIELD DUTY.

Serjeant Piper William Young, 2nd Battalion, The Highland Light Infantry, 1910
Barely visible on the pipe major's unique sporran is the elephant superscribed 'Assaye', a hard-earned
battle honour gained by the 74th in India during the 1st Mahratta War of 1803 – Wellington's
earliest victory. The pipe major's pipe banner bears the old precedence number LXXIV, although the
design of the crown shows that it was made after 1901.
(National War Museum of Scotland)

CHAPTER XV
REGIMENTAL MARCHES (1)
~

The concept of the Regimental March, that is a marching tune associated with one particular regiment, is common to most armies. Such marches are a potent means of creating that sense of a separate and exclusive identity, which is one of the first steps in the process of building up the personal morale of the soldier. In addition, such marches were a method of identifying the unit in the field as well as in the parades and reviews which, until the outbreak of World War II, were a feature of the military life. When the band and drums crashed into the savage 'Ça Ira' of the French Revolution, everyone within earshot knew that a battalion of the old West Yorkshire Regiment was on its way, while one of the most musical and attractive marches of all, 'La Mandolinata', announced the imminent arrival of the Bedfordshires, the old 16th Foot, once known as 'The Peacemakers' because of their alleged lack of battle honours.[1] However, those two regiments were unusual; the great majority of British regiments marched past to folk tunes associated with their home county or area.[2] In most cases, the regimental march was played whenever the battalion 'marched past' in the military sense of the term, that is, when the battalion formally marched past an inspecting officer at the end of a ceremonial parade. It might also be played whenever the battalion marched into barracks or camp at the end of a route march or exercise. There were cases, however, when the regimental march differed from the march past, but these were rare.

For many years, a regiment or battalion could march past to any tune which took its fancy and, to the sorrow of succeeding generations of military sociologists, little or no attempt was made to record when a particular tune was taken into use, or, more importantly, why. Commanding officers and bandmasters were at liberty to order the band to play their own personal favourites or, not perhaps infrequently, the favourite of their wife or some other lady in whom they might happen to be interested at the time.

REGIMENTAL MARCHES (1)

Amidst all the other upheavals of 1881, the subject of regimental marches and tunes for marching past came under review. Regiments were ordered to submit such tunes to the War Office for approval, the object being, it might be assumed, to stimulate the process of unification by ensuring that both battalions of the same regiment marched past to the same tune – a vain hope, as we shall see. In the event, some regiments dutifully complied; but others took no notice, among them the senior regiment in the Army, the Royal Scots, which continued to march past happily to 'Dumbarton's Drums' for the next hundred years, blissfully unaware that their unique march had never been officially approved, an omission which would not have worried 'Pontius Pilate's Bodyguard' in the slightest even if it had been discovered.[3]

Let us take a look at when those splendid tunes were played. Formal parades and inspections had two functions. The first was to allow a senior officer to see the troops under his command and to assess their state of discipline, training and morale This was done firstly by sizing each man up as he passed down the ranks of the parade in succession; secondly, by noting how responsive they were to the word of command, how they handled their arms and how they performed certain formalised manoeuvres on the parade-ground; and, thirdly, by having them marched past him in different formations, so that their individual bearing could be assessed, as well as their confidence and cohesion when moving as a unit.

The second, rarely stated, was to let the soldiers have a look at their commander, on whose professional skill and ability their lives might one day depend. This aspect was stressed in the old German Army, where the parade formation allowed the commander and his soldiers to look each other straight in the eye, unlike in the British, where the soldier was trained to glare fixedly to his front. During the later stages of the proceedings the march past took place, with the commander stationed on a raised platform called the Saluting Base. This let him see the troops as they marched past, and they him. In whatever formation or tempo they passed, the troops saluted by turning their heads towards the commander, looking him straight in the eye as they did so; he returned the compliment by raising his hand to his cap.[4]

As has been noted, in the British Army, where individual eccentricities were still treasured, the march past might be carried out in slow time at seventy-five paces to the minute; and in quick time, at either one hundred and twelve, one hundred and sixteen, one hundred and twenty or one hundred and forty paces to the minute, depending on whether the battalion marching past was a Highland, guards, line, rifle or light infantry unit. Occasionally, one of the last-named might march past in double time at one hundred and sixty paces at the minute, that is, running; and until about 1884, every unit was trained to march past at the 'double' but these days are long gone, and marching past in that dramatic fashion is now regarded as the prerogative of the rifles and light infantry.

The soldiers could march past in one of a number of formations and, assuming that before the parade the battalion had been formed up in four companies of equal strength, it might march past in slow time in Column of Companies, while in quick time the formation might be Column of Companies, Close or Quarter Column, Column of Threes, or Column of Route, depending largely on the time which could be devoted to rehearsal or, more likely, how interested the commanding officer was in ceremonial drill.

In 'Column of Companies', each company marches in line of two or three ranks, the distance between companies being the same as the frontage it occupies, that is, the length of the line of men. This was originally a tactical formation which enabled the battalion to form line by having each company wheel to its right or left, either in succession or all at the same time. 'Close' or 'Quarter' Column was the same, except that the companies stood about seven paces behind each other. This, too, had been a tactical formation, used when the battalion had to move up quickly, but under control, to a place where it could deploy into some other formation.

In 'Column of Threes', the company marched three abreast, with the officers and serjeants on the flanks of the marching soldiers. 'Column of Route' was the same, but with the officers and serjeants at the head and rear of the company, taking up as little road space as possible so that mounted men and vehicles could pass easily.

That, put simply, is how troops marched past, and easy

enough it sounds. In practice, however, the whole procedure was fraught with the possibility of disaster. On the other hand, when all went well, a smart parade could be an exhilarating experience for everyone, participants and spectators alike. The standard of music on such occasions is as important as the standard of drill, as anyone would agree who has seen how the marching guardsmen respond to the magnificent music of the massed bands of the foot guards on the Queen's Birthday Parade in London.

The bands could help here by maintaining a settled and rhythmic beat; not for nothing was the bass drummer in some regiments known as the Time Beater. One who could keep a precise time and tempo was a jewel beyond price. Two such paragons were required, one with the band and the other with the pipes and drums or corps of drums, because both played on ceremonial parades. In the Highland regiments the tendency was for the band to speed up the marching pace of 112 to 116, or even 120 to the minute, while the pipes and drums would pull it back to about 108, their preferred speed for playing marches in quick time. Though both were well accustomed to playing marches, their approach was entirely different and could lead to tense confrontations during the rehearsal period as the bandmaster and band serjeant glowered at the drum and pipe majors, while the adjutant and regimental serjeant major held the ring.

Music, played turn and turn about by the pipe and military bands, provided an impressive backdrop to the ceremonies which attended a formal inspection and march past. The inspecting officer was received with a General Salute, the troops presenting arms and the officers saluting with their swords while the band played eight bars of a slow march at a brisk tempo. Most regiments have a pipe General Salute, but the process of starting up and striking in the Highland pipe, even if covered by the drums, can detract from the impact of the salute as the pipers 'wind' their instruments. With the loss of the battalion's military band, the pipes will have perforce to accept this commitment.

During the inspection, which could take some time, the two bands alternated, the pipe band playing slow marches and the military band what were known as slow 'troops', tunes written in

3/4 or waltz time. Slow troops, in theory, differ from slow marches, the latter being written in common time, although the distinction is now rather academic. No such distinctions are made between pipe tunes in slow time, the majority of which are in 6/8 time, a characteristic time signature in Gaelic song, from which the older slow marches, often called slow airs, are derived. The inspection completed, the necessary orders would be given preparatory to the march past.

Here, however, we are dealing with the Scottish regiments only and the music they played when marching past in slow and quick time. The tunes are set out schematically at Appendix 'A' to the next chapter, and it will be noted that when marching past in slow time, every Scottish regiment plays 'The Garb of Old Gaul'. Cases have been known where some soldiers have believed that 'Old Gaul' was some ancient regimental hero immortalised in music, but the mundane fact is that Gaul was a province of the Roman Empire corresponding roughly to Eastern France and Western Germany. Its natives were reported to have worn a mantle or cloak belted round the body in the style of the 'Feile Mor', the belted plaid of yore. Hence the kilt is the 'Garb of Old Gaul', and hence, too, the words of the opening verse:

> In the garb of old Gaul with the fire of old Rome,
> From the heath-covered mountains of Scotia we come;
> When the Romans endeavoured our country to gain,
> Our ancestors fought, and they fought not in vain.

The composer? One reads of the ideal eighteenth-century man, who could write a sonnet, compose a sonata, fight a duel, elope with an heiress and die at the head of a Forlorn Hope, all with equal nonchalance.[5] Such a man was John Reid, who at his death was a general in the Army, having been commissioned ensign in Loudon's Highlanders at the age of fourteen, later transferring to the Black Watch.

Reid was an accomplished musician and a fine flautist. Between 1770 and 1780, he composed and published a set of minuets and marches. The marches are pleasing and attractive, if not of great musical merit, but they include 'The Garb of Old Gaul'. Reid said that the words were composed in Gaelic by a soldier of the Black Watch. All Reid's marches are of two measures or so, and all are written in ordinary time, 72 paces to the minute.

On his death in 1806, Reid left his considerable fortune to the University of Edinburgh, on condition that a Chair of Music was established and that on the anniversary of his birthday a concert was to be held, at which some of his compositions were to be played in order, as Reid explained, to let the audience hear the type of composition which had been in vogue in Reid's time. The Reid School of Music in Edinburgh University still flourishes; the Reid Memorial concerts are still held on 13th January; and among the pieces played is 'The Garb of Old Gaul'.

Although several Black Watch officers claimed to have translated the Gaelic words into English, credit for the version now current is usually given to another General, Sir Harry Erskine of Alva in Stirlingshire, late of the Royal and 25th Regiments, the Royal Scots and King's Own Scottish Borderers. His second verse is worth repeating:

> No effeminate customs our sinews unbrace,
> No luxurious tables enervate our race;
> Our loud sounding pipe bears the true martial strain,
> So do we the old Scottish valour retain.

So there! The words were first published in 1765, the year in which Erskine died.

The Black Watch have played 'The Garb of Old Gaul' as their slow march since 1769, and it was certainly known in its early days as 'The Highland March', and also as 'The 42nd Regiment's March'. It is therefore a Black Watch tune and, by extension, appropriate only to the Highland regiments, who wear 'The Garb of Old Gaul'.

Victorian bandmasters were great 'improvers', and the simple but heart-stirring tune of 'The Garb of Old Gaul' has been arranged as a slow march, with an introduction of stunning forgetability, the whole rounded off with a trio of equal mediocrity. This, unfortunately, is how it has been published in march-card form, and if played as written the whole appeal of Reid's march can be obscured as the band trudges through the turgid march card.[6]

We come now to the music played by the military or regimental bands for the march past in quick time. These were to be heard more often on the bandstand at the end of a performance rather than on the parade-ground, most regiments preferring to march past in quick time to the pipes and drums. As we have seen, different speeds for marching past were laid down; when played on the bandstand the regimental marches tended to be played rather more briskly, as the bandsmen usually had their getaway timed to the last second, the majority having other irons in the fire, fish to fry, or whatever.

The Royal Scots Dragoon Guards march past to a standard band march inherited from one of their component regiments whose traditions they maintain. That regiment was the 3rd Dragoon Guards, and the march is named simply 'The 3rd DGs'. The Scots Guards play 'Highland Laddie', a tune which is very old, originally called 'Wilt thou play me fair play?'. A journalist at the 1845 Queen's Birthday Parade commented that the Scots Guards marched past to 'The national, but mediocre melody "Will ye go to Inverness?"' – there are several versions of the song – and he compared it unfavourably with the splendid music played by the Coldstream Guards. The same, it must be said, holds good today. Consisting as it does of two simple eight-bar phrases, each repeated, 'Highland Laddie' can become monotonous when, for instance, a battalion in column of route has to be played past.[7]

The Royal Scots, The Royal Regiment, 'First of Foot, Right of the Line and Pontius Pilate's Bodyguard', has, as is fitting, one of the oldest marches on record. It is the renowned 'Dumbarton's Drums'. Lord George Douglas commanded the regiment from 1655 until its recall in 1678. He had been created 1st Earl of Dumbarton in 1675 and was reappointed colonel in 1685.

It was at one time believed that 'Dumbarton's Drums' was the tune of the 'Scots March', played and beaten by the units of Scottish mercenaries serving on the Continent of Europe during the Thirty Years War of 1618–1648, and probably earlier too. We now know that the 'Scots March' was a entirely separate tune. 'Dumbarton's Drums' might well be older than its name suggests. If, as seems possible, the Royal Scots were playing it when they finally reverted to the British service, it appears likely that the association of the tune with the regiment might have begun during an earlier spell in the French service. But be that as it may, the first definite connection between the tune and the name appears to be in a book of Scots songs and airs published in 1724.

When Queen Victoria was born in 1818, her father, the Duke of Kent – he who gave his name to the 'Kenthorn', the keyed bugle – was Colonel of the Royal Regiment. In 1889, the band of the 2nd Battalion Royal Scots played 'The Daughter of the Regiment' as a compliment to Queen Victoria when she took the salute at a review in Aldershot. It is now played by the military band as the march past when Royalty is present. The tune comes from Donizetti's opera of the same name and is the melody of a song sung by the heroine to the soldiers, '*Quel Régiment!*' – 'What a Regiment!' – and very apt it is too when applied to the 1st of Foot, the glorious old Royal Scots.

It is a tradition that all British fusilier regiments march past to 'The British Grenadiers', an allusion to the bursting grenade badge which all share in some form or other. Before the amalgamation of all fusilier regiments outside Scotland and Wales into the Royal Regiment of Fusiliers, it was alternated with a march of closer domestic connections – the Royal Northumberland Fusiliers played 'Blaydon Races', for instance. The Royal Scots Fusiliers played 'Highland Laddie' along with 'The British Grenadiers', and the Royal Highland Fusiliers now couple it with 'Whistle O'er the Lave o't!' – 'Whistle Over the Rest of It!' – the title coming from a Burns song poking fun at the institution of marriage. The tune, as is often the case in Burns's songs, is older, and is also the tune to which the Highland dance '*Sean Triubhas*' – The Shoddy Breeks' – is performed. The dance is said to express the disgust of the Highlanders at being forced to wear trousers instead of the kilt under the terms of the Disarming Act of 1747 – although some of the steps and arm movements, which are claimed to illustrate this disgust, owe more to the ballet training undergone by a prominent Highland dancer of the nineteenth century than to the native Highland tradition.

The links between the Scottish Borderland and the King's Own Scottish Borderers are close and strong, and from the wealth of songs and ballads which is to be found in the Scottish

Borders, the regiment has chosen the air to which Sir Walter Scott's verses from his novel *The Monastery* – set in the Border country – is sung:

> March, march, Ettrick and Teviotdale.
> Why the De'il dinna ye march forward in order?
> March, march, Eskdale and Liddesdale,
> All the Blue Bonnets are bound for the Border.
> Many a banner spread
> Flutters above your head,
> Many a crest that is famous in story.
> Mount, and make ready then,
> Sons of the mountain glen,
> Fight for the Queen and our old Scottish glory!"

The tune to which the words are sung is much older than the words themselves, which originated in the fertile mind of Sir Walter, and none the worse for that! It first appears as 'General Leslie's March to Longmarston Moor', which happened in 1644 and puts it at least two centuries earlier than the words. It is unlikely, however, that the tune was composed specifically to meet that occasion, and it is consequently likely to be older still. Sir Walter refers to it as the 'Ancient air of "Blue Bonnets over the Border",' so clearly he wrote the words to fit the tune, although his second line would scan better if he had left out 'the De'il'. In Watts' *Musical Miscellany*, published in London in 1731, the tune is called 'Black, White, Yellow and Red'; it appears elsewhere as 'Leslie's March'; and in some early pipe collections it is called 'The Fusiliers' March'.[8]

The 'Blue Bonnets', as we might as well call it, is one of the very few marches closely associated with one particular regiment by tradition, custom and practice, but which has been taken up by others, not perhaps so much for its words, which apply logically to the King's Own Scottish Borderers, as for its good rousing tune. *The Monastery* was published in 1830, and it might be assumed that the song and its associated tune became popular as a result.

The Black Watch adopted the 'Blue Bonnets' as their march past in quick time for the Military Band about 1850 and have played it ever since. A surprising choice in view of the tune's provenance, although it has to be said that the soldiers of the Black Watch are more accurately described as 'Sons of the Mountain Glen' than the Lowlanders of the King's Own Scottish Borderers. Although 'borderers' is in this case the more accurate term, as the two are not strictly synonymous, and there are many high hills and lonely glens in the beautiful Borderland from where the King's Own Scottish Borderers recruit their hardy and independent soldiers.

The former Queen's Own Highlanders, amalgamated with the Gordon Highlanders in 1994 to create The Highlanders, had been formed by a merger of the Seaforth and Cameron Highlanders in 1961. It had taken the Seaforth Highlanders from 1881 until 1912 to produce Standing Orders applicable to both battalions. Until then, the 1st battalion, the old 72nd, had marched past to 'The Blue Bonnets', which was recognised in 1912 as a regimental tune, played for the march past in Close Column by both battalions, and also when the band of either 'played off' at the end of a performance, the sequence being 'The Garb of Old Gaul', 'The Blue Bonnets', 'Rule Britannia', and 'Scotland For Ever!', this last being none other than 'Scotland the Brave'.

While most of the great magnates of the Highland had a Gaelic patronymic, the Duke of Gordon's was 'The Cock of the North', for although he owned vast estates in the Highlands, Gaelic was not widely spoken in Aberdeenshire, where his influence was strongest. The march 'The Cock of the North', was played by the military band of the Gordon Highlanders as the march past in quick time. As a march, the tune is well known, although the words sometimes sung to it appear to have more to do with soldiers' vernacular speech than with the folklore of Aberdeen.

The Argyll and Sutherland Highlanders share with the Royal Scots Dragoon Guards the distinction of having a standard band march as their march past in quick time to the music of the band. The Argyll's is 'The Thin Red Line', composed at the invitation of the commanding officer by the doyen of British march composers, Frederick J. Ricketts, under his *nom de plume*, Kenneth Alford. Ricketts was bandmaster of the 2nd Argylls, the old 93rd, from 1908 until 1927. Ricketts based the introduction to his march on the second phrase of the 93rd's regimental call: 'Tippy, tippy 93rd!'. The soldiers' word 'tippy' conveying a certain sense of style, as well as mere smartness.[9] 'The Thin Red Line', although composed in 1908, was not published until 1925, remaining the exclusive property of the 93rd in the meantime. In the Argylls, each battalion had kept its old march past, that of the 93rd being 'Highland Laddie', which, as we have seen, they shared with several others, hence the commanding officer's wish to have a more distinctive march past. The 1st Battalion, the old 91st, as befitted a Clan Campbell regiment, played 'The Campbells are Coming!'.

Notes

1. At the Battle of Famars in May 1793, the 14th Foot – later the West Yorkshire Regiment – were being attacked by the French, whose band was playing the revolutionary song *'Ça ira'*:
"Ah, ça ira, ça ira, ça ira,
à la lanterne, les aristos!
Ah, ça ira, ça ira, ça ira
Les aristocrats, on les pendra!"
The Commanding Officer of the 14th ordered his drummers to strike up 'Ça ira!' and, turning to his men, cried, 'We'll beat them to their own damned tune!' This the 14th did, and made *'Ça ira'* their own.
2. The 1st Battalion Wiltshire Regiment, for instance, marched past to a Wiltshire folk song with the refrain:
'The vly, the vly,
The vly be on the turmut
Dang me oyes, 'ow 'ard Oi troys,
Oi can't keep vly off turmuts.'
3. While in the French service, the officers of *'Le Régiment d' Hebron'* – 'Hepburn's Regiment' – were arguing with the officers of *'Le Régiment de Picardie'*, the senior of the six 'Old Corps' of the French Army, about their relative antiquity. The Picardie officers claimed to have guarded the tomb on the night of the Crucifixion; the Scots retorted that they had been on duty as Pontius Pilate's Bodyguard that night; and that they, in any case, would not have slept at their posts!
4. In drill instructor's vernacular the "'ead'n'eyes' were turned right or left as ordered.
5. When a breach had been battered in the walls of a besieged town, it would be stormed by troops of the besieging force. At the head of the stormers moved the 'Forlorn Hope', consisting usually of an officer and some twenty soldiers, all volunteers. Those who survived the assault were rewarded in some way, usually by promotion; in the case of the officer, without purchase.
6. A street song to the tune of 'Highland Laddie' and popular with Scottish urchins when a Pipe Band passed, began:

A' the bumbees kickin' up a row,
Herrin' Jennie, six a penny

7. In Scottish regiments the first subject and the trio are never played.

8. For a fascinating discussion of the provenance of 'Dumbarton's Drums' and 'The Blue Bonnets' see *The Regimental Records of The Royal Scots (1st or Royal Regiment of Foot)*, J.C. Leask and H.M. McCance (Alex Thom & Co., Dublin).

9. The same phrase was the regimental call of the 1st Battalion Highland Light Infantry.

Appendix
Regimental Marches – Band

'In the Garb of Old Gaul'
Slow March of All Scottish Regiments

The first section and the Trio were not played when marching past or at the conclusion of a band programme.

1st Battalion, The Argyll and Sutherland Highlanders (Princess Louise's), Pipes and Drums, 1978
Her Majesty the Queen is colonel-in-chief of The Argyll and Sutherland Highlanders, and is photographed here
with the pipes and drums of the 1st Battalion. Pipe Major M. MacGillivray displays the Queen's personal pipe
banner with the Scottish Royal Arms. On the other side is the regimental crest of the Argylls. On Her Majesty's
right is the colonel of the regiment, Lieutenant-General A.C.S. Boswell and on her left is Lieutenant-Colonel I.
Purves Hume, commanding officer of the 1st Battalion. (RHQ Argyll and Sutherland Highlanders)

2nd Battalion, The King's Own Scottish Borderers, Pipes and Drums, Dublin, 1913
The Kilmarnock bonnet worn by the drummers and buglers replaced the blue home-service pattern helmet in 1903.
The drum major's scarf plaid is in the Leslie tartan while his sash of office is the usual pattern issued from Ordnance.
The pipers wear the Royal Stuart kilt and scarf plaid; their doublet is blue. (National War Museum of Scotland)

2nd Battalion, The Royal Scots (The Royal Regiment), Pipes, Drums and Military Band, Hong Kong, 1938

Drum Major Degnan is in the act of ordering 'Eyes Front' as the bands pay compliments – perhaps to the commanding officer – at the conclusion of a formal parade. The soldiers are wearing khaki drill jackets, indicating that the occasion has been of a domestic nature. On ceremonial occasions, white drill jackets were worn. The 2nd Battalion, The Royal Scots, formed part of the garrison of Hong Kong when the Japanese invaded in December 1941, the survivors becoming prisoners of war. A United States submarine torpedoed the ship, the Lisbon Maru, in which they were being transported to Japan. The Japanese guards battened down the hatches, trapping the prisoners in the hold. When the prisoners succeeded in forcing open the hatch covers, the guards opened fire. A few survived to reach the shore where they were succoured by Chinese fishermen until their eventual recapture. (RHQ The Royal Scots)

CHAPTER XVI
REGIMENTAL MARCHES (2)
~

Now to the Highland pipe. When marching past in slow time to the pipes, the Scots Guards and the Royal Scots keep 'The Garb of Old Gaul', a tune which is, in places, outside the compass of the pipe chanter and has, consequently, to be rearranged to fit it, never a satisfactory process and, in this case, much to the detriment of the melody. Played as a quick march in common time, however, the tune 'goes' quite well. There exists an abundance of Highland and Scottish airs, some composed for the pipes and others within its compass, which would serve equally adequately as a march past in slow time and would sound less 'contrived' than the modified 'The Garb of Old Gaul'. The drawback to all such tunes, however, is that the bagpipe, with its continuous sound and constant volume, cannot mark the beat as effectively as the military band does so well with its wealth of resources. The drums can help; but slow airs and slow marches on the pipes will always convey associations with the Highland shieling[1] rather than the parade-ground, and are less suitable for parade purposes than the slow troops and marches played by the military band.

But the abolition of the regimental military bands – that had been diminished to absurd proportions latterly – meant that the pipes must assume the band's role, which they could fulfil, of course, if only adequately. *'Mo Dhachaid'* – 'My Home' – is a Gaelic song air, long a favourite with pipers, which is the march past in slow time of the Royal Scots Dragoon Guards, the Royal Highland Fusiliers, and the Black Watch. The Argyll and Sutherland Highlanders play 'The Skye Boat Song', familiar to the layman as 'Over the Sea to Skye', few realising that the song refers to the escape of Prince Charles Edward Stuart in 1746 from Benbecula in the Outer Hebrides to Skye in the Inner Isles, disguised as Betty Burke, maid to the brave and beautiful Flora MacDonald. It has nothing to do with his eventual escape to France. It might be said to be a strange choice for a staunchly Campbell regiment, whose clansmen predecessors   were busily

1st Battalion, The Royal Scots Fusiliers, Gosport, 1912
In the Royal Scots Fusiliers, the corps of drums flourished until the outbreak of the Great War. The pipers led and were followed by the corps of drums and the military band, each taking it in turn to play. This illustration shows the strength of musical resources available to a well-found Scottish infantry battalion in those days when marching was the usual method of progression. When the Lowland regiments adopted the Kilmarnock in 1903, the Royal Scots Fusiliers retained their racoon-skin fusilier cap with a white hackle on the left and the grenade badge with the Royal Arms of England on the bomb in the centre. (Douglas Anderson Collection)

engaged in hunting for the Prince, without success, in 1746 — happily for Scottish myth and romance.

The King's Own Scottish Borderers march past in slow time to a beautiful tune called simply 'The Borderers', composed about a hundred years ago by the pipe major of the 1st battalion, John Balloch, who came from Greenock on the Clyde. The Gordon and the Queen's Own Highlanders used to play tunes composed for the pipes, the Gordons 'Saint Andrew's Cross', and the Queen's Own Highlanders 'The Skye Gathering', the tune named for the annual Highland games held on the island in August.

We break into quick time now, as we discuss the tunes played by the Scottish regiments when marching past to the pipes, those tunes which are known, sung, whistled and played throughout Scotland and, indeed, wherever Scots people foregather. The tune played by the Scots Guards and the Royal Scots Dragoon Guards is 'Highland Laddie', although the Scots Guards call it

'Hielan' Laddie', a Lowland corruption eschewed by the Highland regiments. The comments made about the tune in 1845 still apply, and it is, in any case, a tune about men in the kilt, the dress of the Highland soldier whether he is one by birth or adoption. At one time there were many small regimental quirks about how the tune was played, and, indeed, most regiments had their own little touches which made it possible for a knowledgeable listener to identify the regiment from the setting which was being played. Like several other tunes, notably 'Scotland the Brave', the tune has become standardised over the years as a result of too much massed band playing at Tattoos and the like where, for obvious reasons, all the pipers have to play the same version or 'setting'.

The pipers of the Royal Scots have to cope with 'Dumbarton's Drums' in its pipe setting, which follows the military band arrangement closely – rather too closely, as a young piper might think as he tries to get his fingers round the somewhat intricate melody. 'Dumbarton's Drums' is what a bandsman might call a 'black' tune, meaning that it has a lot of notes; and he would be quite right, as it is one which is difficult to play well, particularly when the drummers are keeping up a brisk one hundred and sixteen paces to the minute, as the regulations for non-Highland regiments require. 'Dumbarton's Drums' is not a pipe tune, although it is hallowed by tradition and by its irrevocable connection with the 1st of Foot. It is interesting, all the same, that the former 9th (Highlanders) Battalion of the Royal Scots, the 'Dandy Ninth' of Edinburgh fame, marched past to 'The Blue Bonnets', not a Highland tune by any means, but one retained when the 7th (Leith) Battalion united with the 9th after the Great War.

The Royal Highland Fusiliers keep up the old tradition, formerly widely observed, of playing one march when marching past in Column of Companies and another when returning in Close Column. In Column, the tune is 'The Blue Bonnets', inherited from the Highland Light Infantry, in Close Column, it is 'Highland Laddie', from the Royal Scots Fusiliers.

'The Blue Bonnets' is the march past in quick time of the King's Own Scottish Borderers, who must be adjudged to have first claim on it. One reason for its popularity is that it is not only an outstanding march for the pipes, but that in the pipe arrangement there are four 'parts' or 'measures', the first two building up to the third, with its insistent 'March! March!' motif. There once was a soldiers' doggerel verse to the first part, which began:

> Lance-Corporal Dugald MacFarlane,
> He is the pride of the second battalion . . .

and the tune might be called for simply by a shout of 'Dugald MacFarlane'. There were also doggerel words to the third measure, which went:

> March, march, over the Border,
> Some of them drunk and some of them sober . . .

As the pipe setting of 'The Blue Bonnets' runs to four parts, whereas the band setting has only two, there is no hint of repetition or monotony, no matter how many times the tune has to be played over, either during a march past or on the line of march. 'The Blue Bonnets' is one of those tunes which features in the repertoire of every piper and every pipe band. However, in Scottish military music nothing is ever simple, and the 5th (Dumfries and Galloway) Battalion of the King's Own Scottish Borderers substituted 'Bonnie Gallowa'', a song which lauds the beauties of their home country, for the third and fourth measures, effectively altering the whole impact of the march, as well as bringing it closer to home.

'Highland Laddie' is the march past on the pipes of the Black Watch, the regiment which has best claim to it. It is mentioned in eighteenth-century accounts of life in the regiment as having had Gaelic words put to it by Mr MacLaggan, the chaplain at the time – in their original state, the Highland regiments were notably strict in religious observance - who also had Gaelic words to 'The Garb of Old Gaul'. It is the Black Watch regimental setting of 'Highland Laddie' which is now universally played, a pity, as the alternatives have their own charm and uniformity is anathema in pipe music. The reason is perhaps that published regimental collections of pipe music all print the Black Watch setting, and now that every piper can read music, it is easier for him to learn the tune from the printed page, rather than 'off the fingers' of an older hand, as used to be the case.

When the Queen's Own Highlanders was formed, the choice of a pipe tune for marching past was eased, ostensibly, by the fact that both the Seaforth and the Cameron Highlanders had done so to the same tune – arguably, the best march past in the Army. The tune is anglicised as *'Pibroch o' Donuil Dubh'* – 'Black Donald's March' – and is probably over five hundred years old. It has associations with both Clan Cameron and Clan Donald, and in several of the ancient versions, which clan triumphs depends on the clan of the singer. In 1816, Sir Walter Scott put words to the tune of the Gaelic song which is, basically, that of the march.

Needless to say, however, all was not plain sailing, as the Seaforth and the Camerons played different settings. A neutral setting was evolved in a laudable attempt to satisfy both sides, always important in the negotiating stages of a regimental amalgamation, but in the event, the pipers of the new regiment took matters into their own hands and simply played the setting they liked best. Nobody noticed!

'The Cock of the North' has immediate associations with the Gordon Highlanders, and was the tune played by Piper Findlater at the storming of the heights of Dargai by the 1st Gordons on the north-west frontier of India in 1897. It is, as we have seen, the patronymic of the Duke of Gordon. However, in the collection of bagpipe music published by Donald MacDonald about 1822, the tune appears as *'Gairm na'n Coileach'*, which means, near enough, 'The Cock's Call', or 'Crow', and what Donald prints are the opening measures of the pipe setting played by the Gordon Highlanders. Until 1932, the Gordons marched past to the ubiquitous and, some might say, hackneyed, 'Highland Laddie'; but in that year 'Highland Laddie' was discarded and 'The Cock of the North' adopted, a change worthy of applause, and one which gave the Gordons an inspiring and distinctive march past.

Before the Gordon Highlanders and the Queen's Own Highlanders amalgamated, the question of how the music of the old regiments should be modified was handed over to a committee consisting of pipe majors and officers with a piping background. The committee recommended that both the *'Pibroch o' Donald Dubh'* and the 'Cock of the North' should be retained as regimental marches, but that the march past should be a tune composed by Pipe Major Donald MacLeod of the Seaforth and

Queen's Own Highlanders called 'The Wee Highland Laddie'. It is in Common or 4/4 time and has the true Highland lilt to it. The Slow March adopted was the 'Trooping the Colour' by Pipe Major G.S. McLennan of the Gordon Highlanders. He having died in 1929, his family agreed that the tune be renamed 'The Highlanders Slow March'.

'Highland Laddie' was the march past of the 2nd Battalion Argyll and Sutherland Highlanders, and we have seen how a march was composed to replace it as far as the military band was affected. The pipes, however, stuck with 'Highland Laddie' until the disbandment of all 2nd battalions in 1948, and to commemorate the old 93rd, as the 2nd battalion had been until 1881, 'Highland Laddie' is always played by the pipes and drums of the 1st Argylls along with their own march past, 'The Campbells are Coming!'.

The English words of 'The Campbells are Coming!' are set to the tune of an old Gaelic song *'Bail' Ionbhar-Aoro'* – the Town of Inveraray, seat of MacCailein Mor himself, the Duke of Argyll, Chief of Clan Campbell. Nobody knows who wrote the words or the tune. They are first mentioned in 1716 and first appeared in print in 1745. Although on the face of things it would seem an appropriate tune for a regiment raised by the Duke of Argyll from Campbell country, it is interesting that the 8th (The Argyllshire) Battalion of the Argylls marched past to 'The Glendaruel Highlanders', a comparatively modern tune composed by the pipe major of the City of Aberdeen Volunteers as a compliment to the family of one of his pupils, who hailed from Glendaruel in Argyllshire.

The Seaforth Highlanders always marched into barracks to 'The Campbells are Coming!' to commemorate the Relief of Lucknow during the Indian Mutiny campaign in 1857. In the garrison in the later stages of the siege of Lucknow were the 78th, the Ross-shire Buffs; with the relieving force were the 93rd Sutherland Highlanders. The force was commanded by Sir Colin Campbell. The night before the relief, Sir Colin asked the pipers of the 93rd to strike up 'The Campbells are Coming!' to tell the besieged garrison, which included many women and children, know that at last the long-awaited relief was at hand. It is not recorded whether the pipers of the 78th were able to identify the tune, or indeed, if anyone heard it, but in remembrance of that kindly gesture the Seaforth began, and continued to observe, the custom of playing 'The Campbells are coming', but, of course, in a setting different to that played by the Argylls.

The tune was anathema to the Cameron Highlanders because of the long years of strife between Clan Campbell and Clan Cameron, and when playing troops past in a massed pipe band the Cameron pipers would stop playing when the tune changed to 'The Campbells are Coming!', and take their pipes off their shoulders to make the point quite clear. The ban was, in fact, quite recent, and had no real standing in tradition, but it was a gesture which everyone enjoyed.

Mention should be made here of the tunes played by the two regiments of 'Scouts', the equivalent of the Yeomanry of the South, the mounted Territorials in which the members rode their own horses. These were the Lovat Scouts and the Scottish Horse. The Lovat Scouts were raised in 1900 by Lord Lovat, whose patronymic was '*MacShimi Mor*', the son of great Simon. The tune played by the pipers was '*Morair Sim*' – 'Lord Simon' – believed to have been composed as a welcome to the 11th Baron on his return from banishment. He, after a life well described as 'of notable duplicity', was beheaded on Tower Hill after the rebellion of 1745, with which he had been unwise enough to have associated himself. '*Morair Sim*' is a strong and stirring march, written 'on the bottom hand', as pipers say, meaning that the low notes predominate in the first measure.

The provenance of the march of the Scottish Horse is, on the other hand, irreproachable. The 8th Duke of Athol, who raised the regiment in 1900, a little later than the Lovat Scouts, married the daughter of Ramsay of Bamff, an ancient Highland family. She was a musician of taste and ability, and when the Scottish Horse were in need of their own march, she sat down at the piano and composed a two-part march in 6/8 time, called simply 'The Scottish Horse'.

From the beginning of the twentieth century there were two Volunteer – later Territorial – units in England composed of Anglo-Scots, and Scotsmen living in England. These were the London and the Liverpool Scottish; the London Scottish coming under the wing of the Gordons and the Liverpool Scottish that of the Camerons, just before World War II. The London Scottish chose to keep their March Past – it was 'Highland

Laddie' – while the Liverpool Scottish also retained theirs – 'The Glendaruel Highlanders'. Mention should be made here of the tunes in strathspey rhythm annotated as 'The Charge' in regimental lists. These so-called 'Charges' are, in fact, the tunes for the march past in double time, which fell into abeyance over a century ago.

In 1968, The Cameronians (Scottish Rifles) chose to be disbanded rather than face amalgamation with another regiment. With, as we have seen, their Covenanting tradition, it is surprising that the 1st battalion, the original Cameronians, marched past – at 140 to the minute – to 'Kenmure's Up and Awa', Willie!'. Viscount Kenmure was the Jacobite leader in south-west Scotland during the rebellion of 1715. He and his followers were defeated at the Battle of Preston in November 1715, Kenmure being captured and executed. Among the Government troops which defeated Kenmure was the Cameronian Regiment, but why a song composed many years later by Robert Burns celebrating Kenmure's exploits was selected as the march past remains a mystery.[2]

The 2nd battalion of the Cameronians preferred to be known as the 2nd Scottish Rifles. The battalion had been raised in Perthshire by Thomas Graham of Balgowan in 1794 as the 90th Perthshire Volunteers, becoming light infantry in 1815. Its march past was a Perthshire tune which the 2nd Scottish Rifles called 'The Gathering of the Grahams'. The correct name was, and is, 'The Atholl Highlanders', and it was composed for and named after the 77th Atholl Highlanders, raised in 1778 by the Duke of Atholl and disbanded after a spectacular mutiny in 1783. There is a tradition that the 90th, which had no pipers until 1884, marched past to 'The Atholl Highlanders' played by the military band, but given the progressive Anglicisation of the 90th in the nineteenth century, this seems unlikely. The tune was clearly composed for the pipes.

The Cameronians (Scottish Rifles) march past in quick time to the military band was 'Within a Mile o' Edinburgh Toon'. The words were written before the tune, but neither the librettist nor the composer was Scots, although the song has been accepted into the Scottish repertoire. Whatever its provenance, the choice of the tune as the march past of a rifle regiment was inspired, and it is one of the sad results of the progressive reductions in strength of the Army that it is heard no longer as The

Cameronians (Scottish Rifles) go past at the rifle pace, always a sight worth seeing – and hearing.

Notes

1. The permanent hamlets and villages in the Highlands were situated on the low ground of the glens adjacent to a reliable water supply. In the summer, it was the custom for the people to move, with their cattle, to the hills, where the grass was fresh. They lived in huts and brushwood shelter, and it was a time for relaxation and enjoyment – 'With sport and mirth and music, sharing in the warm kindness of maidens . . . Hearty were we in the camps and the dram was not a rarity!' (from *Last Farewell to the Bens* by Duncan Ban Macintyre [1724–1808] the Glenorchy hunter and bard. He served in the Black Watch, the Breadalbane Fencibles and the Edinburgh City Guard.)

In the first frosts of autumn, the people moved down to their homes, where the fresh grass was ungrazed. The cattle were then at their best condition and were ready for the move to market in the Lowlands, and export to England.

One of the most beautiful Gaelic songs is *'Maighdeanan nan h'Airigh'* – 'The Maids of the Shieling' – a tune which is featured in the military band arrangement of 'Songs of the Hebrides' and which, if anyone had thought of it, would have made an admirable slow troop or march.

2. The tune of 'Kenmure's Up and Awa', Willie' is almost certainly older than Burns's words. It was published in a collection of pipe tunes in 1848 with several alternative titles, none of which has anything to do with Kenmure or his exploit.

REGIMENTAL MARCHES

Regiment	Pipes		Band	
	Slow	*Quick*	*Slow*	*Quick*
Scots D G	My Home	Highland Laddie	Garb of Old Gaul	Highland Laddie 3rd D Gs
Scots Guards	Garb of Old Gaul	Highland Laddie	Garb of Old Gaul	Highland Laddie
Royal Scots	Garb of Old Gaul	Dumbarton's Drums	Garb of Old Gaul	Dumbarton's Drums [1]
R H Fslrs	My Home	Highland Laddie (Close Column) Blue Bonnets (Column)	Garb of Old Gaul March of the 21st Regiment	British Grenadiers Whistle o'er the Lave o't
KOSB	The Borderers	Blue Bonnets [2]	Garb of Old Gaul	Blue Bonnets
Black Watch	My Home Highland Cradle Song	Highland Laddie	Garb of Old Gaul	Blue Bonnets
Highlanders	Highlanders Slow March	Highland Laddie	Garb of Old Gaul	Cock o' the North Scotland the Brave Cameron Men
A & S Hldrs	Skye Boat Song	Highland Laddie Campbells are Coming	Garb of Old Gaul	Thin Red Line

1 'The Daughter of the Regiment' when Royalty is present.
2 Blue Bonnets/Bonnie Galloway in the former 5th (Dumfries and Galloway) Battalion (Territorial Army).

REGIMENTAL MARCHES: DISBANDED AND AMALGAMATED REGIMENTS AND NON-REGULATION MARCHES

Regiment	Pipes		Band	
	Slow	Quick	Slow	Quick
Cameronians	None [1]	Kenmure's Up and Awa' [2]	None	Within a Mile o' Edinburgh Toon
Royal Scots Fslrs		Highland Laddie		British Grenadiers
Highland Light Inf		Highland Laddie		Whistle o'er the Lave o't
Seaforth Highlanders	Garb of Old Gaul	Pibroch o' Donald Dubh [3]	Garb of Old Gaul	Scotland for Ever!
Gordon Highlanders	St Andrews Cross	Cock o' the North	Garb of Old Gaul	Cock o' the North
Queen's Own Highlanders	Garb of Old Gaul	Pibroch o' Donald Dubh	Garb of Old Gaul	The Moray Firth [4] (unofficial)
Cameron Highlanders		Pibroch o' Donald Dubh	Garb of Old Gaul	Scotland for Ever! The Cameron Men
7/9th Battalion Royal Scots		Blue Bonnets		
8th Batt Argyll & S Highlanders		Glendaruel Highlanders		
Liverpool Scottish		Glendaruel Highlanders		
Lovat Scouts		Morair Sim (Lord Simon)		
Scottish Horse		Scottish Horse [5]		

1 Rifle regiments do not march past in slow time.
2 The 2nd Battalion, the Scottish Rifles, marched past to 'The Gathering of the Grahams', better known as 'The Atholl Highlanders'.
3 Until 1912 the 1st Battalion Seaforth Highlanders marched past to 'The Blue Bonnets'.
4 Composed by J. Ord Hume, Bandmaster of the 1st (Volunteer) Battalion Cameron Highlanders 1900–03 on the themes of 'The March of the Cameron Men' and 'The Nut Brown Maiden'.
5 Composed by the Duchess of Atholl.

APPENDIX
REGIMENTAL MARCHES – PIPES

Highland Laddie
    Royal Scots Dragoon Guards
    Scots Guards
    Royal Highland Fusiliers
    Black Watch
    Argyll and Sutherland Highlanders*

Highland Laddie**

*Played alternately with 'The Campbells are Coming'.

**As played by the Cameron Highlanders.

Dumbarton's Drums
Royal Scots

By kind permission of The RHQ Royal Scots

All the Blue Bonnets are over the Border
King's Own Scottish Borderers

The Wee Highland Laddie   Pipe Major Donald MacLeod
   The Highlanders (Seaforth, Gordons and Camerons)

CHAPTER XVII
REGIMENTAL MARCHES (3)
~

The whole question of the origin of regimental marches is a fascinating subject, and no aspect is more so than the reasons why a specific march was adopted by a particular regiment. Following the massive reductions in what used to be called the 'teeth' arms – the cavalry, artillery and infantry – many of those tunes which were once so familiar were no longer to be heard in public, although at domestic regimental gatherings behind the barrack gates they still tend to be played, primarily for sentimental reasons, as the veterans of the amalgamated or disbanded regiments plead to be allowed to hear again the old tunes to which they had once marched so proudly.

It is, of course, very often impossible to discover why a particular tune was chosen. All regiments have archives of one kind or another: order books, letters and diaries being carefully preserved, usually at the Regimental Headquarters. However, the one priceless regimental archive that is always overlooked is the band library. In the general clearout that accompanies every amalgamation, no doubt, much invaluable information has been destroyed. As a result, much irreplaceable regimental lore is thereby lost.

Into this category of regimental lore falls the question of Scottish tunes played by regiments other than Scottish ones, of which there are a surprising number. Scots tunes were to be found throughout the whole field of British military music, some reflecting the original raising of the regiment or one of its battalions in Scotland, others the influence of long-gone officers and sometimes their wives. They were to be found principally in the infantry, but the cavalry, too, had its share of Scottish music. It is possible to try to read too much into the choice of such tunes; a good tune got played, and nobody worried much where it came from. To this day, one can hear the occasional 'rebel' tune played by the pipes of an Irish regiment.

The 7th Queen's Own Hussars was raised in Scotland in 1690 as Cunningham's Dragoons, and although time and circumstance first weakened and then broke the Scottish connection, on a mounted parade in the days before mechanisation, the 7th Hussars ranked past at the walk to our old friend 'The Garb of Old Gaul'.[1] When marching past dismounted in quick time, the band played 'Bannocks o' Barley Meal', a tune which we will come across frequently when we discuss the 'Duty Tunes', as it features somewhere in the list of most Scottish regiments. 'Bannocks o' Barley Meal' is actually an Irish jig from Leinster, where it answered to the name 'Brian O'Lynn's Breeches'. It is a catchy tune, and Robert Burns put words to it:

> Bannocks o' bear-meal, bannocks o' barley,
> Here's to the Highlandman's bannocks o' barley.

A bannock is a scone made from oatmeal; 'bear' or 'bere' is a strain of barley. Hence 'Bannocks o' Barley Meal'. However, for over fifty years the 7th Hussars played the march under another name, of Irish provenance, 'The Kynnegad Slashers'. Kynnegad is a town in Ireland, some twenty miles west of Dublin on the road to Mullingar, an old British Army station. Under that name, 'Bannocks o' Barley Meal' was the march past of the 1st Battalion Gloucester Regiment, the old 28th Foot. The 28th had acquired their nickname 'The Slashers' in the War of American Independence when, at the Battle of White Plains in 1776, they had captured a heavily defended hill using their short infantry swords instead of the bayonet. The 28th was later stationed in Ireland where, presumably, the drummers picked up the tune – a popular one – and attached to it their own name. And so it became 'Bannocks o' Barley Meal' north of the Border and 'The Kynnegad Slashers' to the south.

The 15th The King's Hussars, when marching past dismounted, did so to a tune called 'The Bold King's Hussar', of which the first eight bars came from the Scots song 'Logie o' Buchan', which concerns a lad being taken from home, perhaps to fulfil the laird's second son's quota of men for rank in a new regiment:

> O, Logie o' Buchan, O, Logie the Laird,
> They ha'e ta'en awa' Jamie wha delved in the yaird;
> Wha played on the pipes and the viol sae sma',
> They ha'e ta'en awa' Jamie, the flo'er o' them a'.

~

When the 15th The King's Hussars and the 19th Queen Alexandra's Own Royal Hussars were amalgamated in 1922, 'The Bold King's Hussar' was combined with 'Haste to the Wedding', the march past of the 19th, and said to be an English folk tune. If it is, it goes well on the pipes, and if the surface is scratched, an Irish provenance seems likely. By Queen Victoria's wish, 'Logie o' Buchan' was played as the slow troop by the band when the Queen's Own Cameron Highlanders trooped the Colour, in a typically nineteenth-century arrangement sorely in need of revision and updating.

In 1903, a list of approved cavalry marches was issued. As well as the regimental marches for mounted and dismounted occasions, mounted always in slow time, dismounted in quick, the list included three tunes for ranking past at the trot and four for the canter. The three tunes for the trot included the strathspey 'Monymusk', an estate in Aberdeenshire. A popular pipe tune, it was composed by Daniel Dow, a music teacher in Edinburgh who died in 1783, the original name being 'Sir Archibald Grant of Monymusk's Reel'.[2] Despite the approved list, the 14th King's Hussars ranked past at the trot to a tune which they called 'Up, Light Loo!' but which is the tune in Strathspey time to which 'The Glasgow Highlanders', a Scottish country dance, is performed.

The tunes for the canter included 'Bonnie Dundee', and 'The Campbells are Coming!'. The tune of 'Bonnie Dundee' is much older than the words of the song, which were written by Sir Walter Scott in the early nineteenth century; but whereas Scott's words celebrate the raising of the standard of revolt against King William in 1689 by the recently created Viscount of Dundee – the 'Bluidy Claver'se' of Presbyterian demonology – the song refers to the town of Dundee on the east coast of Scotland, although Dundee himself was indeed a handsome or 'bonny' man.

Although 'The Campbells are Coming!' was approved in 1903, the 7th Hussars, true to their Scottish origin, had played it for many years previously. The tunes prescribed for ranking past at the canter were actually played when regiments ranked past at the gallop – the spectacular climax to ceremonial parades and reviews in the days of the horsed cavalry.

The Lass o' Gowrie

As some Scottish tunes were shared by several of the old

infantry regiments, it seems better to discuss each case under the heading of the tune rather than the regiment. One of the most popular was 'The Lass o' Gowrie', surprisingly, as there are many better and more lively marches.

The tune of 'The Lass o' Gowrie' was once known as 'Loch Eroch Side'. The original words were set to it by one William Reid of Glasgow. The version now current was written by Caroline Oliphant of Gask, whose father had been 'out' with Prince Charles Edward Stuart in the '45 rebellion, after the failure of which he and his son had been attainted and their home plundered by the Government troops. Caroline – her name illustrates her father's staunch Jacobite loyalties – was brought up in a fervently Jacobite ambiance, and as a young woman she wrote most of the Jacobite songs which are current today – 'Charlie is my Darling', 'Wha'll be King but Charlie', and 'Will Ye no Come Back Again?', to name but a few. In 1806, she married the son of another Jacobite family whose title had been forfeited. This was restored in 1824, as were other titles similarly forfeited, in the sentimental afterglow of King George IV's successful visit to Scotland in 1822, and so Caroline became Lady Nairne, the name by which she is best remembered.[3]

'The Lass o' Gowrie' was the march of the 55th Foot, which was raised in Stirling in 1755. The soldiers, it can be assumed, were recruited from the surrounding countryside and hill-foot villages along the south face of the Ochil Hills and the Highland border. Although there is no specific tradition explaining the reason for the adoption of the tune, it has always been assumed that it was intended to commemorate the Scottish origin of the 55th. In 1782, regiments were allocated to counties. The 55th was affiliated to Westmoreland, much to the disgust of the commanding officer of the time, who is said to have hoped that the 55th might be connected to his own county of Fife on the east coast of Scotland, Westmoreland being on the west coast and south of the Border to boot.

In 1881, the 55th (Westmoreland) Foot was amalgamated with the 34th (Cumberland) Foot to form The Border Regiment. Both battalions then marched past to the highly appropriate 'D'yer Ken John Peel?', he being at one time a well-known huntsman to a foot pack of foxhounds in the Cumberland hills. The 1st battalion coupled 'John Peel' with 'The French 34th', the regiment which had been routed by the British 34th at Arroyo dos Molinos in Spain in 1811. Its band, drums, drum major's staff and music had been captured complete and intact, and thenceforth the 34th had marched past to the march of 'The French 34th'. The 2nd battalion of The Border Regiment coupled 'John Peel' with 'The Lass o' Gowrie'.

'The Lass o' Gowrie' was also the march of the 70th Regiment, which was raised in Glasgow in 1756 and stationed there until 1759. Their facings were originally grey, which led to their nickname 'The Glasgow Greys'. In 1782, the 70th was affiliated to the county of Surrey, but from 1812 until 1824 it bore the name 'The Glasgow Lowland Regiment', thus briefly reflecting its origins. In 1881, the 70th became the 2nd Battalion The East Surrey Regiment. As played by the 2nd East Surreys, the trio of 'The Lass o' Gowrie' was the Lowland song 'Jock o' Hazeldean'.

In 1859, the 57th (West Middlesex) Regiment was ordered to discontinue playing their traditional 'Sir Manly Power' when marching past, as the local General considered it to be: 'All drum and damned noise!' 'The Lass o' Gowrie' was chosen to replace it, and when the 57th and the 77th (East Middlesex) Regiments became the Middlesex Regiment in 1881, 'The Lass o' Gowrie' was chosen as the march past. In 1896, the 1st battalion was authorised to revert to 'Sir Manly Power', the 2nd battalion adopting 'Paddy's Resource', a march composed by the band serjeant of the 77th at the suggestion of the commanding officer during the Crimean War.

'We'll Gang nae Mair tae Yon Toon'

This march was played by the 2nd Battalion The Queen's Royal Regiment, the 1st Battalion The Essex Regiment and the 2nd Battalion The Royal Hampshire Regiment. The first commanding officer of the 2nd Queen's when it was raised in 1858 was a Colonel Bruce, who had transferred from the Highland Light Infantry and introduced this tune as the march past. It was played by both battalions of the Queen's from 1881–1883 'We'll Gang nae Mair tae Yon Toon' appears to have been listed by the authorities as the official march of The Queen's Royal

Regiment even after 'Braganza' was finally approved in 1903.

Nobody knows when the 1st Essex and the 2nd Royal Hampshires took up this march. The pipe tune of the same name is an entirely different melody and is the air of the Burns song 'I'll aye Call in By Yon Toon'. The pipe tune also appears as the first of the 'Four Scottish Dances' arranged by Matthew Arnold. It might have been the title which appealed. Soldiers were not popular in Victorian England – except, sentimentally, when engaged in fighting far away – and the title of the march might well have found an echo in the hearts of the soldiers as they marched out of an unpopular station where, perhaps, the people were unfriendly, the girls unapproachable, and the publicans hostile.

The history of the post-1945 amalgamations and disbandments is long and complicated. Suffice it to say that all 2nd battalions were disbanded in 1947/48; the once proud Queen's Regiment is now, two amalgamations later, The Princess of Wales's Royal Regiment, the two battalions of which represent twelve of the old pre-1881 Regiments of Foot including the Royal Hampshires; and the Royal Anglian Regiment of two battalions has absorbed seven, including the two battalions of the Essex Regiment.

'Corn Rigs are Bonny'

This was the march of the former King's Own Royal Regiment, the 4th of Foot, one of the regiments originally raised to garrison Tangier, part of the dowry brought by Princess Catherine of Braganza when she married King Charles II in 1660. The words of the song are by Robert Burns, and describe the seduction of 'Annie' in a cornfield, a not uncommon event in rural Scotland. Although innocuous to our modern ears, a footnote in a Victorian collection of Scots songs reads: 'As the prevalent idea of this fine song as originally written by Robert Burns renders it unfit to be sung by ladies, or in the company of ladies, a modern version, retaining as much of the old lines as possible, is here presented.'

In 1959, the King's Own Royal Regiment and the Border Regiment were amalgamated to form the King's Own Royal Border Regiment. The march past of that regiment is now 'D'yer Ken John Peel?', followed by 'Corn Rigs are Bonny', 'The Lass o' Gowrie', and once again, 'D'ye Ken John Peel?'

~

'Wha Wadnae Fecht for Charlie?'

There are no seditious connotations about this Jacobite tune as played by the 22nd (Cheshire) Regiment, the last surviving unamalgamated English County Regiment of the Line. It commemorates the conquest of the province of Sind, now in Pakistan, after a hard-fought campaign in which the brunt of the fighting fell on the 22nd, the only British troops involved.

The force, which included Indian battalions from the Bombay Army of the East India Company, was commanded by Sir Charles Napier. At Miani, his little Army, 2,800-strong, defeated a Baluchi force estimated at 30,000. Napier became colonel of the 22nd, and 'Wha Wadnae Fecht for Charlie?' was played for the first time when he presented the regiment with new colours in 1850 at Dagshai, near Simla, in the foothills of the Himalayas. The tune was recognised as the march past of the Cheshire Regiment in 1881; until then, the 22nd had marched past to 'The Young May Moon', an Irish tune with words by Thomas Moore, apparently first performed in 1784.

The tune of 'Wha Wadnae Fecht for Charlie?' is also associated with a Glasgow street song, which went:

> Wha saw the 42nd?
> Wha saw them gang awa'?
> Wha saw the 42nd
> Marchin' tae the Broomielaw?
> Some of them had kilts and bunnets,
> Some o' them had nane ava',
> Some o' them had tartan troosers
> Marchin' tae the Broomielaw!

The Broomielaw was the Glasgow dock from which troopships sailed. The song might refer to the practice of making battalions up to strength with reservists and volunteers from units staying at home when warned for active service overseas. There was often no time to issue the uniforms of their new regiment to the reinforcements, so that an embarking unit might present a somewhat motley appearance.

The 42nd was, of course, the 1st Battalion Black Watch; and the battalion took up the tune and played it when leaving a station. It was played when the 1st Black Watch set sail for the Korean War in 1953.

'Wi' a Hundred Pipers'

'Wi' a Hundred Pipers' is another of the Jacobite songs written by Lady Nairne, although the tune might be an adaptation of an older song. It refers to the tradition that when the Jacobite Army entered Carlisle in September 1745, it was led by one hundred pipers, although the tune they are alleged to have played has not been recorded. The song also mentions the crossing of the River Esk, which flows for part of its course along the border between Scotland and England. After they had waded the river, the Highlanders turned, unbidden, to face Scotland and raised their broadswords in farewell salute.

'Wi' a Hundred Pipers' was the march past of the 2nd Battalion Cheshire Regiment, which had been raised in 1858, until 1881, when both battalions took up 'Wha Wadnae Fecht for Charlie?'. 'Wi' a Hundred Pipers' then became the regimental assembly march, played along with an old Cheshire folk song 'The Miller of Dee', both tunes being 'good going' 6/8 marches.

When command of the 50th (The Queen's Own) Regiment was taken over by Lieutenant-Colonel H.E. Weare in 1869, he introduced 'Wi' a Hundred Pipers' as the March Past instead of the Irish 'Garryowen'. In 1881, the 50th became the 1st Battalion The Queen's Own Royal West Kent Regiment. The 2nd battalion had been the 97th (Earl of Ulster's) Regiment; their march was the Scots air 'Hurrah for the Bonnets of Blue', which was played alternately with 'Wi' a Hundred Pipers' as the march past of the Queen's Own Royal West Kent Regiment.

Although nobody knows why Colonel Weare preferred a Scots tune to an Irish one, his name is worth recording as one of the few which can be quoted with certainty as having introduced a specific tune. The Royal West Kent Regiment is another of those whose traditions are now embodied in the two battalions of The Princess of Wales's Royal Regiment.

'The Maid of Glenconnel'

The 54th Regiment was raised in 1755 by John Campbell of Mamore, later the 4th Duke of Argyll, who had distinguished himself in command of the Argyll Militia fighting on the Government side in the '45. Thenceforth he was always 'Colonel John' to the Highlanders.

The song 'The Maid of Glenconnel', composer unknown, is believed to have been a favourite of Colonel John's wife. It describes the betrayal of 'The Pearl of the Fountain, the Rose of the Valley' by a faithless lover, and warns other maidens to bear her sad example in mind. For whatever reason, it was played so often by the 54th that in due course it became the march past. When the 54th was united with the 39th in 1881 as the Dorset Regiment, 'The Maid of Glenconnel' became the march past of both battalions; and since the amalgamation with the Devonshire Regiment in 1958, it follows 'Widdecombe Fair' as the march past of the Devon and Dorset Regiment.

'The Red, Red Rose'

In 1881, the 47th (West Lancashire) Regiment and the 81st Loyal Lincoln Volunteers became the 1st and 2nd battalions of the Loyal North Lancashire Regiment. The emblem chosen by the Loyals was the Red Rose of Lancaster, so the choice of Robert Burns's song, better known as 'My Love is Like a Red, Red Rose', was perhaps appropriate. The tune to which Burns set his words is 'Graham's Strathspey'.

In 1970, the Loyals amalgamated with the Lancashire Regiment to become the Queen's Lancashire Regiment. 'The Red, Red Rose' has been kept as the regimental march.

The 73rd (Perthshire) Regiment played 'The Red, Red Rose' as its march past for some years before 1881, when it became the 2nd Battalion The Black Watch, and changed to 'Highland Laddie' to conform to the 1st battalion's custom.

'Speed the Plough'

The 'Inverness Country Dance', a Scottish country dance also known as 'Speed the Plough', is performed to the same tune as the march past of the former Suffolk Regiment, the 12th of Foot, which was absorbed into the Royal Anglian Regiment in 1959. The march past of the Royal Anglian Regiment is 'Rule Britannia', once the march past of the Royal Norfolk Regiment, the senior partner in the amalgamated regiment. Each battalion of the Royal Anglian Regiment played its former march past after 'Rule Britannia', so the 1st battalion, formed from the Royal Norfolk and the Suffolk regiments, follows it with 'Speed the Plough'.

'The Dashing White Serjeant'

'The Dashing White Serjeant' was composed by Sir Henry Bishop, an English conductor, arranger and composer who died in 1855. He is also said to have composed 'Speed the Plough'.[4] Both tunes appear to have been appropriated by the Scots for the eponymous country dances. The former Royal Berkshire Regiment marched past to 'The Dashing White Serjeant', while the Grenadier Guards play it for the Advance in Review Order, with which manoeuvre ceremonial inspections used to conclude.

It was also briefly the march past of the 2nd Battalion The Suffolk Regiment at some period before 1898, when both battalions changed to 'Speed the Plough'. In 1841, Bishop was appointed Reid Professor of Music at Edinburgh University, but he refused to give any lectures and was invited to resign two years later.[5]

'Auld Robin Gray'

This beautiful air was the march past in slow time of the 99th Lanarkshire Regiment, which became the Duke of Edinburgh's Regiment in 1874 and the 2nd Battalion The Wiltshire Regiment in 1881. There are two versions of the tune, a traditional four-lined setting and a more elaborate arrangement, which is attributed to the Reverend William Leeves, a Somerset clergyman, and which is used as the slow march by the regiment. The words are attributed to Lady Anne Lindsay, who died in 1825. Despite the provenance of the tune, 'Auld Robin Gray' is accepted as a Scottish song.

The 99th marched past in quick time to 'The Blue Bonnets'; in Close Column, 'Kinloch of Kinloch', another Scottish march, was the tune.[6] The 2nd Battalion Wiltshire Regiment continued to march past to 'The Blue Bonnets', until it ceased to exist in 1948.

In 1959, the Royal Berkshire and the Wiltshire Regiments amalgamated to form the Duke of Edinburgh's Royal Regiment. The amalgamated regiment marched past in Quick Time to 'The Farmer's Boy', and in Slow Time to 'Auld Robin Gray'. In the latest round of reductions, the Duke of Edinburgh's and the Gloucestershire Regiment have been amalgamated to form the Royal Gloucester, Berkshire and Wiltshire Regiment.

'The Caledonian'

The 57th of Foot, from 1881 until 1966 the 1st Battalion The Middlesex Regiment, was raised in 1755, and in 1775 was commanded by Lieutenant-Colonel John Campbell of Strachur, who introduced 'The Caledonian', at one time apparently known as 'The Highland March', although there is nothing particularly Highland or even Scottish about the tune, apart from the so-called 'Scotch Snap' which features in it.[7]

An entirely different march named 'The Caledonian March, or the March of the Die Hards 57th Regiment' appears in *The Gesto Book of Highland Music* published in 1895. It is annotated: 'This march, believed to be of great antiquity, was a great favourite with Duncan MacDonald of Dalness, colonel of the 57th Regiment or Die Hards, one of the heroes of the Peninsular War.' The tune of this march is the same as that of the 'Roussillon March', the slow march of the former Royal Sussex Regiment, raised in 1701, absorbed like the Middlesex into The Queen's Regiment in 1966 and, until 1881, the 35th Foot, otherwise 'The Orange Lilies', from its facing colour. The 35th defeated the French regiment Royal Roussillon at Quebec in 1759, and incorporated the Roussillon, the white plume of Henry of Navarre, in its crest and ultimately in its cap badge. As published in the Gesto book, the Scotch Snap is prominent, but as played by the Royal Sussex the figure was reversed, the long note falling on the beat. History fails to relate either how the 35th came by this tune, or how it acquired its connection with the 57th, nicknamed 'The Diehards' after an incident in the Peninsular War when at a tense moment during the Battle of Albuhera in 1811 their mortally wounded commander, Colonel Inglis, had exhorted his men to 'Die hard, 57th, die hard!'

Mention should be made here of the march known as 'The Highland Piper'. A 'good going' tune in 6/8 or jig time, it was played by the former 1st Battalion The Royal Hampshire Regiment, the 2nd Battalion Gloucestershire Regiment and the 2nd Battalion Essex Regiment. Nothing is known about its provenance or how it acquired its name. The tune is outwith the range of the bagpipe chanter. It may well be of Irish origin and may have been picked up from a fiddler or fifer and have been played by the Corps of Drums in the first instance.

Notes

1. Cavalry 'ranked' past when mounted; they 'marched' past on foot.
2. *Regimental Music of the Household Cavalry and Royal Armoured Corps*, D.H. Mackay (HQ DRAC).
3. *The King's Jaunt*, John Prebble (Collins, 1988).
4. Infomation kindly provided by Mr I.F. Maclaren FRCS (Edin).
5. *The New Oxford Companion to Music*, Wendy Thompson.
6. The tune of 'Kinloch of Kinloch' is that to which 'Blow the Wind Southerly' is sung, but played in quick time.
7. *Regimental Music of the Queen's Regiment*, Lt-Col L.M. Wilson (1980). The 'Scotch Snap' consists of two notes in succession, the first falling on the beat, with the second prolonged at the expense of the first. In Scottish music the proportion is often semiquaver: dotted quaver.

1st Battalion, The Cameronians, Pipe Corporal
His distinctive Glengarry badge consists of the
mullet, a five-pointed star, said to derive from a spur
rowel, and it is the crest of the Earl of Angus, the
regiments first colonel. Below the mullet, a scroll is
inscribed 'The Cameronians'.
(National War Museum of Scotland)

2nd Battalion, The Scottish Rifles, Piper
Pipers of the 2nd Battalion wore the regimental
cap badge, the mullet within a wreath of thistles
above a bugle horn. The glengarry cap in both
battalions was dark green.
(National War Museum of Scotland)

2nd Battalion, The King's Own Scottish Borderers,
Pipe Corporal
Pipers of this battalion wore the old 2nd battalion
forage cap badge, the crest of the Royal Arms of
England, the crown surmounted by a lion passant
guardant, surrounded by a strap and buckle inscribed
'King's Own Scottish Borderers'. The soldiers refer to
their crest as the 'Dug and Bunnet'.
(National War Museum of Scotland)

CHAPTER XVIII
DUTY TUNES AND ROUTINE CALLS

'The Colours are the soul of the regiment, and the band is its voice.' So went the saying of an earlier era. But the Scottish regiments were fortunate in that they spoke – or sang – with two voices, that of the military band and, more relevant to their origins, the music of the pipes and drums and, especially, that of the Highland bagpipe. It might be said that there was also a third voice, that of the bugle; but the bugle spoke on behalf of the Army, whereas the other two played the major part in the projection of the regiment or battalion as a distinct and separate military entity, which each, in practice, was. No two regiments were, in any sense, identical, though there were, of course, similarities; and the same applied to battalions, even to battalions of the same regiment.

The music of a Scottish regiment could be divided into three categories. First, there was the music which was distinctive to itself, the regimental slow and quick marches and, to a lesser extent, the other tunes played when marching past in different formations.

Secondly, there was the pipe music which regulated the soldiers' day in barracks in conjunction, for the most part, with the calls sounded by the bugler. This might be termed the routine music, played usually by the orderly piper – the 'picquet piper' in the Scots Guards – and sounded by the orderly drummer, sometimes called 'the drummer on guard'. In this sense 'orderly' means simply someone on duty for the day or week. The tunes played on the pipes are the 'duty tunes'; those sounded on the bugle are the 'routine calls'.

Finally, there was what might be termed the parade music, that associated with the occasions on which the battalion took part as an entity in ceremonial order, as, for instance, when the Regimental Colour was trooped on the anniversary of some significant event in the regiment's or battalion's history. The occasions on which the Queen's Colour might be trooped were restricted by regulation, one such being her official birthday, but the Regimental Colour could be trooped more or less at will, although it was not a

214

7th Battalion, The Highland Light Infantry, Pipe Major Robert Reid
Pipe Major Reid was the finest piper of his day. During the Great War he had served with the 5th
Battalion in Gallipoli, Palestine and France. He wore his war medals with pride.
(College of Piping)

ceremony to be embarked on lightly, being long and complicated.

We have already discussed the question of regimental marches. This chapter will deal with the duty tunes, the routine calls and, in outline, the parade music. As we have seen, it was the drum which originally provided the background to the military life, both on the exercise ground and in the field, in the first instance alone, but later supplemented by the 'cheerful fife'.

The basic task of the fife was to clarify and enliven the somewhat sombre message conveyed by the unaccompanied drum. One beating can sound very like another to the untrained ear and, by the nature of things, the soldier found it easier to grasp the drum's message if it was accompanied by a tune which he could recognise. The simpler the tune, the better, and better still if it was that of a song the soldiers knew.

The fife and the drum remained the instruments which regulated the daily routine for many years after the bugle had ousted the drum on the battlefield. The drum beatings and fife tunes can be found in manuals and books of instruction up until the Great War, and in some cases the appropriate bugle call is printed as well, indicating that all three might have been used at one time.

It is more difficult to establish when the Highland bagpipe supplanted the fife and drum in the Scottish regiments, as the date by which the fife had disappeared differs between regiments, Highland as well as Lowland. The 1st Battalion Seaforth Highlanders had a drum and fife band in 1885, while the Royal Scots Fusiliers maintained one until the outbreak of the Great War; but other indications suggest that in the majority of the Highland regiments, the fife had gone out of fashion by the end of the Indian Mutiny, that is, about the middle of the nineteenth century.

This surmise is, to some extent, supported by a small manual of regimental pipe music printed privately for the Seaforth Highlanders in 1901. It is based on the manuscript notebook of Pipe Major Ronald MacKenzie, one of the giants of the piping world in his day. MacKenzie was pipe major of the 78th Ross-shire Buffs – which became the 2nd Battalion Seaforth Highlanders in 1881 – from 1861 until 1879. The little manual contains tunes to mark all the principal events of the day, although when the two battalions of the Seaforth Highlanders standardised their pipe music in 1912, some were altered, presumably to allow the inclusion of tunes played by the 1st Battalion Seaforth Highlanders – the old 72nd Highlanders – to take their place in the litany of the 'new' regiment, which had by that time been in existence for thirty years. We may smile; but experience has shown that thirty years is about the time it takes for an amalgamated regiment to shake down.

However, the suggestion that it was not until the middle of the nineteenth century that the pipe tunes began to complement the bugle calls might be questioned in the light of the claims which have been made in the past based on two early order books, both said to date from 1778. The first is that of the Argyll or Western Fencibles – these were regular units raised for home defence and not liable for overseas service – while the second refers to the Earl of Seaforth's Highland Regiment, raised from the MacKenzie clan and territories. The Argyll Fencibles were disbanded in 1783, but Lord Seaforth's went on to become the 72nd Highlanders and, eventually, the 1st Battalion Seaforth Highlanders.

Event	Argyll Fencibles	Lord Seaforth's
Reveille	The Finger Lock	The Macraes' March
Gathering	War or Peace	*Tulach Ard*– 'The High Hill'
Troop	Lord Breadalbane's March	–
Retreat	Glengarry's March	The MacKenzies' March
Tattoo	Mary's Praise	The Head of the High Bridge
Salute	–	The MacKenzies' Salute
Slow March	–	Fingal's Weeping
Quickstep	–	Castle Donan
Charge	–	*Cabar Feidh*
Stimulus before battle	–	The Battle of Strome
Lament	–	The MacKenzies' Lament
Warning before Dinner	–	The Battle of Glenshiel
During Dinner	–	The Battle of Sheriffmuir

All the tunes in the Argyll Fencibles list are from the *piobaireachd* repertoire known to exist at the time, and it is therefore possible that the list is contemporary and genuine. The same cannot be said for that of Lord Seaforth's Highlanders. '*Tulach Ard*' was the slogan or war cry of the Clan MacKenzie, and the tune of that name is also known as 'The MacKenzies' Gathering', but no specifically named 'MacKenzies' March' is recorded. 'The Head of the High Bridge' commemorates the first action of the 1745 rising, in which two companies of recruits of the Royal Regiment were ambushed and captured by a small party of Keppoch MacDonalds led by Donald MacDonald of Tirnadris. The heir to the forfeited Earldom of Seaforth and his followers took no part in the '45, so it would appear unlikely in the extreme that his son, who raised what became the 72nd, would have selected a tune vaunting the prowess of the rival Clan Donald in a rebellion against the House of Hanover, which had but recently restored him to his ancestral title, rank and lands. There are Salutes for the MacDonalds, the

MacGregors and the MacLeods, but none recorded for the MacKenzies as a clan.

Laments in the *piobaireachd* repertoire are dedicated to individuals or, rarely, objects or events, and these usually with some historic associations. There are no 'Clan' laments named as such. The only MacKenzie lament at present known is the 'Lament for MacKenzie of Gairloch'. Similarly, the only MacKenzie salute is the 'Salute to MacKenzie of Applecross. 'Fingal's Weeping' is a slow air – it is the 'Lights Out' call of the Argyll and Sutherland Highlanders – but difficult to march to without drum support. The pipe band was a hundred years away, and in any case slow time was known as 'Ordinary Time' in 1778. No quickstep called 'Castle Donan' is known, and quickstep marches were again two generations away. At the Battle of Glenshiel, which ended the abortive Jacobite rebellion of 1719, the MacKenzies had fled in disorder; and so on.

No one has so far recorded seeing either of those two order books. Lord Seaforth's, one suspects, might derive from a laudable attempt by a later regimental historian to provide his regiment with a flawless MacKenzie pedigree. It seems wise, therefore, to approach this evidence with caution, whereas we can be as certain as it is possible to be in the circumstances that the Duty Tunes played today originated in the nineteenth century, from both oral tradition and from manuscript books of the period.

New Duty Tunes had to be selected when the Royal Highland Fusiliers was formed in 1958 and when The Highlanders emerged some thirty-six years later. The committee formed by the component regiments of the latter referred to on page 124 decided that as the two outstanding composers of pipe music in the twentieth century had served with the former regiments, Pipe Major G.S. McLennan with the Gordon Highlanders and Pipe Major Donald MacLeod with the Seaforth and Queen's Own Highlanders, the Duty Tunes of the new regiment should reflect this unique heritage.

Now to the duty tunes themselves. The sequence in which they were played followed the course of the day. The military day always began early – well before daylight in winter and in the first glow of dawn in summer, the barracks would be stirring. Apart from the sentries, the first soldier to appear might be the junior NCO of the barrack or quarter guards, who rejoiced in the title of 'the NCO marching reliefs', it being his job to post and relieve the sentries every two hours. Armed with the list of early calls, he made his lonely rounds, waking up the cooks, and those who had to be on duty by Reveille, including the orderly piper. The orderly drummer slept in the guard-room, in case a call had to be sounded during the night, perhaps the 'Fire' call:

> There's a fire, there's a fire, there's a fire!
> Run and get some water for to put the blighter [!] out!

Or, in a foreign station or on the 'Frontier', the 'Alarm':

> There's a nigger on the wall!
> There's a nigger on the wall!
> There's a nigger on the wall!

So much for 'political correctness' a few decades back.

The soldiers of the quarter guard would be stirring, too, as the guard orders required them to turn out under arms at 'Reveille, Retreat and Tattoo', properly dressed, for inspection by the guard commander. In a Highland regiment, this could involve changing from tartan trousers, worn after Retreat, into the kilt, ready for the dismounting parade under the orderly officer, sometimes more grandly 'The subaltern of the day', who would be wrestling with his own white spats in his room in the officers mess by Reveille.

At the time appointed for Reveille, the drummer would sound whatever call was in vogue at the time; left to himself he would sound the easier and less taxing 'Rouse' rather than the official Reveille call. The quarter guard would fall in outside the guard-room, in theory at least. If darkness still reigned, or if the morning was more than usually unwelcoming because of fog, rain or frost, an easygoing or 'cushy' guard commander might content himself with shouting the appropriate orders from the guard-room door. The piper would strike up; in most cases, tuning the instrument beforehand might result in a charge of 'creating a disturbance before Reveille', so the piper would stride off on his morning round with his bagpipe truly 'skirling', or out of tune. Lights would come on; the barracks would come to life as the Orderly NCOs of each company banged the barrack-room doors with their morning shout 'Rise and shine'; and the day would begin.

The tune the majority of Scottish regiments play at Reveille is 'Johnny Cope', an arrangement for the pipes of the mocking Jacobite ballad:

> Hey! Johnny Cope! Are ye waukin' yet?
> Or are yer drums a-beatin' yet?

The song was composed by the Jacobite sympathiser Adam Skirling, who had watched from his farm near Haddington, east of Edinburgh, as the troops under General Sir John Cope had been routed by the clansmen of the Jacobite Army of Prince Charles Edward Stuart in September 1745. It is one of the ironies of Scottish military music that 'Johnny Cope' is the Reveille call of two of the regiments in which the unfortunate Sir John – 'a little finical dressy man' – had served, the Scots Guards and the Royal Scots. Despite celebrating a Jacobite victory, 'Johnny Cope' is also played by the Royal Scots, the King's Own Scottish Borderers and Royal Scots Fusiliers, now the Royal Highland Fusiliers, the regiments whose forbears shattered the charge of the Highlanders at the Battle of Culloden in April 1746, in the final throes of the already-doomed rebellion.

The Gordon Highlanders alone of the Scottish regiments play a different tune at Reveille, theirs being 'The Greenwoodside', a more lively air, but equally tricky to play on a frosty morning.

After he had played Reveille, the orderly piper might take his ease until it was time to play 'First Breakfast Pipes', but half an hour after Reveille the orderly drummer would have sounded 'Defaulters':

> You can be a defaulter as long as you like,
> As long as you answer your name!

This summoned the men on 'Jankers' – 'confined to barracks' until 1955, thereafter 'on restricted privileges' – as they paraded at the guard-room for roll call.

'Sick Parade' came next, and a parade it was indeed. For many years it was an article of faith that any soldier who reported sick did so in order to escape some parade or duty, and was therefore malingering, swinging the lead, or dodging the column.[1] Sick Parade was therefore held some forty-five minutes after Reveille, and on the presumption that anybody who was really ill would be forthwith admitted to hospital, the sick soldier had to pack up all his belongings, hand them into store – obtaining a receipt – and then answer the 'Sick' call carrying his 'small kit', i.e. the things he would be likely to need in hospital – shaving gear, for instance, and, of course, his boot brushes and blacking. When the drummer sounded:

> Sixty-six, sixty-four [i.e. soldier 6664],
> He'll never go sick no more,
> Poor beggar, he's dead!

It was the signal for the Sick Parade to 'fall in' perhaps on occasion under the RSM himself, when on a bad morning some time might be spent sharpening up the foot drill of the 'sick', followed by an inspection of their 'small kit', with consequent charges of 'failing to parade with small kit complete when reporting sick'. Despite the foregoing, there was a system by which a really ill soldier could avoid the indignities of the sick parade. An officer's signature on a special sick report secured immediate access to the medical officer. In 1882, the words sung by the Rifle Brigade, to their own 'Sick' call, were:

> Bring out the sick!
> Never mind the dead!

Breakfast came next. No breakfast ration was issued until well into the nineteenth century; until then, a soldier's breakfast consisted of a hot drink, plus any bread he might have managed to save from the previous day's ration of one pound of bread and one of meat, bone in. Given that the previous meal had been some seventeen hours earlier, this was little enough for young bodies to sustain the day's labours on, and, even though the scale of rations had been vastly improved, until after the Great War soldiers were always hungry. Most of their miserable pittance had to be spent either on food or on strong drink, simply to keep the pangs of hunger at bay and recruits would sometimes cry themselves to sleep, not from homesickness, but from sheer hunger.[2]

Officers were not issued with rations, and so had to provide their own food; hence the old saying 'a subaltern's breakfast: a drink of water and a pull at the belt'!

Until the Great War, the soldiers ate in their barrack-rooms. Dining halls had been built in the more modern barracks, but were not popular, the soldiers preferring the homelier and cosier atmosphere of their own barrack-room, where everyone had his own established place in the pecking order, with their own corporal reigning as a more-or-less benevolent father figure. When the bugle sounded:

> Come to the Cookhouse door, boys,
> Come to the Cookhouse door!

the call meant precisely that, the 'boys' in this case being the orderly men detailed from each barrack-room. They paraded at the cookhouse, carrying the appropriate utensils; the cooks issued the meal to them according to the 'number in mess'; and the orderly men carried it back to the barrack-room, where the food would be divided out by the corporal, who would also keep an eye on the table manners of the soldiers, as well as their general behaviour. The language formerly associated with the barrack-room, but now in general use, is a modern development; 'using obscene language in the barrack-room' was an offence; and the first duty of a junior NCO was to 'curb the use of foul and intemperate language'.

The orderly piper took a hand here, and after the bugle call he struck into First Breakfast Pipes, the tune either 'Bundle and Go!' or 'Brose and Butter', depending on the regiment. In the days when a drummer and a fifer played the duty tunes, First Breakfast was 'The British Grenadiers'. The process of fetching the meal was known as 'drawing rations', hence the old doggerel, sung to the trio of the march composed by cavalryman Charles Payne a hundred years ago, 'Punjab':

> Why should I draw rations
> When I'm not the Orderly Man?

The Second Breakfast Call meant that the soldiers were to make their way to their barrack-rooms for the meal, and that the subaltern of the day was starting on his rounds. The bugle call went:

> Oh, pick 'em up, pick 'em up, hot potatoes, hot potatoes,
> Pick 'em up, pick 'em up, hot potatoes, Oh!

The tune the piper played was 'Bannocks o' Barley Meal', or perhaps, 'Bundle and Go!'. The fife tune for Second Breakfast is 'The Roast Beef of Old England', and when the Scotch Duty was abolished in 1816, this must have been the tune played by the fifers of the Scottish regiments.

After breakfast, the orderly man cleaned the utensils and tidied the room for inspection, while the soldiers got ready for parade as the drummer sounded the 'Warning for Parade':

> Just half an hour to do the whole affair,
> Shine up your shoes and brush up your hair,
> My, but you're bonny when you're dressed for parade,
> No Serjeant's eye need make you afraid,
> Just half an hour to do the whole affair,
> Shine up your shoes and brush up your hair.

Universally known as the 'Half-hour Dress', the call might be complemented by the piper playing the appropriate duty tune. Today, the Royal Scots play 'Up and Waur ThemA', Willie'; as did the Queen's Own Highlanders; the King's Own Scottish Borderers, 'Highland Laddie'; the Gordon Highlanders used to play 'Johnny Cope'; the Black Watch 'Loch Tummelside', Loch Tummel being a beauty spot in the Black Watch country; and the Royal Highland Fusiliers 'MacKenzie's Highlanders', a reminder that one of their illustrious predecessors, the 71st Highlanders, had been raised by a MacKenzie, a tune played as a Gathering by the Seaforth Highlanders for the same reason. Before great occasions 'Loch Tummelside' and 'MacKenzie's Highlanders' might be played by the pipers alone, without the drums, and most effective and evocative these tunes sound played like this as did the Gathering tune of the Cameron Highlanders, *Gillean nan Fheile* – 'Lads wi' the Kilt'.

The Quarter Call followed, although in most cases the piper does not contribute, as by then the preliminaries were well under way, and anyone who was not ready was already late! These 'Warning Calls', or 'Sounds preparatory to Turning Out', were important. Within living memory, few soldiers below the rank of serjeant could afford a watch, and the only way they had of telling the time was by listening to the warning calls sounded by the Orderly Drummer before the main events of the day, all of which were preceded by the Half-hour and Quarter Calls.

Until some thirty years ago, the piper played the appropriate duty tune at Reveille, at meal times and at 'Lights Out' only. The modern practice of having the pipe virtually duplicate the bugle calls originated because in the many active theatres in which the battalions were deployed during the so-called 'low-intensity operations' after World War II, the companies were often dispersed in separate operational bases. Good buglers were usually scarce in the Scottish regiments – The Cameronians and the Highland Light Infantry always excepted – so it was easier for the company to be detached complete with its piper, and for him to play the routine calls as well as the duty tunes. It was then a logical step to select a range of specific tunes to cover all the occasions on which the drummer would have sounded a call had one been available, and this led, in turn, to the pipe calls being played along with the bugle calls as a matter of routine.

After the morning's work and duties, dinner followed in the same way as breakfast, often with a different sequence of pipe tunes although the bugle calls remained unchanged. Until the outbreak of World War II, and for a decade afterwards, the day's work virtually ended at midday, it being widely believed that five hours' military training a day was as much as the soldier could be expected to assimilate.[3] However, in this context it has to be borne in mind that the majority of the British infantry was continuously embroiled in the different emergencies and upheavals which characterised the first two decades after World War II, from Palestine in the mid-40s to Borneo in the mid-60s, since when aid to the civil power in Northern Ireland and peace-keeping in the Balkans have taken over as the principal preoccupation of the Army. Therefore, to some extent it was understandable that in between their all-too-frequent operational tours battalions tended to make the most of such periods of relative peace and quiet as came their way.

In the late-Victorian Army, right up until World War II and for some years thereafter, sport in the widest sense of the word filled the afternoons, officers and men taking part together. Everyone was interested in the progress of the regimental teams in the different leagues and competitions which were run by the District Headquarters and Area Commands, more or less all the year round, the aim being to keep the soldiers occupied, busy and fit, and to encourage them to avoid the drinking dens and red-light areas that had been the bane of the old garrison towns.

Bands and music generally had their part to play in the process, too, as most of the soldiers and the majority of the officers were unmarried and lived in barracks. As a result, there was always an audience for the beating of Retreat and Tattoo, which were performed on alternate days by the pipes and drums or corps of drums until the Great War, and once a week thereafter, although the practice varied from regiment to regiment and from station to station.

Retreat signalled the end of the official day. Stores were locked and calm settled apart from the sentry of the quarter guard pacing his beat and the sounding of 'Defaulters' every half-hour by the orderly drummer, those unfortunates being kept busy in one way or another throughout the evening. Soldiers 'walked out' after tea at about five o'clock, but until the general relaxation of discipline, which followed the recruiting difficulties of the 1930s all had to be back home in barracks by the time Tattoo sounded, when the roll was formally called, with all the soldiers at their bedsides, dressed in what was known as 'clean fatigue after Retreat', one of the multitudinous orders of dress lovingly detailed in the Standing Orders, but in this case amounting to jacket and tartan trousers for the most part.

At 2150 hours, 'Defaulters' sounded for the last time and a few minutes later everyone on duty that day formed up for the closing ceremony of the day – 'Staff Parade' – taken by the subaltern of the day or the captain of the week. A similar parade had taken place half an hour after Reveille, which was effectively merely a roll call, but the evening Staff Parade was a rigidly observed ritual. All the NCOs on duty would report that all was in order. In India, the ritual mantra intoned by the battalion orderly serjeant, the senior NCO on duty, might have run: 'The battalion is reported present, sir; all fires are out, all mules secured, all mosquito nets tucked in.' Or words to that effect.

At precisely 2200 hours, the whole parade would be called to 'Attention'; the orderly drummer would be ordered to 'Sound Off!'; he would sound 'Last Post', the degree of expression and the tempo very much depending on the state of the weather. On a wet night in Aldershot, pathos was a bonus, whereas on a fine evening in the gloaming at Fort George in north Scotland, the drummer would give it all he had, earning a rare word of praise after it. Then the NCOs were dismissed, the Defaulters were inspected and that was that, except that fifteen minutes after the 'Last Post', 'Lights Out' was sounded and the piper played his final tune of the day, usually the old Gaelic lullaby *'Cadail, mo Ghaoil'* – 'Sleep, Darling, Sleep!' The soldiers' text ran:

> Sodger, lie doon on yer wee pickle straw,
> It's no' very broad, and it's no' very braw;
> But, sodger, it's better than naething at a',
> Sae sleep, sodger, sleep.

Words that tended to come to mind when settling down for the night in a wartime bivouac under the stars or in the rain, to the mutter of the guns, instead of the piper's tune.

So much for the daily routine, which went on regardless of where the battalion might be stationed, Hong Kong or Hounslow. The effect was to create a background of stability and order, in which everyone knew precisely what was going to happen at any time of the day and what was expected of them. In the soldiers' language of the time, everyone knew 'what they were on'. Climatic conditions might necessitate some adjustment of the routine, as, for instance, during the monsoon in India, but by and large the procedure went on day after day, month after month and year after year.[4]

The system is often criticised by those who have had no experience of it as soul destroying and monotonous, and so it might appear. But, paradoxical as it might seem, it came into its own and showed its value when on active service, particularly after some stern and testing period, perhaps with significant casualties.

After a short spell of complete rest, spent eating and sleeping, the immediate adoption of the well-tried and tested regimental routine, familiar to everyone, not only brought a sense of security and safety, but also reminded everyone that whatever things may have been like 'up there', the regiment and the battalion would go on in its own time-honoured and inimitable fashion, whatever happened. This aspect is brought out superbly in the film *Bridge over the River Kwai* in which, despite the appalling conditions, the battalion commanded by the fictional colonel maintained its morale and spirit by conducting itself as it had always done. And in *Defeat into Victory*, Field Marshal Viscount Slim's account of the campaign in Burma in World War II, he wrote: 'It was our experience in a tough school that the best fighting units, in the long run, were not those with the most advertised reputations, but those who, when they came out of battle, at once resumed a more formal discipline and appearance.'

We now come to Parade Music, that is, the tunes played as the battalion formed up for some ceremonial occasion with the Colours on display. In the British infantry, the Queen's and Regimental Colours were carried by officers, escorted by three serjeants. But, as always, there were exceptions. Escorting the Colours was regarded as an 'honourable duty', and the escort might sometimes be composed of one serjeant, one corporal and one private soldier.

The Colours were always received with a Royal Salute, the troops presenting arms and the band playing the National Anthem. It was the practice in some cases for the Colours to be marched on to some specific march, as attempting to march to 'God Save the Queen', was difficult for the Colour Party, the officers of which were probably nervous enough already.

Each preliminary phase of getting the battalion formed up on parade was accompanied by its own appropriate music. In a Highland regiment, the 'Gathering' might be played at some stage, either by the pipes alone or by a single piper. The officers might be played to their posts to some traditional regimental tune, and as the battalion was being inspected the band and the pipes and drums would play slow marches, troops and slow airs alternately. The music for marching past has already been described, and the dispersal after parade might also have a specific tune, played after the dismissal as the soldiers made their way off parade.

Mention should also be made of what was liable to happen on Sundays. Until well into World War II, attendance at what was called 'Divine Service' was compulsory, every soldier having to declare his – or, rather, a – recognised religion. The daily orders on Saturday would specify the time and place of Church Parade for each denomination on the following day, with an officer detailed by name to march the soldiers to the appropriate church. Once a month there would be a Parade Service at full strength, the troops dressed in Review Order, less rifles but including bayonets. In India, a British regiment went to church under arms, the officers with their swords and the soldiers with their rifles and ten rounds of ammunition. The initial outbreak of the Indian Mutiny had been planned to take place while the British troops in garrison at Meerut were at church, so thereafter no risks were taken.

Considerable pomp and military circumstance accompanied the Parade Service. The Warning Calls were sounded, the battalion formed up according to its formal procedure, and the ritual music was played, including 'Church Call', which was usually the catch or 'glee', 'Hark, the Merry Christchurch Bells', a piece not often associated with the Church of Scotland, which for Scottish units remained the established Church wherever they were serving, so that the Church of Scotland parade was regarded as the commanding officer's, which the pipes, drums and band attended. During the preliminaries, other music of a religious nature might be played; in the Seaforth Highlanders, the national hymns of Austria – 'Glorious Things of Thee are Spoken' – and Russia – 'God, the Omnipotent' – were among the music played.

But, as ever, some had to be different, and in those cases no Warning Calls were sounded or music played while forming up for the Parade Services, or even when marching to the church. The pipes, drums and band would head the column, formed up in 'Beating Order', that is, as if they were going to play, but without instruments, the drum major leading, wearing his sash and carrying his staff. This was fine when the battalion was stationed by itself in some small garrison, but when, as in Aldershot, the Parade Service was followed by a march past the District Commander or some equally senior officer, difficulties could arise. A stoutly Presbyterian Highland battalion that had marched dourly to church without music could find itself in dire straits when sandwiched between an English battalion marching at one hundred and twenty paces to the minute and, breathing down its neck, a rifle battalion at one hundred and forty paces with twenty buglers and a full band blaring forth 'Jellalabad' or some similar march for band and bugles.

The period during which such regimental systems of what was known as 'interior economy' flourished is, to a great extent, over; these very systems themselves are things of the past; and some might say that it was high time too. However, a well-tried and understood routine not only simplified the soldier's peacetime existence, but, sensibly applied, supported him in the not-infrequent periods in war spent out of contact with the enemy by providing him with a familiar and reassuring structure round which he could base his life. So that a wounded soldier returning from convalescence to his old battalion, seeing everything going on as he remembered it and hearing the pipe tunes and bugle calls once again, immediately felt, and often said, 'I'm home!'[5]

Notes

1. 'Malingering' was entered in red on the sick report by the medical officer and, if proved, might lead to an exemplary sentence being awarded by the commanding officer. 'Swinging the lead' comes from the Royal Navy, where, apparently, the sailor who swung the lead – by which the depth of water under the ship's keel was calculated – was deemed to have a easy job. 'Dodging the column' derives from the columns of cavalry or mounted infantry, marching infantry and guns which operated against the Boers in the later guerilla phase of the Boer War of 1899–1902. Such operations involved long, forced marches on little food and scarce water, hence the temptation to avoid them by reporting sick.

2. Personal communication Captain James Murray.

3. 'Half a day's work for half a day's pay!' It has to be said that no one felt particularly guilty. Until the mid-50s the rates of officers' salaries, paid monthly, and soldiers' wages, paid weekly, were derisory, even by the standards of the time. Before the outbreak of World War II, officers were paid in advance, so that when an officer was killed in action, the balance of his salary had to be recovered from his estate.

4. Needless to say, the duty tunes tended to vary between battalions of the same regiment. The range of Duty Tunes played by the 1st Battalion Royal Scots differed from those played by the 2nd, as did the regimental bugle calls. The desire to be different extended even to the uniforms. The 1st Battalion wore a red patch behind the St Andrew in their cap badges; the 2nd Battalion wore green.

5. 'Our home was astride a spur to the east of the Imphal road, at a height of 4,500 feet. There we viewed spectacular scenery; our outlook was over mountains and valleys, as far as the eye could see. A merit of the camp was that it so suited the bugle calls, so well sounded by Corporal Cripps. In such a place, there was an uplifting of spirits on hearing the daily calls, so clearly, within the vastness of that remote world.' *March On! The 2nd Dorset Regiment in India and Burma,* Norman Havers, Square One Publications, 1992

Appendix
Duty Tunes

The Scottish Division of Infantry
The Duty Tunes

Event		RS	RHF	KOSB
Reveille		Johnny Cope	Johnny Cope	Johnny Cope
Breakfast	1st Pipes	Bundle and Go	Bundle and Go	Brose and Butter
	2nd Pipes	–	Bannocks o' Barley Meal	
Dinner	1st Pipes	Brose and Butter	Brose and Butter	Brose and Butter
	2nd Pipes	–	Dornoch Links	–
Tea	1st Pipes	Jenny's Bawbee	Jenny's Bawbee	Jenny's Bawbee
	2nd Pipes	–	–	–
Retreat		Heroes of Kohima	Banks of Allan Water	Battle of the Somme
Tattoo	First Post	Killiecrankie	–	Killiecrankie
Tattoo	Last Post	Lochaber No More	Lochaber No More	Lochaber No More
Lights Out		Sleep, Dearie, Sleep	Sleep, Dearie, Sleep	–
Officers Mess	1st Pipes	Bannocks o' Barley Meal Pibroch o'	Up and Waur Them A' Willie!	Highland Laddie Strathspey and Reel Bannocks o' Barley Meal
	2nd Pipes	Donuil Dubh	Heroes of Vittoria	

THE SCOTTISH DIVISION OF INFANTRY
THE DUTY TUNES

Event		Black Watch	The Highlanders	Argyll & Sutherland Highlanders
Reveille		Johnny Cope	Greenwoodside	Johnny Cope
Breakfast	1st Pipes	Brose and Butter	Brose and Butter	Bundle and Go
	2nd Pipes	—	—	—
Dinner	1st Pipes	Brose and Butter	Over the Water to Charlie	Bundle and Go
	2nd Pipes	—	—	—
Tea	1st Pipes	Brose and Butter	Jenny's Bawbee	Bundle and Go
	2nd Pipes	—	—	—
Retreat		Green Hills of Tyrol	The Kilworth Hills[1]	Green Hills of Tyrol
Tattoo	First Post	Scotland's ma ain Hame	—	—
Tattoo	Last Post	Scotland the Brave	People of this Glen[2]	—
Lights Out		Donald Blue[3]	The Highland Cradle Song	Fingal's Weeping
Officers Mess	1st Pipes	Any 2/4 March	Any piobaireach theme	Pibroch o' Donuil Dubh
	2nd Pipes	Slow air or any piobaireach theme	Captain E.B.B. Towse VC[4]	Any march, strathspey and reel

1. The Kilworth Hills are situated in County Cork, Republic of Ireland.
2. *Muinntir a Ghlinne So*, also known as 'Lord Breadalbane's March'.
3. Go to Bed, you Drunken Soldier', also played by the Scots Guards.
4. Captain Sir Beachcroft Towse VC, KCVO, CBE of the Gordon Highlanders was awarded the Victoria Cross at the battle of Mount Thaba, which took place in April 1900 during the South African War. During a flanking engagement at Houtnek – the Wooded Pass – he was wounded and lost his sight. Thereafter, he devoted his life to the cause of blinded soldiers, and after the Great War was knighted for his work. Pipe Major G.S. McLennan composed his tune.

CHAPTER XIX
REVEILLE, RETREAT AND TATTOO

~

The procedure for the formal beating of Reveille, Retreat and Tattoo differed from regiment to regiment. What follows is an outline of the drill usually observed on these occasions, but it must be borne in mind that the procedure followed by a particular regiment might have variations that are not discussed here. These procedures were very much a matter of custom and practice, but were open to change as conditions altered and expectations grew. For instance, at one time, the performance of all three ceremonies was the prerogative of the pipes and drums, or the corps of drums, as the case might be; but in recent years it became the practice for the military band to parade at Retreat or Tattoo and to play marches, both slow and quick, as well as selections. Now that the military band no longer forms part of the battalion, this practice, which had no foundation in tradition, will no doubt lapse, as will the business of the pipes and drums and the military band playing together, which began as a novelty, but in time came to destroy the individual functions of both sources of music, each of which had so much to offer in its own way. The process also tended to reduce the pipes and drums to the level of the corps of drums in an English or guards battalion as the 'poor relation' of the military band, the bandmaster, as a warrant-officer, outranking the pipe and drum majors. More insidiously, it led to the gradual elimination of the distinctive pipe scale, as the pitch was raised to Bb, and pipe chanters began to be made in the diatonic scale. The beating of Reveille, however, remained firmly the prerogative of the pipes and drums or corps of drums, and it is with Reveille that we will deal with first.

In the days when all soldiers lived in barracks, with the few on the married roll living in quarters adjacent or within easy walking distance, it was the custom for the full Reveille sequence of tunes to be played every morning, but by the end of the nineteenth century it would appear that Reveille was being beaten once or twice a week. The Reveille call on the bugle and,

1st Battalion, The Queen's Own Cameron Highlanders, Pipes and Drums, Tidworth, 1908
Twenty-one pipers, eleven drummers and nine buglers are photographed with the adjutant, Captain
J.G.S. Scovell, seated in the centre. This was the normal strength for a marching, regimental pipe
band before the Great War. The serjeant drummer is George Scotland and the serjeant piper is
William Kinnear. (Queen's Own Highlanders Amalgamation Trust)

1st Battalion, Seaforth Highlanders, Pipes and Drums, Nowshera, Northwest Frontier Province,
India, 1905
The pipe band is formed up in 'Beating Order' read to march on the parade-ground for the regular
beating of Retreat. The serjeant drummer is Andrew Cunningham and the serjeant piper is William
Taylor. The sodiers wear the white drill jacket; officially, a 'sleeved waistcoat'. (Queen's Own
Highlanders Amalgamation Trustees)

in the case of the Scottish regiments, 'Johnny Cope' on the pipes usually sufficing to rouse the soldiers and to start the day. The Royal Scots Dragoon Guards occasionally sound the Reveille call introduced into the 6th Dragoon Guards in 1895, a three part arrangement for six cornets of '*Ach, du lieber Augustin*'.

When the pipes and drums turned out to beat Reveille, it was known as 'Long Reveille', and it is so termed on the relatively few occasions on which it is beaten today. 'The Crimean Reveille' is, as its name implies, a form of Long Reveille which originated in the latter period of the Crimean War, by which time the soldiers were adequately housed and clothed, had enough to eat and were looked after when sick. The Black Watch, the 79th Cameron Highlanders and the 93rd Sutherland Highlanders were serving together in the Highland Brigade, all three camped at Kamara on the heights north-east of the base at Balaclava. From time to time, the pipers and drummers of all three played Reveille together. The sequence of tunes played on these occasions has been preserved, and these are played on the morning of the 15th of every month by the pipes and drums of the Black Watch. This was formerly treated as a parade, and all officers and serjeants attended to hear Reveille beaten in the traditional way, a custom no longer observed now that so many married officers and serjeants live some considerable distance away from the barracks. The other two regiments allowed the custom to lapse, although the Cameron Highlanders had evolved their own Long Reveille sequence over the years, which bore little resemblance to the Crimean Reveille, and consisted of 'The Point of War', 'Johnny Cope', and 'Up in the Morning Early', a sequence which was also played by the Queen's Own Highlanders from 1961 to 1994.

The Gordon Highlanders, which as the 92nd Highlanders joined the Highland Brigade in the final stages of the Crimean War, also beat their own form of Long Reveille, as did the 2nd Battalion Royal Scots. And during the Great War, the Divisional Pipes and Drums of the 52nd Lowland Division, formed on the ill-fated Gallipoli Peninsula after the disastrous opening battles of the summer of 1915 from the surviving pipers and drummers of the twelve infantry battalions in the Division, devised and beat their own Long Reveille. All these regimental Reveille sequences include some reference to the Reveille for the corps of drums laid down in the English Duty, which supplanted the Scotch Duty in 1816.

The Reveille of the English Duty is still occasionally played by corps of drums. It goes by the intriguing title of 'The Mother and the Three Camps'. From earlier sources, it would appear that the Three Camps is in fact what is now called the Point of War. The 1st Camp is the first eight bars of the Point of War; the 2nd, the second eight bars; and the 3rd Camp is the Point of War complete, with some differences in the accents. The 'Three Camps' is played in slow time, the drums rolling throughout; then follows, still in slow time 'The Mother', known to the drummers as 'Old Mother Reilly'; the drums break into quick time with the Scotch [sic] Reveille; and, finally, the Point of War is played as a salute, in double-quick time. The Scotch Reveille bears no relation to the Reveille of the Scotch Duty, but appears as the 'Slow Scotch' in some early American manuals, the 'Quick Scotch' being the Reveille of the Scotch Duty. However, it would appear that those early Reveille sequences varied greatly from time to time and, no doubt, from place to place, and that the tunes played were in no sense laid down. Henry Potter's *Drum Major's Manual*, for instance, notes that other tunes may be substituted for the Scotch Reveille.

The Royal Scots played 'The Point of War' as a salute, as did the Queen's Own Highlanders; the latter also played it as the introduction to their Long Reveille, an echo, perhaps, of the 'Three Camps'.[1] 'The Mother' survives in the Crimean Reveille played by the Black Watch, and was played by the 2nd Royal Scots and the 52nd Lowland Division. 'Old Mother Reilly' to the corps of drums, she is 'Granny Duncan' to the pipes and drums, although the Black Watch sometimes call her 'Old Willy Duncan'. He, possibly, was a regimental character in the past, just as 'Old Mother Reilly' might have been a camp follower or sutler – a seller of drink or food to the soldiers – long ago; a British 'Mother Courage', in fact.

This proves what has long been suspected but never confirmed, namely that the fife and the Highland pipe co-existed side by side in the Scottish regiments, and this musical evidence further confirms that the pipers were not above 'lifting' a tune from the fifers when it suited them.

Another possibility is that when the pipers took the fifers' place in the beating of Reveille, some zealous adjutant might have insisted that they followed the corps of drums sequence and repertoire as far as they were able.

We can now compare the Long Reveille sequences under discussion.

	2nd Royal Scots	Black Watch
Slow	'The Soldier's Return'	'The Soldier's Return'
	'Granny Duncan'	'Granny Duncan'
	'Captain Chisholm'*	'Sae will we yet!*'
	'Sae Will We Yet!'*	'Granny Duncan'
	'Granny Duncan'	
Quick	'The Bowmore Reel'	'Miss Girdle'
	'Johnny Cope'	'Erchless Castle'
		'Johnny Cope'**

	Gordon Highlanders	52nd Lowland Division
Slow	'Jessie Chisholm'	'The Standard on the
	'Granny Duncan'	Braes of Mar'
	'Fingal's Weeping'	'Granny Duncan'
	'Granny Duncan'	'The Soldier's Return'
Quick	'Greenwoodside'	'Galway City'
	'Jessie Chisholm'†	'Johnny Cope'

* Quick Time **One tone up †Strathspey Time

We can see that 'Granny Duncan', the 'Mother' of the Three Camps, is common to all the sequences, indicating that the fife had its place in the Highland regiments, as well as in the Lowland, as the inclusion of the 'Mother' in the Long Reveille of the 2nd Battalion Royal Scots, the Crimean Reveille, played by the Black Watch, and the Long Reveille of the Gordon Highlanders suggests. Although the 52nd Division was composed of Territorial battalions of Lowland regiments – with one exception[2] – it would appear that when it came to devising a Long Reveille sequence, folk memory among the many ex-regular soldiers in their ranks was long enough to recall the playing of 'Granny Duncan' by the fifes of, let us say, the Royal Scots Fusiliers. Although most Territorial battalions before the

Great War raised both pipe and military bands, it is doubtful whether any ran to a corps of drums as well.

'The Soldier's Return' is a song by Robert Burns set to an old tune 'The Mill, Mill, Oh'. The song runs:

> When wild war's deadly blast was blawn,
> And gentle peace returning,
> Wi' mony a sweet babe fatherless.
> And mony a widow mourning;
> I left the lines, and tented field,
> Where lang I'd been a lodger,
> My humble knapsack a' my wealth,
> A puir and honest sodger.

Such a song would be known to the soldiers, and its sentiments would appeal to them, describing as it does the soldier's return to the scenes of his early manhood and the days of his courting, unrecognised at first by his faithful wife; faintly embarrassing to us, perhaps, but even sixty years ago the sort of song which would have been accepted at its face value by Scottish soldiers, miles and years away from home.

'Sae Will We Yet!' was written by Walter Watson, born at Chryston, near Glasgow, in 1780; he died at Kirkintilloch in 1854. His words were set to the tune of 'The Wearing of the Green', to which they fit admirably, although it is ironic that an Irish nationalist tune should have been adapted to such fervently patriotic words as:

> Long live the Queen, and happy may she be!
> And success to her forces by land and by sea!
> Her enemies to triumph, we never will permit,
> Britain's aye been victorious, and sae will we yet!
> And sae will we yet, and sae will we yet,
> Britain's aye been victorious, and sae will we yet![3]

Again, this is a song which would have found popularity among the soldiers, apparently stranded on the inhospitable coast of the Crimea and suffering untold hardships from the climate, the weather and the lack of food and medical care; seeing their comrades die and their battalions, which to many were the only homes they had ever known, dwindle away to nothing under the daily attrition of war. But dogged endurance was the strong suit of the soldiers of that period, and this is the sort of song that they sang.

As regards the other tunes, 'Erchless Castle', 'Jessie Chisholm' and, probably, 'Captain Chisholm', too, are all the same tune, Erchless Castle being the seat of 'The Chisholm', as the chief of that clan was known. 'Miss Girdle' and 'The Bowmore Reel' are the same, and while 'Johnnie Cope' is played in four sections in the Black Watch. The setting is raised one tone up, so that it follows the air of the ballad quite closely. In the Victorian manner, the third and fourth measures take off into a maze of quite intricate fingering, showing that even over one hundred and fifty years ago, the regimental pipers were required to reach quite a high standard of finger dexterity.

Although it can be readily surmised why 'The Soldier's Return' and 'And Sae Will We Yet', with their nostalgic and patriotic associations, have been included, it remains a mystery why the Chisholm tune had such an appeal; like the reel tune, 'Miss Girdle', it is of strictly limited musical merit. Pipe Major William Ferguson of the 7th Battalion Highland Light Infantry, was pipe major of the 52nd Divisional Pipe Band. A noted piper and composer, he published his own collection of pipe tunes in 1939, which included the 52nd's Long Reveille, but like the others, he gave no reason for his choice of tunes. His opening Slow March, 'The Standard on the Braes of Mar', refers to the raising of the standard of the exiled Stuarts in 1715, and, on the face of it, would seem an odd choice for the Lowland Division, consisting for the most parts of staunchly loyal Lowland regiments – and one equally loyal Highland – which played their full part in the defeat of the Jacobites, not only in 1715, but in 1746 as well.

In July of 1855, as a consequence of the arrival of large numbers of fresh troops, the Highland Brigade was expanded and named the Highland Division. The three Highland regiments – the 42nd, 79th and 93rd – formed one brigade; the other consisted of the 1st and 2nd battalions of the 1st Royals and the 72nd Highlanders in their Royal Stuart trousers, the 'red-legged partridges' of contemporary military badinage. Towards the end of the year, the 92nd Gordon Highlanders joined the other three Highland regiments. While the Gordons were complete with pipers and may well have joined in beating the Crimean Reveille along with the other three Highland regiments, the 1st Royals were in the middle of their non-Scottish phase and almost certainly had no pipers. But it is interesting that when the 1st Royals decided to reintroduce pipers in 1881, the Long Reveille adopted by the 2nd battalion should have followed so closely that played by the Highland Brigade in the Crimea some twenty-five years earlier. Those were the days of long, long service, and perhaps someone, somewhere, in the 2nd Battalion Royal Scots remembered what the Highland Brigade had played because, despite the differences in name, the tunes are the same but played in a different order. The 1st Battalion Royal Scots do not seem to have beaten Long Reveille, and in the collection of regimental pipe music published by the Royal Scots no Long Reveille is noted.

The Gordon Highlanders, on the other hand, picked their own tunes, apart from the Chisholm tune and 'Granny Duncan', which they inherited, perhaps, from the fifes.[4] The choice of 'Fingal's Weeping' is interesting. This was the 'Lights Out' call of the 93rd, and later of the Argyll and Sutherland Highlanders. It suits the latter role better; there is a slightly eerie and vaguely menacing ring to the tune, suggestive of the long and bloody Highland history, particularly when heard in Stirling Castle, once the home of the Argylls. Whether played in the gloaming of a fine summer's evening or on a wild and windy winter's night, it made no difference. The flesh crept and soldiers fell silent as the sound of the pipes filled the air.

The second main event of the soldiers' day in the eighteenth century had been the 'Troop', when the battalions had formed up with much time-consuming ritual and pomp before setting off for the day's training. This ritual and pomp once formed part of the complete ceremony of Trooping the Colour, now rarely performed, and is simply a complicated way of forming up the battalion and mounting a guard. For this reason it was no doubt continued for its own sake, but times changed and this complicated procedure was relegated to the Manual of Ceremonial, only to be carried out on special occasions. There is therefore no need to discuss it here, except to note that although the beating of Reveille, Retreat and Tattoo was the function of the drummers, the band played the major part in the Troop.

The original purpose of Retreat was to warn the soldier to return to his company in order to answer to his name at roll call. Tattoo told him to drink up and make his way back to his billet for yet another roll call. Even after all soldiers came to be accommodated in barracks during the nineteenth century, both occasions retained much of their significance. Retreat, as ever, was the signal for the changeover from day to night routine, and thus it became the custom to mount the duties for the night either just before or just after the sounding or beating of Retreat. But at Tattoo, all the rank and file – that is everyone below the rank of serjeant – had to be accounted for, so the roll was still called at Tattoo by the Orderly NCOs of the companies, with the soldiers standing by their bedside in tartan trousers with jackets buttoned up to the neck. Like the roll call at Reveille, this was designed to establish the time at which it was noticed that a soldier had taken French leave, which could be important at any subsequent disciplinary proceedings.

What this requirement entailed, among other things, was the closing of the 'wet canteen', the beer bar, sometime before Tattoo so that the soldiers could make their way back to their barrack rooms. The wet canteen sold only beer, long experience having shown that soldiers and 'ardent spirits' did not mix well. Until after the Great War, the wet canteen was a bare and comfortless place furnished only with tables and forms. Soldiers unable to find a seat sat on the floor. The soldiers drank in 'schools', that is, in groups of friends or 'townies', men from the same home town or district. The schools pooled their cash; beer was purchased in quart pots or cans; the can was passed round the school; and as it grew emptier, some innocent young soldier would be invited to finish it. He had then, by custom, practice and protocol, to refill it; hence 'to carry the can', 'take the can back', 'to be left with the can', all meaning to be left 'holding the can' or taking the blame.

Order was kept by the NCO on Canteen Duty who was, on pay nights, usually a hardbitten serjeant, who would 'peg his granny' – 'charge' anyone, given half a chance – backed up by an equally intractable corporal. On a particularly rumbustious night he might need the assistance of a 'file of the guard', two men with rifles and fixed bayonets, to clear the canteen in time for Tattoo. But normally the closing of the wet canteen was a routine business – the soldiers ran out of money in twenty-four hours – and everyone would have time to listen to the pipes and drums or corps of drums beat Tattoo, usually beaten day about with Retreat.

Over the years each Scottish regiment had devised its own procedure for the beating of Retreat and Tattoo by its pipes and drums. There was no standard procedure in either case, unlike in the German Army where the procedure and music for *Der Grosse Zapfenstreich* was rigidly laid down and observed. The Retreat ceremony might either begin or end with the sounding of the bugle call 'Retreat', sometimes with the bugles sounding in harmony. The regimental flag would be lowered during the call, to be rehoisted at Reveille next morning. At an early stage, a march in 3/4 time would be played, this being the time signature of the regulation drum beating, which the tune had to fit. The drummers would beat the 'Drummers Call', a reminder of the days when it was the signal for the officer on duty to inspect the guard. Before and after the 3/4 march, the drummers would beat three rolls, each rising to a crescendo before dying away. These, too, were inherited from the fifers, and represent what were once called the 'Three Cheers', now known as 'The Pause Notes or Chords', during which the fifers played three ascending chords. This concluded the formal part of the Retreat beating.

Some popular slow and quick marches might follow. A pipe band programme would include a 'set', a sequence of music that would include a strathspey and reel tune, both dances involving a change in tempo and played with the pipers and drummers formed in a circle. At the end, the drum major would formally seek permission to march off from the senior officer present, usually the subaltern of the day, the orderly officer, who would always attend.

Tattoo, on the other hand, had to fill in the gap between the sounding of First Post, usually at 9.30 p.m., and Last Post, usually at 10.00 p.m. These were the calls which had originally marked the progress of the 'Rounds' which visited the sentry posts to make sure that all was well at the beginning of the night. There were two types of Rounds, Visiting Rounds when the subaltern of the day carried out the duty, and Grand Rounds when the field officer or captain were present. The sentries would come to the 'Present' for Grand Rounds; for Visiting Rounds they remained at the 'Shoulder'.

The Tattoo procedure was much the same as that for Retreat, except that the 3/4 march was omitted and the ceremony opened with the First Post call. The procedure would include the three crescendo rolls at appropriate points and invariably ended with the bugles sounding Last Post, after which the pipes and drums marched off without playing. When a corps of drums beats Tattoo, or on the rare occasions when the military band is paraded, Tattoo ends with the playing of the National Anthem after which the bugles sound Last Post. Apart from the sounding of Lights Out, no music was played or bugle sounded until Reveille next morning. A pipe band playing Tattoo omitted the National Anthem, which is outwith the range of the chanter, but did not play after Last Post had been sounded.

The Royal Scots Fusiliers was the only Scottish regiment to observe the custom of having the band play an evening hymn after Tattoo on Sunday nights. There were cavalry regiments which had hymns played by their bands every night, but the reasons for the adoption of such a custom are obscure, and those quoted fanciful. Such customs have fallen into abeyance because of the changed conditions of life in the Army, where the majority of the soldiers are married and many are quartered at some distance from their barracks. To turn out the band, or even part of it, on a Sunday evening just to play a simple hymn tune is not worth the administrative effort involved.

After the Great War, the full ceremonies of Retreat and Tattoo were performed once a week, and after World War II they became rarer still. Retreat, being associated with sunset, tended to become a social occasion when it was beaten, the Officers and Serjeants Messes usually holding some sort of function thereafter, with guests invited to watch Retreat being beaten. Tattoo, on the other hand, fell almost completely into oblivion under the altered circumstances of life in barracks, which became progressively more relaxed as time went on, and calling the roll at Tattoo lost its point as a soldier could stay out all night if he wished, as long as he turned up for parade next morning.

~

The name, however, was usurped by the various military displays that came into existence after the Great War as a result of the withholding of funds for the Armed Services on the pretext that no major war would break out for the next ten years, a principle which was invoked annually until it became clear that such a principle was a fallacy. The most prominent of these displays was the Tattoo at Aldershot, where the bulk of the British Army serving at home was stationed. Ostensibly intended to raise money for Army charities, in time, the Aldershot Tattoo became a way of life and created its own impetus, eventually dominating the lives of the officers and soldiers involved as rehearsals began weeks beforehand. It was a highly spectacular affair. There were military bands, mounted and on foot, as well as massed pipes and drums and corps of drums in abundance. The music was of a very high order.

The Aldershot Tattoo was extremely popular with the public, and special trains and buses ran to Aldershot from all over the south of England. However, for the soldiers involved, it was an imposition they could well have done without. The 'performers' marched to Rushmoor Arena from their barracks, which might be up to four miles away, and back again after the show, sometimes wet through, with all their full dress to clean and prepare for the next night's performance and, in the case of the cavalrymen, their horses to see to as well. Weeks were spent in rehearsal. The long-term result was that after World War II those senior officers who had experienced and loathed the Aldershot Tattoo as a massive waste of military time and effort, saw to it that it never took place again. Its mantle, however, descended on the Edinburgh Military Tattoo, a much less-demanding affair in terms of military involvement.

Before leaving this subject, mention should be made of two other ancient ceremonies in which the drums or the drums and fifes played a leading role. These were known as 'Crying Down the Credit', and 'All Debts Paid'. Both had originated in the late seventeenth century, before sufficient barrack accommodation existed in which to house the soldiers. The troops were therefore billeted on the civilian population, usually in public houses. This was unpopular with the publicans, who believed that the presence of soldiers in the public rooms of the inn drove away trade; and with the soldiers, who believed that the publicans were making fortunes out of the subsistence allowance which the paymaster general paid to the regiment on a per capita basis. The publican provided the soldiers billeted on him with their daily meal. When the regimental paymaster received the money from the paymaster general, he paid out the subsistence allowance to the publicans according to the number of soldiers billeted on them. In practice, the subsistence allowance, which was part of the soldiers' wage, was always in arrears, so the soldiers lived on credit, both in respect of their food and of the bar bills which they inevitably ran up, often encouraged, it was suspected, by the publicans. The soldiers' attitude to the latter is well summed up in the ballad 'Hot Stuff', composed by Serjeant Ned Botwood of the 47th Foot, later the Loyal Regiment.

> Come each death-dealing dog who dares venture his neck,
> Come follow the hero who goes to Quebec.
> Jump aboard of the transport and loose every sail,
> Pay your debts at the tavern by giving leg bail![5]

To 'give leg bail' means to abscond, leaving the infuriated creditors to rue the day. A regulation of 1695 required that whenever a battalion moved to new station, a public announcement had to be made, warning the public and the publicans not to extend credit to soldiers above the rate of subsistence allowance currently in force. This procedure became enshrined as 'Crying Down the Credit'.

The drums beat through the streets to the market place or town square. When a crowd had gathered, the drums beat 'The General', and a serjeant announced in stentorian tones the risk involved on allowing soldiers to run up bills in excess of the subsistence allowance.

When the arrears of the subsistence allowance had been paid to the battalion's paymaster, the regulation stipulated that the innkeepers were to be reimbursed within four days. The drums again beat through the streets to the square, accompanied by the paymaster with his bag of subsistence money and his clerk carrying his ledgers. The drums beat 'The General'; the innkeepers appeared with their accounts made up; the paymaster settled the bills; hence 'All Debts Paid!'. Any balance left over was paid to the soldiers, so that they could settle their own bills as well. In theory, this was supposed to happen before each move; in practice, the subsistence was usually so far in arrears that an officer had to be left behind to collect all outstanding bills and forward them to the secretary at war for payment against the amount of subsistence due.[6]

It was the custom for the drummers to be treated to a drink after each of these ceremonies; in the regimental agent's accounts entries regularly appear 'To crying down the credit, 10/-'.

Notes

1. The French composer Léo Delibes uses the 'Point of War' motif in his opera *Lakmé* as the entr'acte to Act 2. The opera was first performed in 1883. Lakmé, the daughter of a Brahmin priest, is in love with a British officer.
2. The 5th Battalion Argyll and Sutherland Highlanders was the Territorial battalion raised in Greenock on the south bank of the River Clyde, and was therefore, strictly speaking, entitled to be regarded as Lowlanders.
3. *Ord's Bothy Ballads and Songs* (John Donald 1930). The earliest known printing of the melody of 'The Wearing of the Green' was in 1845, although it has been claimed that the words, or a version of the words, date from 1802, shortly after the failure of the rebellion of 1798, in which green in some form had been the distinguishing mark of the rebels, and during which both sides, the Crown forces – the Irish militia regiments in particular – and the insurgents, had behaved with equal barbarity. The tune has been claimed by England and Scotland as well as by Ireland.
4. The Highlanders now play the Gordons Long Reveille.
5. *Songs and Music of the Redcoats*, Lewis Winstock (Leo Cooper, 1970).
6. *The British Army of William III 1698–1782*, John Childs (Manchester University Press, 1987).

APPENDIX

THE POINT OF WAR

From *The Drum Major's Manual*

(by kind permission of Messrs George Potter and Co., Aldershot)

The Point of War, which is also played at the start of the Long Reveille and Retreat, is a survival from the old drum and fife beatings, the 'Scotch Duty' and the 'English Duty' which existed separately until 1816 when they were combined in the interests of uniformity in the Army.

The 'Military Discipline' of 1759 gives details of the ceremony of Trooping the Colour, and at the stage when the Ensigns receive the Colours' . . . the Captain gives the Word of Command "Present Your Arms", upon which the Grenadiers present the arms and the Drummers beat a point of war . . .'

The Point of War, as a drum beating, was therefore a compliment to the Colours of the regiment. The tradition remains unchanged today in that, when the Regimental Colour is accorded a General salute, it is still accompanied by The Point of War.

The evolution from a fife to a pipe tune dates from the mid 19th Century when the pipes replaced the fifes on parade, but continued to play the old fife music.

246

The Point of War
Pipe

Drum beating as above.

The Crimean Reveille

CHAPTER XX
THE MILITARY FUNERAL

~

In the garrison towns in the years before World War II, one of the most impressive ceremonies which might be encountered was the funeral conducted with full military honours. The cortège wended its way through the streets, either in slow time with the band playing as it left the hospital or approached the cemetery, or in quick time in utter silence, the only sounds the disciplined crunch of the marching feet, the rumble of the gun carriage bearing the coffin and the clopping of the gun-team's hooves.[1]

The funerals of all, officers or soldiers, were conducted according to the procedure set out in the King's Regulations.[2] General or private, the ceremony took the same form. There were only two points of difference. The first was that a general officer was given a gun salute, from nineteen 'guns' – blank rounds – for a field marshal down to thirteen for a major general. For everyone else the regulation parting salute was given by twelve soldiers who fired three blank rounds from their rifles over the open grave at the end of the service.

The other difference was in the size of the escort; a complete battalion in the case of a lieutenant-colonel in command, three hundred soldiers if he was not; two hundred for a major; down to twelve for a private. The escort paraded under arms and was entirely distinct from the firing party, which consisted of a serjeant, a corporal and twelve private soldiers, and which fired the parting salute. The strength of the firing party remained the same whatever the rank of the deceased. There was no restriction on the number of mourners. A private was accompanied to his grave by all the officers and men of his own company, together with any of his friends or 'townies' from other companies or from anywhere else for that matter. The pipes, drums, military band and bugles attended all funerals at full strength. Review Order was worn, and it was a point of honour with each soldier to turn out as immaculately as possible.

There were certain drill movements peculiar to the occasion. When on the march in slow time, rifles, swords and lances were carried at the 'Reverse' – under the left arm, sloping downwards, point or muzzle to the rear, the right arm stretched behind the body to grip the weapon with the right hand. At the halt, the soldiers armed with swords and rifles stood at the position known as 'Rest on your arms reversed', a complicated movement which ended with the point or muzzle resting on the left toecap, hands clasped over the butt or hilt, head bowed. Well performed, these were impressive movements and lent a due sense of solemnity to the occasion.[3]

A legacy, perhaps from earlier times in India and the West Indies where disease could decimate a battalion in a matter of days, was that death was a 'tabu' subject in the barrack-room and any reference to it was soon stifled. By the same token, the drill movements involved were only rehearsed when required, and even then, never within barracks, the soldiers detailed to attend under arms being marched, along with the bearer party – the soldiers who carried the coffin to and from the gun carriage – to some out-of-the-way spot where the drill could be practised out of sight. Similarly, the funeral music was never rehearsed. The military band played the 'Dead' marches at sight, and while the pipers would run over the tunes on the practice chanter, they would not 'put them on the pipes' until the ceremony itself. 'The Flowers of the Forest', for instance, was only ever played when the occasion arose; the tradition, or perhaps the superstition, was that if played out of its proper context, the lament would soon have to be played in earnest.[4]

The funeral cortège, or procession, would form up at some place near where the coffin lay. The bearer party, eight soldiers of the same rank as the deceased, would carry the coffin to the gun carriage, which was a field gun and limber modified to carry it. In the days before mechanisation, the gun carriage would be drawn by its team of six horses, matched for size and colour, the three drivers mounted on the nearside horses, with the gun commander or number one, a serjeant, also mounted. The drivers would have carefully groomed their horses, their 'long-faced chums', while the limber gunners would have polished the gun carriage until everything gleamed and shone. On the coffin, covered by the Great Union, were placed the dead soldier's cap, belt and sidearm – his bayonet or sword, or his dirk had he been a piper, a drummer or a bandsman.

The coffin was received with the firing party and escort at the 'Present', the first and last time the soldier would be paid this compliment, usually reserved for officers of field rank, that is, above the rank of captain. With arms reversed, the escort set off in slow time, followed by the firing party, with the pipes, drums, and military band immediately in front of the gun carriage and the bearer party on either side it, flanking the coffin. The drums were muffled by loosening the snares and were draped with black crêpe. Crêpe also covered the drum major's staff, which he, too, carried reversed under his left arm with the head of the staff to the rear.

If the deceased had been a mounted officer or soldier, his horse was led immediately behind the gun carriage, by clean white handkerchiefs through the bridoon rings, while his spurred riding boots were placed in the stirrups, heels to the front. Affecting and appropriate when the deceased had been wont to ride the horse in the course of his duty, this custom descends into mawkish sentimentality when observed merely for effect.

No music was played until the cortège was clear of the place where the coffin had lain. Most deaths occurred in hospital, so to spare the feelings of patients who might themselves be gravely ill, the pipe and military bands were silent until out of earshot. The pipes and drums would play first; pipe music abounds in suitable laments and evocative slow marches, which are usually played more slowly than the official slow march tempo of seventy-five to the minute, which could cause difficulties when the military band, trained to observe the correct tempo strictly, took over with one of the 'Dead' marches. Once on the move, however, the cortège would break into quick time after each band had played once. In quick time, no music was played, and the soldiers under arms carried their rifles at the 'Trail', parallel to the ground but reversed, rifle butts foremost.

Approaching the cemetery, the cortège broke into slow time once again and, at this final stage of the journey, it was customary for Handel's 'Dead March in Saul' to be played, all the drums rolling throughout, the bass drum marking every seventh beat only. On arrival at the graveside in due course and order, in which all those in front of the gun carriage in the order of march lined the route to the grave, the funeral service followed, the firing party and escort resting on their arms reversed. And, in a reversal of the usual practice at a similar civilian burial, the mourners wore their head-dress throughout. Indeed, at a military funeral, all the usual observances were turned on their heads.

At the end of the service, the firing party discharged three blank rounds over the open grave in which the coffin now lay. These three rounds symbolise the Trinity. The custom is an ancient one, as Shakespeare knew when he wrote, in the final scene of *Hamlet, Prince of Denmark*:

> Let four captains bear Hamlet like a soldier to the stage;
> . . . and for his passage, the soldier's music and the rites of war Speak loudly for him . . . Go, bid the soldiers shoot!
> (*A Dead March; after which a peal of ordnance is shot off.*)

This was perhaps the most impressive part of the whole ceremony: between each volley, music was played. In the Scottish regiments, a piper, or pipers, played four bars of the first measure of the old, old lament now called 'Lochaber No More' after each of the first two volleys and the whole of the second measure after the third. In the 1st battalion of the Highland Light Infantry, however, the buglers sounded 'Retreat', eight bars after each of the first two volleys and the remainder of the call after the third. In regiments with corps of drums, one chord might be played after the first volley, two ascending chords after the second and the salute, 'The Point of War', after the third. In others, the first eight bars of 'The Point of War' might be played between each of the first two volleys, with the whole salute after the third. Custom and practice varied between regiments, and even within a battalion the procedure might differ from time to time. There is evidence that even in Highland battalions, 'The Point of War' might replace the piper's lament, which itself was by no means restricted to 'Lochaber No More'.

After the third volley had been fired and the third piece of music played, the 'Last Post' was sounded, with the firing party at the 'Present', the officers saluting, the other mourners at

'Attention'.[5] After a short pause, the buglers sounded 'Rouse', and this closed the ceremony. The parade then formed up for the march back to barracks. In some cases, it was the custom for the pipes and drums or the military band to strike up immediately with the most stirring march they knew. Life had to go on. In others, no music was played during the march home.

The density of traffic and the pace of modern life have meant that, apart from the ceremony at the graveside, much of the associated procedure can no longer be carried out. Before World War II, it was quite common for retired officers and veteran soldiers to be buried with full military honours years after they had left the service. But even if these public rites are no longer appropriate, soldiers are given the best possible send-off by their regiments, even if circumstances dictate that only the graveside service can be performed. However, the three volleys and the sounding of the bugle are the very core of the military funeral ceremony, and they in themselves suffice to send the soldier on his way in a manner which does honour both to the soldier and to his calling.

The solemnity with which a regiment took leave of its soldiers who had died in its service in peace was reflected in war, where, even if the soldier had to be buried hastily within sight and sound of the enemy with the only music the 'monstrous anger' of the guns, the occasion was approached in a spirit not far from reverence by his comrades, rough as they tended to be in those harsher days. The grave might be only inches deep, but a crudely fashioned cross would appear and, amazingly, some small floral tribute, often in the most unlikely places. And, as soon as possible, when out of the line, some form of memorial service would be held, with few men absent and fewer still with dry eyes as the piper played his farewell lament.

Formal memorial services commemorating some wartime triumph or tragedy, the exploits of some personality distinguished in war, or a senior officer of the Armed Services frequently include the latter part of the military funeral service in which a bugler sounds Last Post and Rouse, and both have acquired certain gloomy, not to say funereal, connotations as a result. It is salutary to reflect that in former days both calls were sounded and heard every day by the majority of soldiers and that at military funerals they were sounded as a farewell tribute to a comrade of whose life they had been an integral part, not as a deliberately contrived increment to the grief and sadness inherent in the occasion. Drummers and pipers who tended to be selected to perform frequently at memorial services were sometimes surprised, almost bewildered, at the emotion their playing and sounding unleashed, even in hard-headed Scotland. Some grew cynical; one Highland drummer, a brilliant bugler, on being exhorted to do his best at a memorial service in the Scottish National War Memorial in Edinburgh Castle, responded thus: 'Dinna worry, sir; I'll ha'e them a' greetin' afore I'm hauf wey through the Last Post.'

Critics of the Remembrance Sunday ceremonies complain much at the 'militaristic' nature of the occasion, with bands, bugles and servicemen under arms and veterans wearing their medals. But this is the way in which, for centuries, the armed services of the Crown have taken leave of, and have done honour to, their fallen comrades who have been denied the privilege, common to all, of a decent death, faced with the support of their friends and families, and a dignified and reverently conducted burial in their own home country. Long may the tradition continue.

'Go! Bid the soldiers shoot!'

Notes

1. The horses which pulled the gun and limber were the gun team; the soldiers who fired the gun were the gun detachment.
2. 'King's Rules and Regulations for the Army', usually referred to as KRs, set out in detail the procedures to be followed in most circumstances of contemporary Army life. They were not absolute, however, and officers were responsible for ensuring that their provisions were not blindly applied when local conditions clearly rendered the letter of the regulations inappropriate.
3. 'Reverse arms'; and 'rest on your arms reversed' were devised for the funeral of the Duke of Marlborough in 1722. *An Outline of British Military History*, Cole and Priestley (Sifton Praed, 1936).
4. Planning and foresight are among the first principles of good staff work but can be carried to extremes. It was not unknown for rehearsals of the funeral drill and practice for the music to be ordered as soon as a soldier was placed on the dangerously ill list.
5. The custom of sounding 'Last Post' over the grave appears to have been regularised in 1885. Prior to that date, accounts of military funerals mention the playing of the 'Dead March in Saul' but no reference to the sounding of 'Last Post' is made. However, the tradition may be much

older, as regulations often endorsed custom and practice retrospectively. 'Ceremonial 1912' specifies 'Last Post' only. 'The Manual of Ceremonial 1950' prescribes the sounding of 'Rouse' after 'Last Post', the firing party remaining at the 'Present' and officers saluting.

OVERLEAF: 2nd Battalion, The Argyll and Sutherland Highlanders, Regimental Funeral, The funeral of Colour Serjeant Mullen, who died in Hong Kong in 1933. The pipes, drums and military band approach the cemetery, the band playing the regulation Dead March in Saul; the drums, muffled and draped, rolling throughout − note the drum major's staff, draped and carried 'reversed'. The pipers are diverging to the right and left so they can line the final few yards of the route. The nearer soldiers are at 'reverse arms', those further away 'rest on their arms reversed'. (RHQ Argyll and Sutherland Highlanders)

CHAPTER XXI
THE MARCHING BANDS
~

The first duty of the bandmaster is to produce a good marching band. *Standing Orders, The Durham Light Infantry.*

We have seen how the development of metalled roads made it possible for formed bodies of troops to cover long distances on foot, marching in step and cadence. Even with experienced and seasoned soldiers, however, the rhythm will vary and the step become ragged, leading to unnecessary stress and fatigue for the marching men. The solution lies in the provision of marching music; and, in this respect, the British Army, in which each battalion had its military band, supported by a corps of drums and fifes, bugles, or pipes and drums, was in a better position than, for instance, the German Army, where the regimental band had to be shared by the three battalions that comprised a Continental regiment.

With the growth of the rail network in Victorian Britain, troops could be readily moved about in specially chartered trains, and when a battalion moved from one military station to another the journey was made by rail and not by march route along the roads. Even before rail travel became general, units had frequently been moved by sea, or even by canal boat, rather than by road. The relief of the garrisons of Stirling Castle and Fort George were also effected by sea, there being a river port at Stirling and a deep-sea anchorage off Fort George.

This ready availability of alternative methods of moving troops about the country made long marches on home service largely unnecessary, except on training and exercises. But in India, the spiritual home of the British Army for well nigh two centuries, marching was the preferred mode of progression even when travel by rail would have been quite possible.[1] In many cases, the troops, both Indian and British, were marched from one station to another so that the native population might rest assured that the power and might of the *Sirkar* was intact and omnipresent.

257

2nd Battalion, The Royal Scots Fusiliers, Khyber Pass, Northwest Frontier Province, 1927

Ho! Get away, you bullockman, you've 'eard the bugle blowed,
There's a regiment a'comin' down the Grand Trunk Road! ('Route Marching', Rudyard Kipling)

The battalion is on the line of march from its old station at Landi Kotal in the Khyber Pass to Ferozepore in the Punjab, headed by the pipes and drums. The military band is positioned halfway down the column so that everyone can hear it. On a march of this length, many battalions prided themselves on not matching a single step without music. The battalion will join the grand trunk road at Peshawar. (RHQ Royal Highland Fusiliers)

258

~

Another function of those long marches was simply to get the soldiers fit. Life in an Indian cantonment, the military settlement, could plumb the very depths of tedium. For health reasons, soundly based on experience, the barracks were built several miles from the Indian town or city, always firmly out of bounds to the British soldiers. Within the cantonment, what passed for all the amenities of the military life were provided, and a soldier needed to do nothing for himself except clean his rifle, which no Indian was allowed to touch. Apart from the morning's routine training and drill, a soldier could, in theory, spend the rest of the time in or on his bed. Few did, however, and the great majority took an active part in some form of sport and athletics. There were those who read widely and others were interested in Indian history and folklore. For recreation, there was the coffee bar and the wet canteen; 'India' pale ale was so called because, in theory, it would stay drinkable even after the voyage to Bombay. After the Great War, there was also the garrison cinema, but outside the tight little circuit of cantonment life lay two temptations: the local toddy shop selling 'arrack', the country spirit, its effect both instantaneous and semi-lethal, but cheap; and the 'sand rats', the diseased crones, also cheap but eventually lethal, who lay in wait to trap the unwary soldier who was mildly drunk and at a loose end after the canteen had closed.

A battalion could spend long years in India, and this had its effect in many ways. Until World War II, a soldier could spend up to eight years there without any home leave; his enthusiasm for and interest in life could wane progressively as he 'sweated on the boat with the tartan funnels'. In the early days of the Far East War, the uneven performance of battalions of famous regiments which had simply been 'too long abroad' owed much to this factor.

Inevitably, things like band instruments had to be repaired, and in the early days of the British involvement in India, the cost and distance precluded sending them home. Thus arose the race of band *mistris* or Indian carpenters and handymen who, not lacking in either skill or ability, could repair and restore the band's instruments at practically no cost. Not content with mere repair, some could make a perfectly passable and playable instrument, brass or woodwind, so there was no need for a band to become ineffective through lack of instruments. Drums, and their repair and maintenance, were child's play to a competent *mistri*, and even bagpipes were within their capacity, using the local *sheesham* wood, these lacking perhaps in tone when compared with the home product, but perfectly acceptable in a pipe band. In this way, the pipe bands of the Indian regiments could be equipped at an affordable cost, using the products of Indian craftsmen, the founders of the firms of musical instrument makers in India and Pakistan, which now export their goods all over the world.

The battalion of the regiment serving abroad was kept up to full strength by drafts of trained men from the battalion at home, so there were always plenty of soldiers in the 'foreign' battalion. Although the drummers and bandsmen, the pipers and the buglers, tended to form their own fairly exclusive little coteries within the battalion, there was always some contact with the 'dutymen', the soldiers in the ranks, particularly those who came from the same city or district. It might happen that a bored soldier might try his hand at beating a drum, blowing a bugle, playing a flute or a practice chanter. Half in fun, he might try to master the instrument or at least to knock out a tune. The drum major might hear of him, spot a 'prospect' and have him transferred to the drums as a learner; so too might the band serjeant; and so too might the pipe major. Indeed, it was not unknown for a keen pipe major to hold evening classes for aspiring pipers, both to train replacements for the 'time-expired' pipers going home, as well as to give those interested something constructive to do in their ample spare time.

This is how it was possible for the corps of drums of a line regiment in India to turn out, fifty-strong, to beat Retreat once a week; and for a pipe band of twenty-five pipers and fifteen drummers plus twelve buglers, to beat Tattoo on the barrack square, outside the officers mess or on the *maidan*, the central open space in the cantonment, for the benefit of the local Indians. The instruments were readily and cheaply available; the only restricting factor might be the provision of the correct piper's, drummer's or bandsman's clothing, but this could also be easily copied by the regimental *dhursi*, the tailor, and his minions – again at a fraction of the price charged at home for such items.

So life in the cantonment went on, enlivened now and then by the odd sporting or athletic success. There might be, too, the periodic domestic scandal, never infrequent in the military life where young, bored and frequently attractive women lived surrounded by strong, healthy and often personable young men. And every now and then some young soldier, depressed, lonely and far from home, would take his own way out, to be buried with all the panoply described in the previous chapter.

But one day the news would break that the 'Glenwhorple Highlanders' were to exchange stations with the 'Blankshire Fusiliers' several hundred miles away.[2] The commanding officer might decide that this would be an excellent opportunity to stretch his soldiers' legs, and would apply for permission to proceed by march route, which was usually granted, particularly if the route lay through some part of the country where there might be some threat to law and order, either through political activity, always volatile in India, or from the 'Goondas', 'Badmashes' and 'Dacoits', the hooligans, criminals and bandits, the perennial scourges of rural life in the remoter areas, even in the 'British Time'.

A hundred years ago, in Kipling's heyday, the wives and children of the soldiers would have travelled with the battalion, sitting on the baggage waggons, but in the later days the families would have moved by train, under the general control, it was hoped, of some luckless subaltern, whose burden would be eased by the existence among the families of a recognised 'pecking order' which might or might not reflect the rank of the husbands and fathers concerned, but which was, none the less, effective. Provided the harassed officer kept on the right side of the leading wife, all would, in its own way, go well.

At last, the great day would dawn. As the corps of drums beat 'The General', always played instead of 'The Mother and the Three Camps' on the morning of a move, or the pipes and drums beat Long Reveille, first light would see the soldiers falling in on their company parade grounds; answering their names as the roll was called, important because absence from a specific duty might be charged as desertion; and when the pipes played the 'Gathering', or the bugles sounded 'General Parade' or the 'Advance', marching on to the battalion parade ground to form up for the road. In India, the soldiers would be wearing light marching order, with water bottles filled, and haversacks; on the transport would be their packs and '*Dhurri* bundles', the soldiers' bedding roll, never mentioned in accounts of Army life in India but a vital part of the soldier's possessions, consisting of a rough fibre mat, rolled round his mosquito net, blankets and change of clothing. Heavy baggage went by train, under the control of the baggage guard.

In the years between the wars, Highland soldiers would be in the kilt, others in shorts. Both would wear boots, puttees and hosetops, and it came as a surprise to see how colourful a sight a battalion of an English county regiment, the very core of the British infantry, made on parade, with its coloured hosetops, maroon, blue, grey or green, often with contrasting garter flashes; khaki drill shorts pressed and starched; and the silver-grey shirt issued in India with polished shoulder titles. Highland regiments, too, were something special, the Black Watch with Lovat-green hosetops and matching puttees, others with fawn puttees and hosetops, white puttee tapes and regimental garter flashes. All wore the Wolseley helmet as head-dress with badge, patch and hackle, the *pagri* with coloured folds inserted; rather heavy, and replaced in some orders of dress by the pith hat, much lighter and equally gorgeously adorned. For all the fun poked at the 'topi' by the uninitiated, it was a smart and soldierly head-dress, and when wearing it the soldiers looked the part, and, as a result, acted it, too.[3]

At length, all the preliminaries completed, the commanding officer, mounted on his charger, would order: 'By the right, quick march!' With a crash of drums the march would get under way, the pipes and drums playing 'Happy We've Been a' Thegither', or the fifes 'The Girl I Left Behind Me', both tunes usually inappropriate in India, but played nevertheless, tongue in cheek, the younger officers perhaps exchanging a knowing wink when certain houses on the outskirts of the Cantonment were passed.[4] Nobody would be particularly upset to see the last of the old station; but in barrack-room folklore, it would soon be looked back on as the soldier's paradise. The present station was never a patch on the last; but the next one was going to be the best of all!

The pipes and drums or corps of drums would head the battalion column, perhaps preceded by the pioneers, the battalion's tradesmen, traditionally, the men who cleared obstacles from the road. In this case these would be bullock carts, camels, sacred cows and women with huge loads of firewood on their heads and babies on their backs. The women, and their attendant toddlers, 'chickos' to the soldiers – an interesting survival from the Peninsular War – would be moved firmly with rough but friendly kindness. The British soldier never ceased to deplore the women's place in Indian society, and was not averse to making his opinion clear to their menfolk. The Indians' attitude to and treatment of animals similarly roused the soldiers' ire and contempt and, in earlier days, might have led to physical chastisement.[5] However, in the later stages of British rule, it was an offence punishable by court-martial to lay a violent hand on an Indian, however humble.

'March at Ease' would be passed down the column, rifles would be slung and the mounted officers would dismount, their chargers being led behind them. It was a point of honour with them to march every step of the way, except when the column 'Marched to Attention', when the officers would mount again. This was ordered when the battalion passed the quarter guard of another, which would turn out and 'present arms', the bugler sounding the 'guard salute'. The soldiers of the other battalion, far from 'chiyacking' at the marching troops, would be at rigid 'attention', facing the column. Each company, with rifles at the 'slope', would give an 'eyes right' to the quarter guard, which would be at the 'Present'. The same thing would happen when some senior officer turned out to see how the Glenwhorple Highlanders were taking the march, and when troops marching the other way were encountered. All this came under the heading of 'Compliments on the Line of March', usually punctiliously observed, as this was one of the ways in which the battalion would be graded, both officially and unofficially.

Halfway down the column came the military band, both sources of marching music being at full strength. The battalion might take up to half a mile of road, so the music had to be audible. The bands played alternately; when one was nearing the end of its stint, its bass drummer would give his drum four almighty thumps – the 'double tap' – which was the signal for the other band to get ready to take over. Whichever band was due to play and whatever it was going to play, two introductory three-pace rolls were beaten by the drummers and the percussionists of the band. These three-pace rolls are all that remains of the 'English Cadence', one of the recognition signals by which troops made their identity known in earlier times. They were not regulation, and each regiment could have its own system, the drummers of the foot guards beating a five-pace roll and others a seven-pace. The old Queen's Royal Regiment, the 2nd of Foot, took pride in turning out twelve side drummers with their corps of drums, which was always outstanding in smartness and musical skill. The cry was: 'Here come the Queen's; a seven-pace roll and a cloud of white blanco!'

Each band would play for about ten minutes; the pipes and drums would play a four-part march five times through; the corps of drums or the military band would play their march card three times over. The column halted at ten minutes to every clock hour, making five playing sessions in all. At each halt, the order of march would be changed so that each company had a chance to march directly behind the music. Pipers memorise all their tunes, so that the pipe major could order whatever tune took his fancy at any particular stage of the march, although certain popular tunes were demanded by the soldiers. A pipe march such as *'Cabar Feidh'* – the 'Stag's Antlers' – never palled, being full of Highland fire and life. The most popular tunes were in common, 2/4 or 6/8 time. The odd retreat march in 3/4 or 9/8 time might also be thrown in, although 3/4 is a sleepy time signature for a march. The beatings played by the side drummers of the pipes and drums were simple by modern standards, but were designed to maintain a regular marching rhythm, rather than to display the drummers' virtuosity. The bass drum of the marching era was a formidable instrument, so that its pulse might be heard down the length of the column, even though the sound of the music itself was faint. But no matter how hard the bass drummer hit his drum, the laws of acoustics would see to it that the rear of the column was always half a beat behind the front, so that the battalion never looked as if it was in step.

The corps of drums and the military band played from march cards of a size convenient for carrying in a pouch or 'card case'. The earlier corps of drums had played simple two-part quickstep marches, rather like those played by the pipers, but as time went on and the range of instruments available to the corps of drums was increased by the appearance of more sophisticated flutes and piccolos, in different keys and pitches – there was even a bass flute – so march compositions for the corps of drums became more ambitious and marches on the same melodic scheme as those composed for the military band became popular. The flute players wore a lyre-shaped card holder strapped to their left wrists which held their music. Most band instruments were fitted with a similar lyre. Some drum majors made their flute players memorise all their marches in the same way as the side drummers, with the new entrants among the drummer boys having to learn a new march card every week. Of course, this was not possible with the military band because of the number and complexity of the 'inside' parts, but most bands had certain 'dark marches' that all the bandsmen had memorised and that were used when, say, a draft had to be played from the station early in the morning or late at night. On the line of march, the band serjeant would ensure that all the bandsmen had the music for the day's march handy and in the proper order. The aim was not to repeat a march on any one day; but, inevitably, over a long march the same tunes would be heard every day, and so the 'dutymen' came to know them well and to acquire their own preferences. Some of the tunes had doggerel words put to them but, contrary to received wisdom about the musical tastes of the 'brutal and licentious', these tended to be quite innocuous.

An even and steady marching pace enabled the soldiers to relax while marching, paradoxical as it might sound, something quite possible given well-fitted boots and a moderate load. The rate of progress was three miles in the hour. So, allowing for the ten-minute halt, the distance actually covered was two and a half miles in an hour, a rate of progress which trained and seasoned soldiers could keep up for an almost indefinite period, although it was usual to halt one day in four. The tempo worked out at one hundred and eight to the minute, the same as the 'quick step' of the eighteenth century, an even swinging pace which became instinctive after a time. Of course, it was possible to march faster, and in the case of the light infantry and rifle regiments a faster step was kept up, not the regimental pace of one hundred and forty to the minute, but certainly faster than one hundred and eight or even one hundred and twenty. The observation made by a Scottish medical officer – himself a piper attached to an English light infantry regiment – to the effect that this increased speed led to more sore feet and blisters than the regulation one hundred and eight was not well received.

One of the trials of route marching in India, which bore especially heavily on pipers and bandsmen, was the insistence on what was known as 'water discipline'. The object was to control the consumption of water by the soldiers, prudent enough when water was short, but often carried to extremes. To put it simply, water was conserved by forbidding the soldiers to drink from their water bottles. Despite protests from the medical officers that the human frame, unlike that of the camel, was not adapted for storing water and that the moisture lost through sweat had to be replaced, permission to drink was only grudgingly given, and then when essential to avoid heatstroke casualties.

This could lead to real physical distress. Even in the Indian winter, the midday sun was hot. Often the road led arrow straight for mile after mile, with nothing to break the monotony of the red ochre Indian plain save for the occasional wayside temple or, more rarely, an Indian village, apparently deserted under the noon sun. 'Mad Dogs and Englishmen' was based on fact. Now and then a bullock cart, complete with slumbering driver, might potter along in the opposite direction, giving scope for the wits in the ranks, but as the heat of the day intensified, all indigenous activity ceased. But still the march went relentlessly on, the bands playing alternately and the big drum thudding out the step as the furlong stones slid by.

The contrast between the music of the two bands could be quite marked, as the pipes tend to drone along, the volume and the sound constant, the 'dynamics' – the light and shade – imparted by the drums beating 'piano' and 'forte' to alternate eight-bar phrases – what the pipers call 'parts' – the leading, or solo, drummer taking the 'piano' part, the whole corps, the 'forte'. From the rear of the column, it could be difficult to tell which tune the pipers were playing, as the configuration of the instrument throws the sound of the pipe chanter, on which the melody is played, forward.

With the military band, on the other hand, the phrases are distinct, the volume varies and the structure of the march, in its component parts of introduction, first subject, bass solo and trio

lends further variety. The range of available marches is wide and
includes many that are not too exacting to play and were
therefore suitable for playing during a long march. Those the
soldiers enjoyed hearing were not always those the bandsmen
enjoyed playing, and the commanding officer, too, might have
strong, if musically uninformed, views about the sort of music
his band should play. One such, 'The Fizzer' to his soldiers,
directed that only Scottish tunes were to be played by his band
on the march. The battalion found the going very hard and dull
as it slogged out the miles from Parachinar on the Afghan
Border down the Kurram Valley to the rail head at Thal, as the
military band, like the pipes, droned through Scots ballads like
'The Rowan Tree', 'Duncan Gray' and 'John Anderson, my Jo,
John', and the like, instead of 'Belphegor', 'Punjab' and 'The
Light of Foot', all firm favourites with the soldiers.

The endurance shown by the pipers, drummers, and
bandsmen more than matched that of the dutymen, and
occasionally there might be a friendly contest between the two
bands. When the 2nd Battalion Seaforth Highlanders marched
from Nowshera in the north-west frontier province to Lahore in
the Punjab, covering some two hundred and fifty miles, at one
stage the pipes and drums played for the full fifty minutes
between halts without a break. Not to be outdone, the military
band did the same at the next stage, which was just before the
long midday halt. The battalion in fact halted two furlongs
beyond the two and a half mile point so the military band were
deemed to have won, much to the chagrin of the pipers. Well
might the regimental journal for the period compliment 'our two
magnificent bands'.

As the day wore on, so would the ranks fall silent, and it was
at this stage that the music came into its own. The mounted
officers' chargers would now be carrying the younger of the
drummer boys, and the tunes played by the bands would become
less formal, the pipes perhaps with 'The Black Bear', in which
the drum beating had a silent bar where the soldiers were
encouraged to shout or 'hooch', while the military band might
try some current hit popular with the soldiers. For reasons of
professional pride, the end of the day's march had to be done in
style, regardless of the distance covered, the weather or who was
looking on – if anybody. So the column would halt, sort itself

out, brush off some of the dust and, marching at 'attention', step off with the pipes playing the appropriate tune for entering barracks. This was sometimes the march past or some other tune of significance, 'Scotland the Brave' being a popular choice. Before being dismissed, the battalion might be put through some drill movements, just to make sure that there was some energy in reserve.

It could sometimes happen that a battalion might find itself faced with a long march while its military band was away on some lucrative or important engagement and, consequently, the pipes and drums or corps of drums was the only source of marching music available. The great advantage which these had over the military band was that they could be split into their component parts and still remain musically effective. But whereas the pipes and drums could form two pipe bands, the corps of drums could go one better. All the drummers could sound the bugle as well as play the flute or drum, so a system was devised in which half the buglers sounded eight-bar march phrases alternately with the flute players. The flutes would play an eight-bar phrase, only the leading drummer beating; then the bugles would sound for another eight bars, all the drummers beating. It was also possible to split the corps even further, and for the music to be played continuously by the minimum number of two buglers, two flute players, and two drummers.

In the light infantry and rifles, the bugles were the only alternative to the military band, and because of the strain on the buglers' embouchures - their 'lip'- they were usually split into two equal sections, sounding alternately. The Cameronians and the Highland Light Infantry also had pipers, and *HLI Chronicle* carries complaints from the companies of being 'fobbed off' with two buglers instead of two pipers. The 1st HLI had no drummers until 1908, but there is no record of how the battalion managed to march to the sound of the pipes alone, without any percussion to mark the beat.

It was, in many cases, a matter of regimental pride never to march a step without music, the pipes and drums or corps of drums and the military band playing alternately all the way. Consequently, there was little scope or need for the soldiers to sing on the march and, perhaps because of this, the British Army lacks the tradition of organised singing as was such a feature of the German Army where the soldiers were taught during their training to sing the traditional marching songs; or the Russian, where the command 'singers to the front' would be given as the troops approached a village. The small battalion corps of drums, lacking even a bass drum in the case of the Germans, could do little more than set the step for the leading files. The requirement for music to maintain the step and cadence was filled by the voices of the soldiers themselves, and extremely impressive the sound could be. This is not to suggest the British soldiers never sang, but that there was never any co-ordinated official attempt to teach them to sing on the march.[6] The British soldier sang in his barrack-room, in the wet canteen, round the camp fire in bivouac and, indeed, he may have sung on the march, but the evidence of 'The Old Contemptibles', the British Army of 1914, was that singing on the march came in with Kitchener's Army.

However, in the later nineteenth century, there had been a vogue in the British Army for what were called 'Song Marches'. This reflected the German influence, where many of the marching songs were given the same treatment, with an introduction, a first section and a bass solo. The trio consisted of the tune of the song, and when these marches were played in that form in camp or bivouac and on the march, the soldiers came in on the trio. The celebrated Gottfried Piefke, Director of Music of the 8th Life Grenadier Regiment of the Prussian Army, was fond of constructing his marches round a soldier's song.

At the time of the Second Afghan War of 1878–1880, a popular song was 'Her Bright Smile Haunts Me Still'. This was incorporated in a Song March in the German style as was 'Jessie's Dream', which was based on the Indian Mutiny story of Jessie Brown of Lucknow, who had dreamed she had heard the pipes of the relieving force, thus encouraging the garrison to maintain its resistance until relief finally did arrive. These two song marches can be heard every year as the folk of Selkirk in the Scottish Borders celebrate the riding of the Marches, when the bounds of the common lands are traversed by a mounted party of the townsfolk escorting the standard bearer carrying the burgh flag. It appears that about a hundred years ago a retired Army bandsman was appointed to the town band, and it seems likely that he introduced these marches, now regarded by the people of Selkirk as part of their cultural heritage and sung with gusto in the course of the common riding every year. A far cry from a Prussian barrack square.

The French Army solved the problem of marching music quite simply and logically. The soldiers did not march either in step or formation. Each man took his own pace, carried his pack however he liked, and walked along in a group with his friends as he pleased. A French officer was asked by a British general why his men did not march in step like the British; he retorted, 'I suppose, *mon Général*, that all your men are the same size!'

Notes

1. 'Thus the Duke of Wellington: "As to marches, that is not, I should say, our men's 'forte'. In India, they become good marchers from necessity; changing one's quarters five or six hundred miles off makes a good marcher at once; but in England we are in the habit of conveying them by steamboats or canal boats and never letting them walk. First, it saves public money, that is one thing, and then it saves commanding officers trouble."' *Conversations with the Duke of Wellington*, Stanhope (John Murray, 1889).
2. The 'Glenwhorple Highlanders' were the subject of an eponymous song mocking the style and pretensions of the Highland regiments.
The chorus ran:

> Heugh, Glenwhorple hielan'men!
> Great strong whusky-suppin' hielan'men!
> They were reid heided hairy leggit hielan'men
> Slansh-a-va Glenwhorple!

3. Until 1943, the sun was treated as hostile. Sunbathing was forbidden. The topi was worn until the early evening – usually until Retreat – and only the knees and lower arms were exposed. After Retreat, slacks and long sleeved shirts were worn to prevent mosquito bites and consequent malaria. When the Afrika Korps landed in Tripoli in 1941 all the *Landser* – 'Tommies' – sunbathed by order, acquiring deeply tanned bodies. This was noted with envy by the British, who, learning by experience that their heavy suntan in no way inhibited the Germans' military performance, soon followed suit. The topi became an object of derision, and 'shorts only' by day remained the rule as long as the East of Suez commitment remained. The risk of melanoma or skin cancer seems to have been discounted, but many a veteran has had cause to rue the example of the Afrika Korps as he strips off to have his solar keratoses – skin cancers – 'zapped' with liquid nitrogen.
4. Students of the period should not be misled by the many accounts of

Army life in India which suggest that it was officered by saints and manned by stallions. But every sexual preference, proclivity or aberration could be accommodated in an Indian town or city, given a bit of notice. The Indian city was always out of bounds and was patrolled by the Military Police, but with a little forethought and planning, the risk of detection was slight, as each establishment maintained an efficient early warning system. In the major cities, red light districts flourished, Grant Road in Bombay and the Diamond Market in Lahore being world famous.

The above does not seek to justify or excuse the utter misery of life for the low-caste Indian prostitute, sold by her poverty-stricken family into virtual slavery, to end, diseased and starving, as one of the 'sand rats' lurking in the shadows round the rifle range. And, any soldiers managed to live happy, fulfilled, but celibate lives during their Indian service.

5. The wrath of the soldiers was invariably aroused when a typical Indian family group passed down the column, headed by father riding on the donkey, mother trudging in rear carrying the baby, the toddlers trailing behind her. When not under the immediate eye of an officer, the soldiers would turn the father off the donkey and seat the mother, baby and the smallest toddler on the patient donkey's back.

6. Singing on the march sounds easy, but it is a skill which has to be taught, as invariably the singers progressively accelerate the tempo unless they are trained to sing on the beat.

2nd Battalion, Argyll and Sutherland Highlanders, Military Band, West Indies, 1927
Bandmaster F.J. Ricketts and his band taken at the start of the 93rd's foreign tour of service.
Appointed to the battalion in 1908, Joe Ricketts left shortly after to take up the appointment of
director of music of the Plymouth Division Royal Marines. Under his pen name, Kenneth Alford, he
remains the doyen of British march composers. His compositions include 'Colonel Bogey' and 'The
Thin Red Line', now the regimental march of the Argyll and Sutherland Highlanders. Note the
distinctive sporran worn by the bandsmen, white with two black tassels and a white, metal cantle, the
band serjeant's has a more elaborate cantle. Mr Ricketts wears a badger-head sporran, worn by
officers and serjeants at their own expense. The pipe major and two pipers stand in the back row, and
these three could have sustained their own piping and dancing item during a performance, while two
pipers and two bandsmen might have performed a foursome reel to the pipe major's playing.
(RHQ Argyll and Sutherland Highlanders)

1st Battalion, The Queen's Own Cameron Highlanders, Fyzabad, United Provinces, India, 1931
The military band on the flag march that took the battalion some two hundred miles through the Gonda district of the United Provinces in January 1931. It was the annexation by the British of the Kingdom of Oudh – in which Gonda was situated – that was one of the causes of the Indian Mutiny of 1858/1859. (RHQ Queen's Own Highlanders Amalgamation Trustees)

CHAPTER XXII
MUSIC IN THE MESS

~

Besides the provision of music for parades and on the line of march, the military band, the pipes and, to a lesser extent, the drums also played a part in the social activities of the battalion, from the all-ranks dances, which took place from time to time, to the more formal functions in the officers and serjeants messes. Over the years, the serjeants began to assimilate their mess customs and traditions to those of the officers, to the extent of devising their own formal mess uniform and closely following the procedure of the officers mess. Therefore, it will suffice to describe those functions which took place regularly in the officers mess until a few decades ago, although it must be borne in mind that the lifestyle of the regimental officer was no longer as privileged as it had been up to the outbreak of the Great War. The social changes brought about as a result of that war and accelerated by those of World War II had meant that the private income demanded by most regiments of their aspirant officers had been scaled down to conform to the reduced financial base from which the vast majority were operating, and many lived on their military salary alone.[1]

Once a week there was band night, to which officers might invite private guests. As the name implies, the military band attended, though not at full-parade strength. Playing in the officers mess was a military duty for the bandsmen, as band night was for the officers, attendance being compulsory for those living in mess. Mess 'undress' was worn with 'strapped trews' instead of the kilt. One or two of the pipers might attend, playing a couple of 'sets' round the table after the meal, during which the band had played selections. The procedure on band night was a modified form of that followed on the regimental guest night, a much more formal and formidable affair, for which band night was often a rehearsal.

The regimental guest night was, as the name implies, a social occasion on which official guests were invited to dine with the officers, the costs being divided and paid according to rank, the seniors paying the highest share. Full mess dress was worn, for Highlanders the kilt and its associated accoutrements. The military band attended at concert strength, with the pipe major and his four best pipers, while some of the drummers might be involved in the preliminaries. Half an hour before the time set for dinner, the drummers would sound 'Officers Dress for Dinner' outside the mess, and one or more of the pipers would play 1st Officers Mess Pipes according to regimental custom. These were warning calls, but woe betide the officer who was not present in the anteroom in full fig when 1st Pipes sounded. All officers were hosts for the evening and hospitality demanded that all be present to welcome the guests.

In due course, the guests would begin to assemble. It would never have done to arrive too early, and the more nervous would have been hiding until the moment was right. On the other hand, it would have been disastrous to have arrived after the principal guest, possibly a general officer, so a nice balancing of factors was involved.

As the hour for dinner struck, the drummers would sound the 'Officers' Dinner' call. Regiments often sounded their own special First and Second Mess Calls on these occasions. In the years before the Great War, many officers had shot and hunted on the Continent and had been impressed by the calls and fanfares sounded by the foresters, gamekeepers and huntsmen during the hunt, before and during the lunch break and at the end of the day. Some brought home with them the music of a particular call that had caught their fancy; others persuaded the bandmaster to compose calls in the same musical idiom, more evocative of the woods and forests of France and Germany, perhaps, than of the grouse moor and the deer forest, but still effective and conveying the sense of occasion. The calls might be sounded on open horns by the brass section of the band or by the drummers on bugles with the chromatic attachment.   The Mess Call was followed by 2nd Officers Mess pipes; the mess serjeant announced that dinner was served; the band would play 'The Roast Beef of Old England', the old Mess Call from *The Drum and Flute Duty*; and, headed by the commanding officer and the principal guest, the officers would troop into the dining-room, where the mess silver, accumulated over centuries, would be laid out in all its splendour, with the Colours uncased and displayed, crossed, on the wall.[2]

The 'Roast Beef' over, the chaplain – always referred as 'Padre' regardless of his denomination – said grace, each officer standing behind his chair. After grace, sometimes in Latin and occasionally in Gaelic, the meal began, the band launching into a concert march such as 'Marche Militaire Française' from Saint Saëns' *L'Algerienne* rather than some veteran of the parade-ground. So the evening rolled on, the band steadily working its way through the programme, probably not one of any great depth, as the object was to provide background music, not to entertain an audience. The pipers, tucked away in some back room, smoked and talked piping, unless someone had a pack of cards in his pipe box, when a few hands of solo whist and pontoon – 'Vingt et Un' – might be played to help while away the waiting period until the band serjeant sent word that the time for the National Anthem was approaching, when a quick tune up would ensure that any disasters were unlikely.

At the end of the meal, the port decanters were placed in front of the mess president, officially the President of the Mess Committee and the officer appointed to run the mess, sitting at one end of the long table, and the vice president, appointed for the evening, at the other. Having somehow brought the table to order, often more difficult than it sounds, the president would rise and intone, 'Mr Vice, The Queen!'; Mr Vice rose in his turn and announced, 'Gentlemen, The Queen!' in, he hoped, the appropriate tone of relaxed formality which he had been practising in his room ever since he had been warned that he had been 'chosen' to play the part of Mr Vice for the evening. All rose, the band played the National Anthem and the toast was drunk, entirely without dramatics. Customs varied; in some cases officers of field rank added 'God bless her!' to the toast; in others, this was anathema, as it was in the Royal Artillery. There were regiments, originally raised as marines, which drank the toast seated, as is the practice in the Royal Navy, whether because the loyalty of naval officers was never in doubt or because the space between decks was so low that nobody could stand up without banging his head remains unclear to this day. In certain Highland regiments, the place settings included finger bowls, not for use, but so that they could be cleared away before the Queen's health was drunk, lest any neo-Jacobite among the officers pass his glass over his finger bowl, thus indicating his attachment to the 'king over the water'. This made a good talking point for an officer seated next to a stranger, or one who might be heavy-going conversationally. Other healths might be proposed; each Scottish regiment has a royal colonel-in-chief, whose health would be proposed and drunk. If a foreign officer was present, the health of his Head of State would also be drunk, and his National Anthem played. But, unlike the Royal Navy and the Royal Air Force, there would be no speeches!

However, on occasions deemed to be suitably auspicious, when the health of the colonel-in-chief or some other illustrious friend of the regiment was proposed, 'Highland Honours' might be called for. In its original form, this involved everyone standing, one foot on their chair, the other on the table, glass raised. There followed an arcane ritual in which the glass was raised, lowered, held out to the right and then to the left as the company chanted in Gaelic 'In with her, out with her, up with her, down with her!', 'her' being the glass. Finally the health was drunk with acclamation, the glass drained and then smashed against the wall so that no lesser health might be drunk from 'her' again. As drunk in the mess, however, Highland Honours consisted only of standing with one foot on the table and one on the chair and drinking the health with acclamation. Only very rarely were the glasses smashed. It was good fun, all the same!

In Victorian times, and indeed much later, the serious business of the evening then began. This was, quite simply, drinking. Over the years, things steadily improved, and every generation was able to claim that in its time it had seen a great reduction in the amount of liquor consumed, not only in the officers mess, but also in the serjeants mess and the wet canteen. In the earlier days of Queen Victoria's reign, the majority of the officers were unmarried and lived in the mess. They dined together every evening, usually at seven o'clock, but as one young officer of the 1840s recorded, 'We seldom rose from the table before midnight.' He went on, 'Mulled port in a great silver jug was placed on the table after dinner and drunk out of claret glasses, a very insinuating satiable liquor, but bad to get up on in the morning.' But: 'Late nights and heavy drinking were never allowed to interfere with duty, and no excuse was ever admitted for being late on parade and drill.' This last remained true; and even in much later times, care had to be taken to remember the next morning's commitments as the port circulated after dinner in the mess, for to be absent from parade because of the night before was to lose face all round, quite apart from any semi-official action which might very possibly ensue.

After the Queen's health, in came the pipers, playing a march, kilts and plaids swinging as they circled the table clockwise. Sometimes the same march of entry is always played, in other cases a different tune each time. After a couple of circuits the pipers would halt behind the commanding officer's chair and break into a strathspey followed by a reel; then, back into a contrasting march, twice more round the table, and out. The pieces played by the band were, by custom, never applauded; but it was acceptable to acknowledge the pipers' contribution to the evening by rapping the table with the knuckles, hand clapping being considered unofficer-like in this context.

It was now the turn of the pipe major to play the *piobaireachd*. Since the days of the civilian bandmaster it had been the custom for the bandmaster to join the officers after the Queen's health had been drunk and to take port with the commanding officer. An experienced bandmaster knew that if he did not succeed in making his exit before the pipe major came in, he would be stuck there for the whole *piobaireachd*. Also, his chair would be in the pipe major's way and, as relations at that level were generally slightly strained at the best of times, a formal complaint to the mess president next morning would be inevitable. So with profuse thanks to the commanding officer, the bandmaster would escape as the pipe major began his first circuit of the table, playing the *Urlar*, the ground or theme of his *piobaireachd*.

Piobaireachd tunes vary in duration between seven and twenty minutes, and there are more of the latter than of the former. The music itself is formal and stylised and, like all classical music, it is difficult to understand. It is also very slow and, to the uninitiated listener, monotonous. Boredom can set in early. Until relatively recently, it was considered permissible for conversation to be continued during the piping, including the *piobaireachd*, but in recent years, the realisation has spread that the music has its own appeal, and for the sake of good manners, if nothing else, it should be listened to in silence. But whereas in the old days the pipe major had no compunction in curtailing the piece, now he is expected to play the whole tune. The pipe major reciprocates by choosing a shorter *piobaireachd*; and the younger officers place bets on how many times he goes round the table.

After the *piobaireachd*, the pipe major marches in for his ceremonial dram, poured for him into the regimental quaich by the commanding officer, sometimes, if he knows the form, by the principal guest. The pipe major then proposes a toast in Gaelic. If he is not a native Gaelic-speaker himself, he will have been coached by one of the Gaelic-speaking pipers. Nobody in the room will understand a word he says; but provided he ends with the Gaelic '*Slainte!*' – 'Good health!' – nobody will mind, for this is the cue for everyone to respond with a reciprocal cry of '*Slainte!*', and to drain his glass. In some cases, the pipe major carries out the rite of turning the quaich over to show that he has emptied it and of kissing the base; in others, this was regarded as a bogus Highland ritual of the sort devised to impress tourists. The pipe major then salutes and stalks out, to return a few minutes later at the head of his pipers for the second 'set'.[3]

The officers might then rise and make their way to the anteroom, where, after a pause, some basic Scottish country dancing might be attempted, remarkable more for strength than skill, and if someone was swung off his feet, so much the jollier. All officers were taught the popular country dances and were given some instruction in Highland dancing as well, at an hour which left them free for their ordinary duties. The scene in the film *Tunes of Glory*, where the officers are turned out at 0630 on a winter's morning to practise and improve their dancing, is wholly authentic.

Eventually, the party would draw to a close, the band and pipers to enjoy the luxury of a late Reveille and a free morning. There would be extra duty pay for the cooks and waiters and aspirin and 'Bombay Oysters' for those officers who needed them at breakfast.[4] A fair amount would have been drunk, but without incident, and any dirty washing would be done regimentally. The historian of a Highland regiment has described the unwritten code, which applied to everyone, as the difference between 'drink taken' and 'drunk'. With 'drink taken', a soldier would be told to shut up and go to bed; a 'drunk' would be locked up. An officer might fall against the furniture, but notice would be taken if he fell over it.[5]

~

Of course, there were any number of variations in the way in which the regiments conducted their regimental guest nights and how the pipers came in, when and what they played. Sometimes they marched out anti-clockwise to show the reverse side of the pipe banner, which each piper carried on the bass drone of his instrument. This well-meant practice ignores the ergonomics of the Highland bagpipe. The vast majority of pipers play 'on the left shoulder', that is the drones are carried on the left, so that when the piper marches anti-clockwise, the decorative cords, tassels, and ribbons worn when the instrument is 'dressed' brush lightly along the tops of the heads of the seated company unless the dining-room is big enough to allow the pipers to march close to the wall.

A pipe banner is a small guidon – a fish-tailed flag with the corners rounded off – the field or ground being in either the tartan or the facing colour of the regiment, the banner displaying its badge or crest. It was formerly the custom, and still is in some cases, for an officer to have a banner made when he is first appointed to command a company, and for the banner to display his personal armorial bearings or coat of arms. There has been much erudite discussion with the Lyon Court, presided over by the Lord Lyon King of Arms, the ultimate authority on such matters in Scotland, about the precise form the armorial bearings should take, but in these modern days the officer who has inherited or who has been granted his personal achievement of arms is a rare bird; although all officers, by virtue of the commission they hold from the Sovereign, are considered to be armigerous, that is, eligible for the grant of Arms, the process is not inexpensive, so few take up the option.

The colonels-in-chief of the Scottish regiments usually possess their own personal pipe banners, in many cases presented to them by their regiment, and these are carried when they are present. Similarly, towns and burghs, and now regions and districts, which have strong connections with their local regiments have also presented pipe banners, with their crest or coat of arms on one side, and the regimental devices on the other. The pipers of the Black Watch only carry banners when playing indoors, as was also the custom in the Gordon Highlanders. The other Scottish regiments wear banners on State and ceremonial occasions, which can be disastrous when it rains. The Queen's Own Highlanders had no personal banners, a custom inherited from the Cameron Highlanders where, as in the Scots Guards to this day, only regimental banners were permitted to be carried.

In conclusion, it perhaps ought to be made clear that a regimental guest night is now a rare event, and an officer might wear his mess dress only once or twice in a year. For all that, these were splendid occasions of the nature that remain fresh in the memory, and if their day is passing, then regimental life is the poorer as a result, such occasions stressing the vocational nature of the military life, in which it was a privilege to share. And not only the officers; for the soldiers involved would mention the pride they felt in belonging to an organisation that was capable of mounting an event of that nature with such style and such panache.

Notes

1. 'The regiment I hoped to join, the Royal Scots Fusiliers, was an expensive one; but it had shortly to cut expenses to the bone to allow the sons of former officers to join it. It was the same everywhere.' *The Uneven Road*, Lord Belhaven (John Murray, 1955).
2. The mess silver consisted of table cutlery, candelabra, cups, tankards, trophies of all kinds and, invariably, an elaborate centrepiece for the mess table, plus glasses and crockery. All these items either had been presented to the mess or had been purchased by the officers at some time or another. The silver belonged to the officers mess and not to anyone else, least of all the Government. The officers bore the heavy cost of insurance themselves.
   A steady and trustworthy old soldier was appointed 'silverman', which excused him from parades, guards, and other duties, and brought him 'extra-duty pay', subscribed by the officers. He slept in the silver-room in some cases; in others, the keys were handed to the orderly oficer every night for safe-keeping. The silverman might well have been sent to one of the major firms of silversmiths to be trained in the care of the silver, in which he often became expert. A junior officer would be appointed to supervise the silverman, and to learn the history of the different pieces that made up the collection. Periodically, all the subalterns would be taken to the silver-room, and would be lectured on the provenance of the silver, so that when asked by a guest about some piece, they would be able to give a sensible answer; in theory, anyway!
3. The Gaelic toasts proposed by the pipe major varied, each regiment having its own traditional forms, usually ending with the words 'Slainte do'n Bhan-Righ! Slainte!' – 'Health to the Queen! Health!' Others might be 'Slainte do'n Bhan-Righ; agus slainte do'n ise daoine – uasal!' –'Health to the Queen and her gentlemen!' i.e. the officers; or, somewhat equivocally, 'A

'*dhaoine – uasal agus luchd na'n Gaildhealtachd, gualainn ri gualainn!*' –
'Gentlemen and Highlanders, shoulder to shoulder!' The regimental toast
of the Seaforth Highlanders and, until 1994, the Queen's Own Highlanders
was, however, sheer poetry in either language.

> Tir nam Beann, nam Gleann, 's nam Gaisgeach;
> Far am faighear an t'eun fionn,
> 'S far am faigh am fiadh fasgadh.
> Cho fada's chitear ceo mu bheann
> 'S a ruitheas uisge le gleann
> Mairidh cuimhne air éuchd nan treun.
> Slàinte agus buaidh gu bràth
> Le Gillean Chabair Féidh
> *Cabar Féidh gu bràth!*

> The land of the Bens, the Glens, and the Heroes,
> Where the ptarmigan thrives
> And the red deer finds shelter.
> Whilst mist hangs over the mountains
> And water runs in the glens,
> May the deeds of the brave be remembered,
> And health and fortune ever be
> With the lads of Cabar Feidh!
> *Cabar Feidh gu brath!*

'*Cabar Feidh*' was the patronymic of the Earls of Seaforth, Chiefs of Clan
MacKenzie, 'Sons of the Bright One'. The clan badge was a stag's head, as
were the cap badges of the Seaforth and Queen's Own Highlanders. '*Cabar
Feidh*' means simply 'Deer's Antlers'. So much is lost in translation – '*Cabar
Feidh gu Brath*' means literally 'The deer's antlers for ever' – that the Gaelic
term is invariably used. The Seaforth Highlanders referred to themselves
as '*Cabar Feidh*', and when three cheers were called for, a fourth was added
– 'And one for *Cabar Feidh*!', a custom continued by the Queen's Own
Highlanders.
4. The 'Bombay Oyster' was a raw egg in Worcestershire sauce, once
favoured as a quick morning-after cure for a sore head brought about by
over-enthusiastic drinking. Recipes varied, and as India faded from the
group consciousness it lost its popularity as more advanced remedies
became available. In some Indian Army officers messes it had been the
custom to serve mulligatawny soup at breakfast on the morning after to
clear the heads and palates of the recovering officers.
[5]*Proud Heritage; the History of the Highland Light Infantry*, Lt. Col. L.B. Oatts.

APPENDIX
OFFICERS MESS CALLS

The Royal Highland Fusiliers Officers Mess Call
Scored for open horns, but now sounded by trumpets and trombones

(By kind permission of RHQ The Royal Highland Fusiliers)

The Seaforth Highlanders Officers Mess Call

Sounded by 3-9 drummers on the bugle with the chromatic valve attachment
(By kind permission RHQ Queen's Own Highlanders)

2nd Scottish Rifles, String Band, Landi Kotal, Khyber Pass, India, 1929
In addition to the military band, the 2nd Scottish Rifles could also supply a thirty-piece string
orchestra. The majority of the bandsmen were 'double-handed' i.e. they could play a stringed
instrument in addition to their own. The band provided the marching and parade music, while the
string band played at the officers mess and gave orchestral concerts. (S.J. Sellwood Collection)

1st Battalion, Black Watch, Military Band, Flanders, 1915
Look well on these men, the original 'Old Contemptibles'; their like was never to be seen again.
In 1914, the 1st Battalion, Black Watch, had gone to France with the 1st Guards Brigade
and suffered very severely at the Battles of the Aisne and first Ypres. Most Scottish regular battalions
had revived their pipes and drums by early 1915, but the Black Watch was unusual in resuscitating
the military band as well. All the bandsmen had been trained as stretcher-bearers before the war, and
this photgraph of the much-reduced band suggest that their primary role was under the regimental
medical officer, seen here with the commanding officer. (RHQ Black Watch)

1st Battalion, The Queen's Own Cameron Highlanders, Pipes, Drums and Military Band, Flanders, 1918
Although by early 1915 the pipes were sounding again for the 1st Camerons, the pipe band was not re-formed until a year later. The military band rejoined the battalion in January 1917, as by that stage of the war, the pipe and military bands were not employed in the trenches, except in emergencies or to carry ammunition and rations to the rifle companies. (Queen's Own Highlanders Amalgamation Trustees)

CHAPTER XXIII
Music in War
~

As originally envisaged, this book was to have included accounts of the part played by music in the Scottish regiments during the wars of Imperial expansion in the nineteenth century and the two major wars of the twentieth. It quickly became clear that if justice was to be done to the contribution that military music – in all its forms – had made to the successful outcome of these operations, the book would have been twice as long. This course was impracticable for a variety of reasons, principally the sheer size of such a book. This chapter seeks to summarise the part played by music during the period between the outbreak of the Crimean War in 1854 and the beginning of the Great War; the Great War itself; the brief period between the wars; and World War II.

The middle and later decades of the reign of Queen Victoria saw many operations of varying intensity on the periphery of what became the British Empire. These minor and often short campaigns are usually lumped together under the heading 'small wars'. But however insignificant they might have seemed to the man on the Clapham omnibus, the politician in Westminster, or to later military historians, from the standpoint of the lonely British soldier on sentry in the stifling Indian or African night, armed with a rifle likely to jam and bayonet liable to bend at the moment of truth, there was nothing minor or insignificant about his personal situation. Glib references to the Maxim gun 'which we have got and they have not' obscure the facts.

The British were invariably outnumbered. The enemy was invariably brave, aggressive and determined, 'fighting for all the good God gives anyone to fight for': his home, his country and his way of life.[1] He was by nature a close-quarter fighter, trained and equipped with that object in view. Hardy, abstemious and able to cover vast distances at speed: such were the military characteristics of the Pathans of the north-west frontier of British India, the Zulus of the Natal border in South Africa and the 'Ansar', the followers of Al Mahdi al Muntasser – The

Expected One – in Sudan. All were merciless; prisoners taken alive were commonly tortured to death, so that wounded men had to be recovered whatever the cost.

The British were compelled to keep their forces concentrated. Small detached parties and isolated outposts became hostages to fortune. The campaigns were conducted at the end of long and vulnerable communications. Rations were monotonous and lacked nutrition; water was dirty and often fouled; medical care was primitive by modern standards. Clothing was unsuitable;[2] footwear wore out; rifles jammed; and bayonets, the last resort of the infantry soldier, buckled and bent. It was entirely possible for the Gatling to jam, the colonel to die; for the regiment to be blinded by dust and smoke; and fortunate is the soldier who has never felt that 'England's far, and Honour a name'.[3] But, for whatever reason, the ranks did rally and the soldiers stood and fought it out, rank by rank, where they stood. So the British civilian, secure in his music hall, might well sing:

> And when we say we've always won
> And when they ask us how it's done
> We'll proudly point to every one
> Of England's soldiers of the Queen!

It is in the field of pipe music that we find traces not only of the two major wars in which the British were involved in the decade of the 1850s, the Crimean War and the Indian Mutiny, but also reminders of those far-off and almost-forgotten campaigns.

The Crimean War itself gave us 'The Battle of Alma', by Pipe Major William Ross of the Black Watch, although he himself was not present at the battle. Unknown composers produced 'The Heights of the Alma', and 'Sir Colin Campbell's Farewell to the Highland Brigade'. The Indian Mutiny followed closely, producing one march, 'The Siege of Delhi'. An incident at the siege of Lucknow, when a Scots girl in the sorely beleaguered and outnumbered garrison heard in a dream the pipes of the relieving force, led to the composition of another, 'Jessie Brown of Lucknow', although there are grave doubts about the incident as there is conflicting evidence. In both cases the composer is unknown.[4]

Now for the 'small wars'. The little-known Ashanti War of 1873, in which the Black Watch took part, gave its name to 'The Black Watch March to Coomassie', composed by Pipe Major John MacDonald. Coomassie or Kumasi was the chief town of the Ashantis, and the pipe major was known thereafter as 'Coomassie John'. The Second Afghan War of 1878–1880 involved the 72nd Highlanders, the 92nd Gordon Highlanders and, to a lesser extent, the 78th Ross-shire Buffs – who, like the 25th King's Own Borderers, were condemned to fret on the line of communication. The opening battle at the Peiwar Kotal produced a 72nd tune, but the celebrated march from Kabul to Kandahar at the end of the campaign was to go unrecorded, perhaps because by that stage there were very few pipers surviving.

From the Egyptian campaigns of the 1880s and 1890s there emerged 'The Highland Brigade at Tel-el-Kebir' by Piper John Cameron of the 2nd Battalion Highland Light Infantry.

Operations in 1897 on the north-west frontier of India gave rise to the most celebrated incident in the history of regimental piping when Piper Findlater of the 1st Battalion Gordon Highlanders, wounded in the legs, played his comrades to the assault on the Heights of Dargai with the old Gordon tune 'The Cock of the North'. For this he was awarded the Victoria Cross, the country's highest award for gallantry in battle. Estimable as his action was, Findlater was to motivate a host of would-be imitators, many of whom were to die emulating his example in the hope of winning the coveted award, the first at the Battle of the Atbara in the Sudan the very next year.[5]

The South African War of 1899–1902 produced a Retreat march in 3/4 time by Piper John Maclellan of the 1st HLI called 'Magersfontein', the only instance of a tune commemorating a defeat. The Highland Brigade had been led by an inept commander into what turned out to be a butcher's shop, and had suffered severe casualties before withdrawing in disorder. John was awarded the Distinguished Conduct Medal for rallying his comrades by blasting out 'MacKenzie's Highlanders' during the first intensive burst of fire. In the previous engagement at Modder River, the 1st Argylls played a vital part in breaking the tactical stalemate in which the attacking British lay and suffered in the sun, every move attracting accurate fire from the invisible

Boers, hence 'The 91st at Modder River', yet another example of the affection in which the old precedence numbers were held twenty years after their official abolition. The boot was on the other foot at Paardeberg a few months later when the Boers who had so roughly handled the Highland Brigade were compelled to surrender at that place. Who composed the marches 'Modder River' and 'Paardeburg'? Nobody knows! 'Magersfontein' and 'The 91st at Modder River' are frequently heard today, the first when a pipe band beats Retreat, the second on the competition platform and at recitals – a fine tune it is, too!

The Great War was the last in which soldiers were to sing on the march. 'Tipperary', usually associated with the pre-war Army, had appeared in 1912, and was out of date when war broke out, according to a veteran of the 2nd Royal Welch Fusiliers.[6] It was taken up, however, by the New Armies and is now the song most associated with the Great War and the men who fought in it, along with 'Pack Up Your Troubles', the tune taken over and sung by the German Army as *'Weit ist der Weg zurück ins Heimatland'* – 'It's a Long Way Home'. With the outbreak of the war, the British public began to take a belated interest in its Army, and some were disappointed to learn that the songs the soldiers sang were not always worthy of the noble cause in which it was believed they fought, particularly when a clergyman witnessed a column of troops on the march singing lustily:

> Send out the boys of the old brigade
> To keep old England free.
> Send out my brother, my sister or my mother
> But for Christ's sake don't send me!

A movement then began to compose songs of a more elevated nature for the soldiers to sing, none of which excited anything except derision. The movement spread to Scotland.

John Maclellan's mother came from the island of Jura off the west coast of Argyll, and before his enlistment with the Highland Light Infantry he had composed a march which he called 'The Bens of Jura'. During the South African War he renamed his march 'The Highland Brigade's March to Heilbronn'; after the war, the 1st HLI moved to Egypt, where his march became 'The Burning Sands of Egypt'. On the outbreak of the Great War, a

Scots clergyman familiar with the melody of the march set to it, in augmented form, a poem, 'The Road to the Isles', which it was hoped would appeal to Scottish soldiers as a marching song. For this purpose its 'kailyard' sentimentality ruled the song out, but as 'The Road to the Isles' John Maclellan's march became popular on the concert stages and in the drawing-rooms of Scotland and indeed Britain, to the extent that today his march is played in slow time and is invariably called for as 'The Road to the Isles', except in the Argyll and Sutherland Highlanders where it firmly remains 'The Bens of Jura', while to the Highland Light Infantry and their successors the Royal Highland Fusiliers it is still, equally firmly, 'The Burning Sands of Egypt'.

The story of military music in the Great War deserves a book of its own, one which has yet to be written. Accounts tend to feature the exploits of individuals, particularly pipers, which led to the award of the higher decorations for gallantry. Yet music played an important part in the reconstitution of the shattered battalions of the Old Army after the opening battles of 1914, and in the formation and training of the vast New Armies summoned to the colours by the minister for war, Lord Kitchener. He had decided that these new soldiers were to be formed into 'Service' battalions of the existing county regiments rather than into *ad hoc* units striving to come to terms with modern war without benefit of ancestry.

As part of the process of learning how to be a soldier in the shortest possible time, it was soon discovered that men responded to a bugle call far more positively than they did to the shout of an NCO, however stentorian, the bugle representing the disembodied voice of authority, whereas the NCO was just another man, shouting. The distinctive regimental bugle or trumpet call, preceding as it did all the routine calls in camp or quarters, reinforced the feeling of community and continuity fostered by the badges of the glorious old regiments which each New Army battalion wore, in whose history they came to feel they shared and to whose list of battle honours they were to contribute.

The infantry was by far the strongest element in these new armies, and the infantry covered ground on foot. The well-tried system of march discipline evolved in the decade before 1914 required a steady pace and a compact column. In this essential training, music had an important part to play. So, whenever possible, every unit, regular, territorial, or new Army, provided itself with a source of martial music as an aid not only in the training for war which marching epitomised but also in the creation and enhancement of morale by 'exciting cheerfulness and alacrity in the soldier', not least by making the march past of the regiment familiar to every wartime soldier. Not for nothing did C.S. Forester in his novel *The General*, make his hero 'labour long and hard to see that every battalion had its band'.

The New Armies were 'blooded' at the Battle of the Somme, fought from July to November 1916, in which the heavy casualties suffered by the British were offset by the equally severe losses on the German side.[7] A grim resolution replaced the uncaring optimism of the first two years. The 'out since Mons' look was no longer fashionable.[8] Discipline was tightened, attention was given to the appearance of the rear-area troops, saluting was insisted on out of the line and marches had to be carried out in the regulation manner. Some regular battalions sent home for their military bands to complement their pipes and drums. The 1st Black Watch had kept theirs going throughout; the 1st Camerons, serving in the same brigade, sent home for theirs in January 1917. The band arrived minus the bandmaster, kept with the reserve battalion to train learners and band boys against the day when peace would reign and the band would reform.

The early stages of the Great War were to see the full effects of the Findlater/Dargai syndrome when battalions assaulting the German trenches were eagerly played into action by their pipers. Piper Laidlaw of the 7th King's Own Scottish Borderers won the Victoria Cross at the battle of Loos in 1915 for rallying his badly shaken comrades with the regimental march 'All the Blue Bonnets' and leading them over the top playing the regimental charge 'The Standard on the Braes of Mar'. The casualties among pipers were inevitably severe, as the regular battalions had already found out in the early days of the war, and so it became customary to leave the pipers and drummers out of the trenches and to deploy them to play the battalion up to and down from the line. Mention must be made, however, of Drummer Walter Ritchie, 2nd Battalion Seaforth Highlanders. On the first morning of the Battle of the

Somme in July 1916, he stood on the parapet of the trench under heavy enemy fire continually sounding the regimental call and the 'Charge'. Ritchie was awarded the Victoria Cross, one of the few drummers to have been decorated for gallantry in the drummer's primary role, although many others, pipers, drummers and bandsmen, were to earn awards while acting as message-carriers and stretcher-bearers.

The Germans asked for an armistice in 1918, and the process of rebuilding the regular Army began forthwith. In the years immediately following the Peace of Versailles in 1919, the Army had to meet many commitments, but by the mid-1920s a fairly settled life began. Funds were limited, with consequent restrictions on training and equipment. Music came into its own once again, and the giant military bands, corps of drums and pipes and drums began to reappear. There arose the military displays involving large numbers of troops, the Aldershot and Tidworth Tattoos and the older-established Royal Tournament – originally an assault-at-arms or competitive display of military skills – becoming popular summer attractions drawing large crowds and taking up much military effort that would have been more profitably spent on combined training had funds been allotted for the purpose.

The outbreak of World War II saw the military bandsmen revert to their primary role as stretcher-bearers and medical orderlies, while pipers – in excess of the pipe major and five – and all the drummers went back to fight in the ranks. The defeat of Dunkirk saw most of the pre-war bandsmen, pipers and drummers taken prisoner of war, so that when the Prime Minister, Winston Churchill, ordered 'let the bands play!' there were few bands to obey, and in some regiments the military band had become almost non-existent. But the 'good' band regiments that had set about reconstituting their military bands by identifying and employing the appreciable numbers of competent musicians who had been called up for the statutory three years or the duration, all at once found themselves in constant demand to play at the street marches and public concerts. These were held to boost support for this or that aspect of the complex business of winning the war, designed to foster civilian morale and to stress that everyone was in this together and that everyone had a valued part to play, as, indeed, most had.

Under wartime conditions there were units which had little opportunity, or even desire, to organise their own domestic sources of military music either for parade or for recreation, and life in such units could be dull indeed, without even a bugle call to mark the passage of the day. But every Scottish battalion contrived to form, complete and maintain a pipe band, often with great difficulty. Instruments were hard to come by, but old and long-silent bagpipes were dragged from under the beds of veteran pipers and aged relatives and put in playing order. The same applied to the drums; the 2nd Battalion Royal Scots Fusiliers borrowed the drums of the Enniskillen Pipe Band, carried and beat them round half the world and restored them to their rightful owners after the war.[9]

By 1939, marching in the old sense of the term had become a thing of the past, although the soldiers still covered long distances on foot. The chances of hostile air attack, even at home, were real and ever present, long columns of troops and vehicles being particularly vulnerable. Also, the roads had to be left clear for the vastly increased numbers of vehicles, the British Army being unique in having no animal transport at all, except in the Far East where roads were few and mules still had an essential role to play.

As a result, the infantry were compelled to move in single file, leaving the crown of the road free for lorries and staff cars, the latter often passing at speed and covering the 'poor foot' in mud or dust depending on the theatre and season. Every soldier was thus left alone to grapple with his own thoughts, and marching was no longer a group activity where each might draw support from the sense of comradeship stimulated by the old, close-order marching formations. Inevitably, singing on the march died out. There was little point in the company piper playing on the march when only those nearest could march to his tune. However, the Highland pipe is an outdoor instrument. The sound of the pipes carries far, and told everyone within earshot that the Scots were on their way and in good heart. And thus was fostered that sense of being in some way special, which every Scottish soldier shared, and which communicated itself to every Englishman, and there were thousands, drafted into the Scottish regiments in the course of the war. Almost to a man, they acquired many of the characteristics of their Scottish comrades for better or, in some cases, worse.

Although three Scottish Divisions, comprising some twenty-seven infantry battalions plus supporting troops, were deployed in the later stages of the war, there were also many Scottish battalions that served beside battalions of the old English county regiments. It could come as a surprise to a young Scotsman raised in the 'wha's like us' tradition to find that a battalion of the hitherto despised 'swede bashers' could be as proud of its heritage as any 'Jock' battalion and could, indeed, regard Scottish soldiers and battalions with a nice blend of amusement and condescension in roughly equal measure. Equally, the Scottish 'hard men' were chastened to discover that the products of the industrial cities of Yorkshire and Lancashire, though less quick to take or simulate offence, were as formidable in a brawl as those of Govan and the Gorbals, and that, when roused, even the stolid English west countryman could give as good as he got, and often better.

Many such battalions had maintained and were as proud of their corps of drums as any Scotsman was of his pipe band, and many a Scot came to enjoy their gentle music, inspiring in its own way and with a wider range than the Highland pipe, forever screaming defiance or wailing in grief. The music of flute and drum heard far from home as the tropic sun went down at Retreat could be touchingly evocative of the milder English countryside, in telling contrast to that of the pipes, which recalled a bloodier history and a harsher land.

Since the early stages of the Great War ,the pipe bands had been kept out of the line, but in World War II, the forward battalions of the 51st Highland Division had been played into battle by their company pipers at the Battle of El Alamein in October 1942 as a matter of deliberate policy. The reconstituted 51st was in action for the first time since the original Division had surrendered at St Valery in France in 1940. If the battle were to be won, the spectre of 1940 had to be exorcised, and all the Divisional resources were deployed to that end. There were casualties; Piper Duncan MacIntyre of the 5th Black Watch was found dead next morning, drones on his shoulder and bag under his oxter, just as he had fallen. The practice did not became general, all the same, although pipers played where possible on the march. Possibly the last piper to play his company into actual battle in the traditional manner was Piper John Laidlaw of the 1st Battalion Cameron Highlanders at the Battle of the Ava in Upper Burma in April 1945. The word had gone out that the battalion was soon to be relieved and the officers and soldiers of the company were determined that on this last occasion they would stand up and go forward in the old style.

The music of pipe and drum played an important part in the process of pulling a Scots battalion together after a difficult battle, a period when it is vital not to leave the soldiers with time to brood over their lot, a hard one for an infantry soldier in any warlike situation. The sound of the pipes was associated in everyone's mind with stability and normality, three meals a day, and nights in bed. This held good for the bugle, too, the voice of disembodied authority. A bugle call could transform a crowd of exhausted and apprehensive men, susceptible to every rumour, into a functioning unit. And when the bugle was followed by the familiar Duty Tunes, and when the pipes and drums, however small, were beating Retreat and Long Reveille as they had done in happier times, then the process of recovery was accelerated, and was completed sooner than if everyone had been left to mull resentfully over the law of averages and their prospects in the next battle. It was a sensible commanding officer who reinstituted the peacetime routine as soon as possible – sympathetically applied with due regard to circumstances.

This was important, too, when reinforcements – the US Army term 'replacements' is perhaps more accurate here – had to be absorbed. These tended to arrive after dark, and were tired, bewildered and dreading the future. The later stages of their journey always seemed to lead past a hospital with its queue of ambulances or a cemetery with its rows of freshly dug graves. After these and other similarly depressing experiences, to join a battalion working efficiently to a well-established routine meant that the apprehensive new arrivals felt that at least they would have a chance. Scottish regiments were good at this, accustomed as they were to make the most of their own unique features: their background and their history.

So, in the places where the fighting was fiercest and the casualties highest – north-west Europe in 1944–1945 – the pipe bands were left with the rear echelons to carry out their principal task: the maintenance and enhancement of the morale of the soldiers, especially those recently arrived as reinforcements, fearful of the unknown future, some with death already in their eyes.[10]

It was this music that was to catch the popular imagination in the later years of World War II, as the massed pipes and drums of the 51st Highland Division paraded in Tripoli and Tunis during the successful North African campaign of 1942–1943. After the war, performances by the pipes and drums of all three Scottish Divisions, the 15th, 51st and 52nd, were to set their seal on the many victory celebrations.

Many pipe tunes were composed during both the Great War and World War II, the majority of which were to prove ephemeral. From the Great War a Retreat march, 'The Battle of the Somme' in 9/8 time – i.e. with the regulation three beats in the bar – features in the repertoire of most pipe bands, military and civilian, while some individual pipers include 'The Taking of Beaumont Hamel', one of the 51st Highland Division's great victories in the closing stages of the same battle, in their recitals. 'The Battle of the Somme' is usually attributed to Pipe Major William Lawrie of the 8th Argylls. His successor as pipe major, John Maclellan of Magersfontein fame, composed 'Beaumont Hamel'.

From World War II, 'The Heights of Cassino', a reminder of one of the bloodiest and bitterest battles of the Italian campaign, has taken the pipers' fancy. It was composed by Pipe Major Donald MacRae of the 2nd Cameron Highlanders, one of the battalions which suffered there. 'The Heroes of St Valery', where the original Highland Division was compelled to surrender in 1940, is also played occasionally. It came from the pen of Pipe Major Donald MacLean of the 2nd Seaforth Highlanders, captured at St Valery.

Less frequently heard are 'El Alamein', composed by Pipe Major William Denholm of the Royal Scots, and 'Wadi Akarit', by Piper William MacDonald, 5th Seaforth Highlanders, both harking back to battles fought during the final North African campaign. Although tunes were composed to commemorate feats of arms in the Far East, none have stood the test of time, except 'The Heroes of Kohima' by Piper John Stewart of, curiously enough, the Royal Artillery, 'that great, bitter, battle', as the Japanese called it, played at Retreat by the 1st Battalion Royal

Scots, one of two Scottish units to have taken part. The other was the 1st Battalion Cameron Highlanders whose Pipe Major Evan MacRae celebrated the victorious advance of the 14th Army in 1945 with the march 'Over the Chindwin'. Only one march, composed by Pipe Major Donald Ramsay and named for the part played by the 10th Battalion Highland Light Infantry in the climactic crossing of the River Rhine by the Allies in 1945, emerged from the north-west European campaign. As the Scots Guards alone of the Scottish regiments maintain the corps of drums tradition, the several marches composed in that idiom and named for battles in the Great War do not fall into this purview.

After World War II, national commitments world wide required that conscription, introduced just before the outbreak of the war, be continued. This was a new experience for the Army in peacetime and was to have its effect on the music of the regiments, particularly on the pipes and drums.

Notes

1. 'We were at their hearths and homes . . . and they were fighting for all the good God gives anyone to fight for.' Major Frederick W. Benteen, 7th US Cavalry. He was describing the fighting spirit shown by the Cheyenne and Sioux warriors during the Battle of the Little Bighorn, 25 June 1876, 'Custer's Last Stand', quoted in *Son of the Morning Star* by Evan S. Connell (Picador, 1984).
2. The soldiers wore their greyback flannel shirts and serge coats and trousers for weeks if not months at a time, and, as an American historian of the Zulu War comments, 'in those days before deodorants' they smelled somewhat in consequence. It is a fact, however, that in such circumstances nobody notices. *Like Lions They Fought*, Robert J. Egerton (Weidenfeld and Nicolson, 1988).
3. The words went:

> The sand of the desert is sodden red –
> Red with the wreck of a square that broke:–
> The Gatling's jammed and the Colonel dead
> And the regiment blind with dust and smoke,
> The river of death has brimmed its banks,
> And England's far, and Honour a name
> But the voice of a schoolboy rallies the ranks
> Play up! Play up! and play the game!

Sir Henry Newbolt, 'Vitäi Lampada' 1897
The Gatling gun was the first serviceable machine-gun. It was made

possible by the invention of metal cartridge cases, and was deployed in the Zulu War of 1879 and the Egyptian campaigns of the 1880s. The single shot Martini-Henry rifle introduced in 1871 used the same cartridge as the Gatling. Damp could penetrate the cartridge cases, causing misfires, and the base of the cartridge case could break away from its body, leaving it literally jammed in the chamber.

4. The tale, apocryphal though it proved to be, caught the imagination of the Victorian public, and Jessie's dream provided the inspiration for a large and graphic painting in which Jessie, hair streaming in the breeze, proclaims that relief is at hand. There followed an epic poem, a stage play and a song 'Jessie's Dream', still sung during the riding of the Marches in the Scottish Border town of Selkirk, as well as the pipe march.

5. Piper James Stewart, 1st Cameron Highlanders.

6. *The War the Infantry Knew*, J.C. Dunn (ed) (Cardinal, 1989).

7. *The Smoke and the Fire*, John Terraine (Leo Cooper, 1992).

8. *Into Battle; a Soldier's Diary of the Great War*, Sir John Glubb (Cassell, 1977). Sir John describes how by 1917 'the war had become a way of life'.

9. The 2nd RSF carried and beat the Enniskillen drums in South Africa, Madagascar, India, Persia, Egypt, Syria, Sicily, Italy, Palestine, France, Belgium and Germany.

10. When replacements joined an infantry platoon, some experienced soldiers claimed to be able to sense which of them would soon be killed. They were right disconcertingly often.

2nd Battalion, Seaforth Highlanders
LEFT: Drummers, 1913. The drummers are stepping out on their way back to barracks for dinner after practising in an adjacent area. Their drums are slung over the shoulder by the 'back carriage', then the usual way of carrying them on the march when not playing. Sixth from the left, broadly smiling, is Drummer Walter Ritchie. (Queen's Own Highlanders Amalgamation Trustees)

BELOW: Pipes and Drums, France, June, 1916. Drummer 'Wattie' Ritchie stands third from right in the middle row. Over his shoulder is slung his bugle. Two days later, on the first day of the Battle of the Somme, he stood on the parapet of the trench under intense enemy fire and repeatedly sounded the 'Regimental Call' and the 'Charge'. Ritchie was awarded the Victoria Cross, survived the war and became drum major. (Queen's Own Highlanders Amalgamation Trustees)

1st Battalion, The Queen's Own Cameron Highlanders, Military Band, Aldershot, 1939
In war, bandsmen reverted to their role as stretcher-bearers, and the bands stationed in the Aldershot
Command competed annually for the Connaught Ambulance Shield. In 1939 it was won by the 1st
Camerons. Band Serjeant Robert Mackenzie, team captain, is seated behind the shield; on the right
sits Bandmaster Douglas A. Pope; and on the left, wearing the strapped trews, is Regimental Serjeant
Major A. Cooper. Douglas Pope went on to become a lieutenant-colonel and also the director of music,
Coldstream Guards. (Queen's Own Highlanders Amalgamation Trustees)

The 51st Highland Division,
Victory Parade, Tripoli, 4 February 1943
The massed pipes and drums of the Highland
Division play for the march past of the Black
Watch contingent as they approach the
Saluting Base where Winston Churchill, Prime
Minister, will take the salute. It will be noted
that half the pipers are not playing. Such was
the length of the marching column that each
half of the massed pipes and drums had to play
in turn so that the music might be continuous.
(RHQ Black Watch)

301

CHAPTER XXIV
The National Service Years

~

When World War II ended in 1945, the residual commitments that Britain had to sustain precluded any possibility of an early end to the system of compulsory military service, which had been introduced a few months before the outbreak of war in 1939. The situation was eased by the decision of the post-war Labour Government to grant what amounted to independence to India, with the consequent partition of the sub-continent between India and the much smaller state of Pakistan. The removal of this commitment meant that the requirement for infantry battalions was reduced, and this led to the disappearance of all 2nd battalions, except in the foot guards, thus halving the prospects of promotion within the regiment at a stroke and leading to much pain and grief, as the cadres of the two battalions – the regular officers and soldiers – which under the British system hardly knew each other and had certainly never served together, were forced to settle their long-cherished differences and to learn to co-exist amicably, a process which took some years.

Military bands were divided into two categories, staff and regimental. The bands of the larger corps of the Army such as the Royal Artillery, Royal Engineers and the Royal Corps of Signals, as well as those of the household cavalry and the foot guards were major staff bands and were led by a director of music.[1] Those of the smaller corps, such as the Royal Army Medical Corps and the Royal Army Ordnance Corps were minor staff bands, but were also led by a director of music. A major staff band paraded some sixty-six-strong, except for those of the household cavalry, which were smaller. Minor staff bands consisted of thirty-plus musicians. Regimental bands were those of cavalry regiments and infantry battalions. Until the late 1980s, these were of the same strength as the minor staff bands but were led by a bandmaster. Directors of music were officers; bandmasters were warrant officers 1st class. Instrumentalists in staff bands were musicians; in the cavalry and infantry they were

*ABOVE: 1st Battalion, The Royal Scots (The Royal Regiment), Pipes and Drums, Edinburgh, 1948
The Pipes and Drums are leading the old guard from the esplanade of Edinburgh Castle. The drum major
is flourishing his staff, as was expected and encouraged in those days, but it is now an accomplishment seen
no more. (RHQ The Royal Scots)*

*BELOW: 1st Battalion, The Queen's Own Cameron Highlanders, Cameron Barracks, Inverness, 1954
The inspection of dress and 'turnout' preceded every full dress parade or outside engagement. As pipe
banners are being carried, the occasion must have been important. Note the golden eagle feather in the
Glengarry caps. Eighth from the left stands Corporal J.D. Burgess, later pipe major and MBE, a leading
piper of his generation. (Pipe Major Andrew Venters)*

bandsmen. Under the 1994 reorganisation, all bands will be led by directors of music and the divisional bands of infantry will be at minor staff band strength.

The national service net was widely cast and it yielded many aspiring young musicians, most of whom were delighted to spend their two years perfecting their knowledge and widening their experience. The major staff bands were able to attract a number of promising young musicians of high quality by reason of their contacts with the professional musical world, as could the bands of the household cavalry and the foot guards, where string players 'doubling on brass' were always welcome, as one of their duties was the provision of string orchestras to play during State functions. Much the same went for the bands of the Royal Artillery, whose musicians were required to play a string as well as a wind instrument, and whose orchestra was more in demand for outside engagements than its military band, splendid though the latter was. The bands of the line battalions, restored to their parent units at the end of the war, could not offer the same inducements and, as a result, went through a lean period, having to rely on soldiers on regular Army engagements; but there still came forward a steady trickle of youngsters with musical inclinations, recruited by word of mouth and willing to enlist in order to take advantage of the opportunities for acquiring a sound musical education, which service in a line band offered. As time went on and the well-tried system of sending bandsmen to the Royal Military School of Music for a year to learn to master their instruments had its effect, matters gradually improved, although much, as ever, was to depend on the interest taken in the band within the battalion or regiment, particularly by the commanding officer.

During the war, the British people had been starved of colour and pageantry and, also, to a lesser extent, of music. Although there was a reaction, inevitable after a long and hard-fought war, it was against the cult of militarism and not in itself anti-military. However, the enthusiasm shown for the revival of the pre-war military displays and tattoos was surprising, and it was during this period that the Edinburgh Military Tattoo was conceived – its first modest performance took place in 1948 – as part of the Edinburgh International Festival. South of the Border, similar events proved popular, and the Royal

Tournament was soon revived, while a large-scale tattoo at the White City in London replaced the old Aldershot event. During the national service period, there were always plenty of men available to take part in those displays. It was not uncommon for a draft of national servicemen to be retained at their regimental depot after completing their training in order to provide the cast for some historical re-enactment or, in the Scottish regiments, to take part in a Highland or country dancing display. This worried the national service soldiers not at all; they had to be in the Army for two years, and to dance at the Edinburgh Tattoo was welcomed as a 'good skive'.

No tattoo was complete without a display by the massed pipes and drums, in the same way that no finale was complete without its massed military bands. Fine; but while every bandsman had been taught to read music and could attempt a score at sight, this was an accomplishment scorned by the average piper or drummer. For generations pipe tunes had been passed from one Army piper to another either by ear, or 'off the fingers', while the drummers had memorised their beatings round the table on which they practised. In this primitive method of transmission even the simplest tunes and beatings tended to become garbled, and in this corrupt form passed over the years into the regimental folklore as the correct way to play the tune or beating. The result was that no two Army pipe bands played 'Highland Laddie' in the same way, and neither was prepared to change.

A step in the right direction had been made in 1934, when the Army Piping Committee published *The Army Manual of Bagpipe Tunes and Drum Beatings*, with the avowed intention of standardising a selection of the better known and more popular pipe tunes, so that when pipe bands were detailed to take part in a tattoo, the tunes and beatings could be selected in advance from the manual, and all the pipers would turn up playing the same version of the tunes and all the drummers would have learned all the beatings. This did not mean, however, that all the pipers hastened to learn to read a pipe score. The tunes were still taught by ear by the pipe major, who had learned to read music at the Army Piping Class, while the others picked it up off his fingers.[2] One unexpected result was that the settings in the manual tended to supersede the traditional regimental settings, so that, for instance, the older styles of 'Highland Laddie' drifted into oblivion. Much the same happened to the drum beatings, although the situation was easier in that the same beatings could be played to different tunes with the same time signature, particularly in strathspeys and reels. The 3/4 beatings began with the old regulation Retreat beating, but by 1934 its provenance had long been forgotten. The increasing sophistication of civilian pipe bands and the excellence of the standards they were reaching was to make the Army Manual beatings not only redundant in the post-1945 years, but positively ludicrous.

In the decade after the end of World War II, all Army pipes and drums, corps of drum and military bands in the marching role were still equipped with rope-tension drums. The rope-tension drum had a fine resonant sound. It looked good. Its shell could be polished or emblazoned and the ropes themselves kept white. The tension of the drumheads was, however, relatively poor, but their great disadvantage was that in wet or even damp weather the batter head was liable to split, putting the drum out of action, so that in most cases a shower of rain put paid to the pipes and drums and corps of drums as a functioning musical unit.

In 1930, a rod-tension drum had been produced by a leading firm of instrument manufacturers, designed with the needs of the civilian pipe band specifically in mind. In competition in the following year, the one pipe band which had equipped itself with these new-type drums swept the board, and it became essential for any pipe band competing seriously to follow suit if it wished to remain in the hunt for trophies. The pipers of these leading bands were highly competent musicians, to whom the tunes played by the military bands were so simple as to be boring and, as a result, what pipers call 'the heavy stuff' tended to be heard more and more at the top level. The standard drum beatings were designed to be used with any tune in the same time signature, but did not suit the more intricate and demanding tunes which were being played in competition, as indeed the pipe band of the 2nd Highland Light Infantry had done as early as 1916.[3]

As civilian pipe bands were not marching bands in the military sense, their drummers had the freedom to experiment and to break new ground, and in this they were influenced by the jazz and dance bands which were widely heard and imitated as radio, 'the wireless', became more generally available. Whereas the Army drummer was required to master rolls, accented rolls, the paradiddle, the flam, the drag and the triplet, by the end of the 1930s, civilian pipe band drummers were using 'a wide variety of rudiments, linked together, played in unusual sequence, accented in the "wrong" places, and had already produced a style which was exclusive and specialised.'[4]

In 1936 there appeared *Standard Settings of Pipe Music of the Seaforth Highlanders*, which included the Duty Tunes played by the regiment and a wide selection of tunes of great variety and of no great technical difficulty. Priced at 3/6d. (17½p) it was not cheap in the context of the times, and its impact was probably greater in the civilian piping world – it had lots of tunes in it – than in the Army, where each regiment and, indeed, each battalion, had its own well-established set of tunes and its own way of playing them, and although a copy of the 'Seaforth book' might be held in the pipe store, scant attention was paid to it. However, this was an imaginative step, which was followed by the Scots Guards *Standard Settings*, the first volume of which appeared in 1954. The Scots Guards were fortunate in that the copyright of the six books of pipe music published by Pipe Major William Ross, MVO MBE, the doyen of Army pipers between the wars, was made over to the regiment by his daughter. The Scots Guards *Volume 1* thus contained most of the classic tunes in the 'small music' repertoire. The trend was reinforced when the Queen's Own Highlanders published their *Standard Settings* soon after the formation of the regiment after the amalgamation of the Seaforth and Cameron Highlanders in 1961. *Standard Settings* of the Royal Scots and Gordon Highlanders soon followed.

In the same way as young conventional musicians were attracted to the well-established staff bands, so were young pipers and drummers of correspondingly high quality attracted to the 'good' pipe band regiments, which, for their part, went out of their way to arrange for the better prospects to spend their two years' national service where they would be accepted and appreciated. Consequently, piping in the regiments was to reach a standard which was sadly impossible to maintain once national service had ended. But the most lasting effect of this period was on the drummers of the pipe bands, where the young national service entry, trained to the heights of virtuosity taken for granted in civilian pipe bands, simply laughed out loud when confronted with the drum scores published in the 1934 Army Manual. These were not only outdated by civilian standards, but were also redundant, as in the post-war Army the days of the marching bands were over, never to return. Circumstances had changed; at home, the increase in motor traffic had made marching on the public road positively dangerous; while overseas, although there was plenty of marching, it was carried out through the jungles of Malaya or over the mountains of Korea rather than along the long, straight roads of India.

The impact of those young, highly skilled and dedicated pipe band drummers led to an immeasurable rise in drumming expertise. It would be wrong to suppose that this was welcomed. To senior regimental officers this syncopated drumming was 'jazz', with all the decadence the term implied for them, while to drum majors, brought up in the days of the old Army Manual beatings, it was too clever by half. But it appealed to the drummers, and in time the modern approach was to supersede the traditional military style. The process took some time, however. The Army was still equipped with rope-tension drums, splendidly painted and emblazoned in the traditional style, which displayed the Royal Arms on a background of crossed Colours under a label bearing the name of the regiment with the battle honours set out on both sides. It was becoming the fashion on privately purchased drums, however, to replace the Royal Arms with the crest or device of the regiment. Impressive as they looked on parade, such drums now belonged to the Dark Ages as far as the young national service drummers were concerned.

The rod-tension drum had been under continuous research and development in order to meet, or even keep pace with, the demands of the leading drum artistes, for that is what they were. Eventually a drum was to appear which had a 'brilliant snapping tone', but which had the volume necessary for pipe band work in the open. This further increased the dissatisfaction verging on scorn with which Army pipe band drummers regarded their rope tension drums. The situation was to be solved, paradoxically, by a piper. The chief – and only – instructor at the Army School of Piping in Edinburgh Castle was Pipe Major J.A. MacLellan of the Queen's Own

Highlanders, who submitted a paper pointing out that the development of a modern side-drum technique in the Army was handicapped by the substandard drum issued from Ordnance, and that as the need for bands to provide music for long columns of marching troops had disappeared, there was no longer any justification for the provision of drums designed primarily for that purpose. Increasingly, too, regiments were buying rod-tension drums from commercial sources at great expense and were leaving the Ordnance-issue drums in store, the money the Government had paid for them being therefore wasted. So skilfully did the Pipe Major deploy his arguments and exploit his connections that his paper was accepted, and for the last thirty years rod-tensioned drums of playable quality have been provided from official sources. The standard of Army drumming, in the pipe bands at any rate, has correspondingly risen.

It has been noted previously how the drum and fife combination was derived from the units of Swiss mercenaries that fought on the Continent in the fifteenth and sixteenth centuries. The tradition still flourishes in Switzerland itself, particularly in the town of Basle, and the distinctive Basler style of playing the drum has also had its effect on Scottish drumming, which had its critics in that it was felt that it was becoming over-elaborate, a tendency which now seems to have been curbed. As far as pipe band drumming in the Scottish regiments is concerned, the drawback has been that now everything is subordinated to sheer technique, and the impeccably drilled and immaculately dressed drummers of the past are now no more than a memory.

The day of the super-confident and flamboyant drum major is also over, and most are content merely to march in front of their bands, giving the minimum of signals. The staff was no longer either flourished or thrown, until the myth became current that there was a 'tradition' against such adventures, which precluded the staff leaving the drum major's hand, or the crown on the head of the staff being inverted. This was, of course, utter nonsense, but it would be over-reacting to become too upset over the demise of flourishing the staff. The practice is regarded by the foot guards as 'unsoldierly'; and so the guards system of staff drill has become universally accepted as correct, perhaps, it might be said, with considerable relief.

The last national servicemen were called to the Colours in 1960, and by 1962 all had returned to civilian life. By no means all had regarded their two years in uniform as a waste of time, and one of the results of the conscription period was that throughout Scotland there had been created a network of former national servicemen who had good memories of their experience, especially those who had served overseas. This was especially the case with pipers and drummers, and even to this day competing pipers of the national service generation will often wear the cap badge and tie of their old regiments. However, the strength of the pipe bands was rapidly reduced by the departure of the national servicemen, which in the case of the newly amalgamated regiments was exacerbated by the fact that two regiments' worth of soldiers left, while only one regiment's worth came in.[5] The military bands, with their larger regular component, were not so badly affected.

The disappearance of the national servicemen exposed the meagre base on which the Army pipe band rested, and it was clear that action had to be taken to rectify the situation, despite the inevitable resistance aroused by any suggestion which involved increased expense. At that stage, the accountants were not wholly in control of the armed services – their day would come, all the same – and once a well-reasoned case had been submitted with appropriate support, the cause of Army piping took a leap forward with the appointment of a director of Army bagpipe music with commissioned rank to the Army School of Piping at Edinburgh Castle with a remit that covered all the aspects of military pipe music.[6] At the same time, a system of instruction was instituted that created a series of progressive courses designed to foster talent while encouraging the more moderate performer to work at improving his own standard of playing. This system has so far survived the current round of cost cutting, and has ensured that the standard of piping in the regiments is probably higher than it has ever been since national service ended. It is now possible for a piper to reach commissioned rank in the same way as a bandsman, the appointment of Director of Music having carried commissioned rank since 1927.

From 1962 onwards, with reduced manpower available, a far closer control began to be exerted over how soldiers were employed. With increasingly severe financial stringency there began an intense scrutiny of what each soldier was doing, to an extent which officers of the older school, when what the commanding officer did with his battalion was regarded as his business, found difficult to accept. Those days were long past, however, and a band, pipes and drums of eighty on parade was no longer a feather in a commanding officer's cap. Instead, questions were asked about the 'misuse' of soldiers, and it was of no avail to point to the number of marksman's badges on the pipers' sleeves.

The heyday of the musical and ceremonial side of the Army was drawing to its close.

Notes

1. The household cavalry at this time comprised The Life Guards and the Royal Horse Guards (The Blues) and the foot guards, the 1st or Grenadier Regiment of Foot Guards; the Coldstream Guards; the Scots Guards; the Irish Guards; and the Welsh Guards. In 1969 the Royal Horse Guards were amalgamated with the Royal Dragoons (1st Dragoons) to form The Blues and Royals (Royal Horse Guards and 1st Dragoons). In 1993, The Life Guards and the Blues and Royals amalgamated to form the Household Cavalry Regiment.
2. The Army Piping Class was organised by The Piobaireachd Society, a group of influential Highland professional men and landowners devoted to the research and publication of *piobaireachd* music. Students were detached from their regiments for an intensive course of study lasting eight months under a tutor selected and paid for by the Society, those completing the course successfully being placed on the potential Pipe Majors Roll. This system continued until 1958 when the Army took over responsibility for the instruction and the Army School of Piping was instituted. Since 1919, the course had been held in Edinburgh Castle, where the Army School of Piping was situated until 1999. Now known as the Army School of Bagpipe Music and Highland Drumming, it occupies modernised and commodious accommodation in the Redford Barracks complex in Edinburgh. The Director of Army Bagpipe Music has assumed responsibility for all pipes and drums training in the Army, and the school is now, after nearly a century, adequately staffed in both the musical and the administrative fields.
3. In an open pipe band competition held in France in 1916, the 2nd Battalion HLI played the march 'Leaving Glenurquart', the strathspey 'Maggie Cameron' and the reel 'Duntroon', a programme which would not have disgraced a first-grade pipe band seventy years later.
4. *The Rise of the Scottish Style of Side Drumming*, W.G.F. Boag (unpublished).
5. In 1958, the Royal Scots Fusiliers and the Highland Light Infantry were

ordered to amalgamate to form the Royal Highland Fusiliers. In 1961, the Seaforth Highlanders and the Queen's Own Cameron Highlanders amalgamated to form the Queen's Own Highlanders (Seaforth and Camerons). In 1971, the Royal Scots Greys (2nd Dragoons) amalgamated with the 3rd Carabiniers (Prince of Wales's Dragoon Guards) to form the Royal Scots Dragoon Guards (Carabiniers and Greys). The 3rd Carabiniers had been formed in 1922 by an amalgamation of the 3rd Dragoon Guards (Prince of Wales's) and The Carabiniers (6th Dragoon Guards). In 1994, the Queen's Own Highlanders and the Gordon Highlanders amalgamated to form The Highlanders (Seaforth, Gordons and Camerons).

6. The first incumbent of the post was, appropriately, Captain John A. Maclellan MBE.

CHAPTER XXV
The End of the Story?
~

In prosperous times it has always been difficult to recruit the army up to its authorised strength in peace. Recent years have been no exception. It may also be the case that soldiering and all that it entails no longer appeals to the young men of 21st century Britain, as has been suggested. But since World War 2 soldiering has ceased to be a solely male preserve and women soldiers are now established as equals throughout the army, particularly in the Military Band context. The Pipes and Drums of infantry battalions is a different matter. Their operational role is as the machine gun platoon, and they are extremely good at it. Women are at present excluded from front line service with the Infantry and the Royal Armoured Corps, though there can be little doubt that the definition of what constitutes the front line will soon be amended. In the peace-keeping operations in which the army has been involved in the seven years since this book was first published women have played an active and indeed indispensable part. However, veterans with vivid memories of the squalor of life in the front line as well as its dangers may wonder how women will fare in a situation from which few men emerge unscathed, physically or mentally.

That aside, during the same seven years the army has continued to contract and the process seems likely to continue. The Highlanders now represents three of the famous old regiments which have featured so prominently in these pages. The Royal Scots and the King's Own Scottish Borderers narrowly escaped a similar fate some years ago. Indications are that the process may well continue and it has been suggested that further infantry amalgamations are inevitable in view of the apparent inability of the army to attract recruits.

Difficulties in infantry and Royal Armoured Corps recruiting now mean that playing pipers rarely enlist. The Army School of Bagpipe Music and Highland Drumming now trains pipers and drummers from scratch. By means of a well thought out and progressive series of courses the School continues to turn out competent performers well able to take their place in the Pipes and Drums of their battalions. An encouraging feature, much against the trend, has been the appearance of pipe bands in the Royal Armoured Corps and Royal Artillery. The 4th Royal Tank regiment was recruited from Scotland and maintained a pipe band. When the 4th was disbanded, the pipe band was posted intact to the 1st Royal Tank Regiment where it continues to flourish. The Queen's Royal Irish Hussars' pipe band was likewise absorbed into the Queen's Royal Hussars. The 40th Field Regiment Royal Artillery, to which Scottish recruits are now posted, also maintains a pipe band, trained at the Army School. In all those units the pipe band is highly thought of and much respected, indicating perhaps that the desire on the part of the soldiers to have their own 'in house' music has been underestimated. At the Edinburgh Military Tattoo the massed Pipes and Drums continue to be a major attraction, followed closely by the massed Military Bands.

When the establishment of the infantry battalion was reorganised some thirty years ago, no provision was made for the pipe major and five pipers who had been borne extra to the establishment of Highland battalions since 1854 and Lowland and Irish since 1918. For whatever reason, this was a major oversight, and one that could easily have sounded the death knell of regimental piping given the intensity of operational and other commitments faced by the regiments. That it has not proved to be so has been due to the regiments themselves, who against all the odds have refused to allow their Pipes and Drums to wither on the vine, and who by a nice combination of determination, skill, and cunning have contrived to keep them active. A major part in this process has been played by the Army School of Bagpipe Music, supported throughout by a succession of right-minded Commanders of the Army in Scotland. Piping in the army is in good shape.

Mention should be made, however, of the prominent part played in the history of army piping over the years by the small but significant number of officers who have played the Highland bagpipe. While all officers are expected to take an interest in the pipes and drums, it has always been acceptable for officers to play. Though they rarely attained the heights of virtuosity, the influence of those officers ensured that piping flourished in the regiments. Also, tribute should be paid to those officers who did not play, but loved and cherished the sound of the pipes and the music and spectacle of the pipes and drums. Many attained high rank, and so the cause of piping has never lacked its advocates. However, much will always depend on the attitude and interest of individual commanding officers.

On the musical side, perhaps things have not gone so well. When the military band of a Scottish regiment went on tour in the years between the Wars and in the decades immediately following World War II, it was customary for the pipe major and four pipers to be included and for the pipers to perform a couple of Highland dances to the pipe major's playing, one in each half of the programme. It also became standard practice for the pipers to contribute a selection before and after the interval, and 'ten minutes with the pipers' – and a good ten minutes at that – became a recognised feature of the programme. These novelties enabled the band to charge a higher rate, which secured a share of the fee for the pipe fund and included the pipe major and the four pipers in the general share-out of the spoils, the 'playing-out money', at the end of the season. Also, they gave the bandsmen an always-welcome break, eased the lot of the bandmaster in compiling and rehearsing his programmes and went down well with the audience.

In the decade before the Great War, Bandmaster Ricketts of the 2nd Argylls introduced an item in which the pipe major played a selection, with the band acting as what would now be known as a backing group. No doubt a musician of Mr Ricketts's calibre was able to overcome the difficulties caused by the incompatability of the pipe scale with its differing intervals and indeterminate pitch with the standard major scales. Less-happy results ensued when these difficulties were imperfectly understood and the pipe major stood happily blasting out some simple tunes on a flat instrument while in the background the bandsmen ground out a series of sustained chords and 'humchucks'. The inevitable happened; someone had the idea of having all the pipers join in and, then, by the process of extension, the whole pipe band. The idea was far from universally accepted and the majority of the Scottish regiments disapproved, except, as was claimed at the time, those neither of whose bands was fit to be heard on its own. But at the Edinburgh Military Tattoo it became accepted that during the finale the pipes, drums and military bands combined to play 'Scotland the Brave' in a setting which apparently had been played between the wars by the bands of the Highland Light Infantry. True or false, the HLI got the blame!

One result was that the correct pipe setting of 'Scotland the Brave' fell into total oblivion. Another was that the practice of the military and pipe bands playing together began to be adopted here and there, but only when 'Scotland the Brave' was played. However, in 1970, in what was to be their swan song before their amalgamation with the 3rd Carabiniers, the bands of the Royal Scots Greys included, at the pipe major's suggestion, an arrangement for band and pipes of the hymn *Amazing Grace* on their farewell disc. The tune is that of a traditional Highland hymn in 3/4 time, simple but evocative. The impact of this item was one of the musical surprises of the century. Despite its shortcomings – the pipes throughout were slightly flat – *Amazing Grace* captured the popular imagination, including that of the knowledgeable but fickle pop generation, and soared to the top of the record sales and made a lot of money for the regiment.

Whereupon the floodgates opened. The band and pipes combination became the rage, as bandmasters strove to produce a successor to *Amazing Grace* in the hope that their offering, too, might repeat the success of the Greys. But the secret of the Greys' triumph lay in the melody which, whether authentically Highland or not, had the true Highland tang to it, and this, of course, suited the pipe scale, which the majority of the succeeding compositions apparently failed to take into account. The Greys' band arrangement, too, did not compete with the melody, but was content to let the pipes carry it without interference, clashing chords or counter melodies.[2]

The long-term effect of *Amazing Grace* was to make the band and pipes combination respectable and, in time, it began to be considered acceptable for both to sustain complete Retreat programmes: marches, slow airs, strathspeys and reels were all played by the pipes and drums, while the military band droned along in the background. As long as the military band confined itself to the backing role, the effect was bearable; but when arrangements became overambitious, the result could be distressing to the ear, as when the massed bands of the Scottish

Division marched past a Royal personage with the pipers playing 'Highland Laddie' and the band 'The Cock o' the North', the first in 2/4 time, the second in 6/8. The art of counterpoint requires that the result should make musical sense. Worse was to come when it became common practice for the pipes and band to form up in alternate files, even on ceremonial parades and occasions, and for both to march, formed up thus, with everybody blowing their heads off, Queen Victoria's 1871 ruling, that 'the pipers must always lead', being conveniently discarded. This was a result of the diminished strength of the military band, which was no longer able to compete on its own.

This practice, now common in even the best piping regiments, completely ignores, of course, the character of the Highland pipe, which contains within itself its own sustained chord accompaniment in the shape of the drones. Also, it has also lent weight to the current process, largely the result of the incorporation of the Highland pipe into folk groups, whereby the unique and distinctive pipe scale – which gives the instrument its own particular character – is being adjusted gradually to conform to the scale of Bb Major or even, in some cases, B natural. A devotee of the Highland pipe, as a result, might view the departure of the military bands with a certain amount of equanimity, as it will leave the music of that truly noble instrument paramount in the Scottish regiments, in the same way that it will restore the 'cheerful fife' to its legitimate place in the regiments of England and Wales.

There was an interesting development in the pipe band sphere in the decade from 1970, when regimental pipe bands began to take part in civilian piping competitions. There had been some doubt as to the propriety of this step, as it might have been detracting from the reputation of the bands of distinguished regiments to have them enter and then not be placed in the prize list. It was soon discovered that the effort needed to compete with the good civilian pipe bands was considerable, and this led to an increased appreciation of the dedication and commitment of the leading civilian pipe bands, all of which practise and train in their own time. Although regimental pipe bands tended to do well in the lower grades, the occasions when top-class honours were taken were rare, and with the ever-increasing pressure of modern military life, its complexity and intensity, it became apparent that while playing in pipe band competitions undoubtedly increased the standard of expertise, this could only be maintained at the expense of military standards. In recent years, the participation of regimental pipe bands in the contests run by the Royal Scottish Pipe Band Association has almost ceased. Distance, too, has played its part, the costs of travel being prohibitive.

In some of the English divisions, the decision to concentrate the regimental military bands into one or two divisional bands had been pre-empted, and a welcome side-effect was the realisation that the regimental music associated with the component units of the division would have to be paid particular attention if it was to survive. In the case of the former Queen's Regiment, the music of the component regiments, with its history, had already been recorded in a handbook which included the solo cornet parts of all the marches, slow troops and anthems. Invaluable to the student of military music, this has ensured that whatever happens, the melodies of those marches will survive, because it is extremely unlikely that all the copies of the handbook will be destroyed, whereas a fire in the wrong storeroom, as invariably happens, can result in an irreplaceable segment of a regiment's history being lost for ever. Also, private efforts are being made to record the music of the regiments, particularly in the case of those affected by the recent round of amalgamations. Surely the time has come for the Royal Military School of Music to assume the responsibility for collating, arranging and playing the ancient traditional music of the British Army in the same way as the band of the Garde Républicaine de Paris does for the French. The role is too important to be left to the surviving divisional bands.

Over the last few decades, the Army has changed to such an extent that the military band has lost its very reason for being. It has been suggested that the bands might once again have reverted to their original role in providing music for social occasions, but in those days the band was supported entirely by the officers. But, it would be difficult to make a case for the same thing to be done at public expense, especially these days, when anyone, including any soldier, can hear his favourite music at the flick of a switch and amplified music can be hired for any social function. The complete reappraisal of what were once regarded as the lynchpins of the daily routine has led to their abolition, as there was no longer any need for them. Officers and soldiers alike are able to live out of barracks, some a long way off, as most are married and there is no longer that core audience within the barrack gates who would make a point of listening out for Last Post when the 'ace' drummer or bugler was sounding the call. There is no point in beating Long Reveille if nobody has to get up nor of beating Tattoo when any soldier can live more or less where he pleases, provided he turns up on time with the right gear. The only marching that is done is when a guard of honour parades for a short distance through the streets.

Bandsmen and musicians, male and female, are now recruited into the Corps of Army Music. After their initial recruit training they are posted to the Royal Military School of Music at Kneller Hall where they are taught to play a selected instrument. After a year's tuition, they are then available for posting by Headquarters Army Music to a band as required and according to their instrument. Infantry divisional bands consist of a director of music commissioned as an officer on time promotion, a bandmaster, who is a warrant officer class one, and thirty-five musicians. The band of the Scots Guards, with its role carrying out prominent public duties in London, has forty-nine musicians. Promotion prospects within the corps of Army music are therefore excellent.

The Scottish Division of Infantry has two bands, both based in Edinburgh; the Lowland, wearing tartan trousers, scarf plaids and the Kilmarnock bonnet; and the Highland, in the kilt, scarf plaid and feathered bonnet. The tartan worn by both is the Government or Black Watch and the doublets are scarlet, faced blue. The present organisation relieves the regiment and the bandmaster from the responsibility for recruiting, which could always be difficult. The fact is, however, that with the best will in the world, the regiment is now divorced from its music and, as a result, many of old tunes are being lost. Under modern conditions the turnover in officers and men is rapid. Memories are short, and when a ceremony has to be mounted, perhaps after a gap of several years, it can happen that there is no one still serving who can remember how it was done last time.

So, the Army, though much attenuated, goes on, still to the

call of the trumpet and bugle, and with the music of fife and drum and pipe and drum, to cheer it whenever it feels the need to refresh itself at the wells of history. And in the background, there will still be the divisional bands to dispense their inimitable music, whose rarity will lead to a yet deeper appreciation of the part it played in the brave days of yore when the scarlet ranks marched, swore and sweated their way over half the world; and the bugle sounded, the drums beat and the flag was lowered as the sun set, from Hong Kong through India and Egypt to Gibraltar; from Gibraltar to Bermuda, across Canada to Vancouver and from Vancouver back to Hong Kong. Those, indeed, were the days. And fortunate indeed are those old soldiers of the Scottish regiments, an ever-dwindling band, who saw the last of them, and for whom their regimental music, in all its variety and glory, was an integral part of their daily lives.

Notes

1. 'He [the Permanent Under-Secretary] knew all about the Army and nothing at all about war.' *Chink*, Lavinia Greacan (Macmillan, 1989).
  The Permanent Under-Secretary is the head of the civil service as distinct from the military component of the staff of the Ministry of Defence. 'Chink' was Major General Eric Dorman-Smith, a staff officer at the War Office in 1934.
2. Mention must however be made of the pipe tune and band arrangement of 'The Sands of Kuwait', composed after the Gulf War by Piper Gordon MacKenzie of the Queen's Own Highlanders which more than satisfies these requirements. Sadly it is never heard today.

1st Battalion, The Black Watch (Royal Highland Regiment), Armed Forces Day, Berlin, 1981
During the occupation of Berlin there was great competition between the Allies to put on the most impressive display on Armed Forces Day. Who better to uphold the reputation of the British Army for style and impact than the glorious old 'Black Watch of the Battles, First in the Field and Last to Leave' seen here as the Pipes, Drums and Military Band, blasting out the Regimental March 'Highland Laddie', lead the battalion past the saluting base? (RHQ Black Watch)

SELECT MUSICAL BIBLIOGRAPHY

Ashworth, Charles S., *A new, useful, and complete system of drum beating* (Not known, 1812).

Barty-King, Hugh, *The Drum* (Royal Tournament, 1988).

Blom, Eric & Cummings, David, *The New Everyman Dictionary of Music* (Revised) (Dent & Sons, 1992).

Bruce, George B. & Emmett, Dan D., *The Drummers and Fifers Guide* (W.A. Pond, New York, 1865).

Cassin-Scott, Jack & Fabb, John, *Military Bands and their Uniforms* (Blandford, 1978).

Combre, Marcel, *Sonneries d 'Ordonnance Officielles et Réglementaires* (Marcel Combre).

Diack, J.M., *The Scottish Orpheus* (Paterson's Publications).

Fairrie, Lt-Col Angus, *The Piper's Day* (RHQ QO Hldrs, 1991).

Fayeulle, R., *Marches et Refrains de l'Empire* (Robert Martin, 1964).

Fuld, James J., *Book of World Famous Music* (Dover Publications, 1985).

Gordon, W.J., *Bands of the British Army* (Belmont-Maitland, 1970).

Hulbert, James, *The Complete Fifer's Museum* (Simeon Butler, 1811).

Jacobs, Arthur, *Dictionary of Music* (Penguin Books, 1990).

MacDonald, Keith Norman, *The Gesto Collection of Highland Music* (Oscar Brandsetter, 1893).

Mackay, Major D.H., *Regimental Music of the Household Cavalry and the Royal Armoured Corps* (HQ Royal Armoured Corps).

Moeller, Sanford S., *The Moeller Book* (Ludwig Music, 1956).

Ord, John, *Bothy Songs & Ballads* (John Donald).

Pares, Gabriel, *Anciennes Marches et Refrains de l'Armée Française* (Andrieu Frères).

Potter, Henry, *Drum Major's Manual* (Henry Potter, 1905?).

Scott, John, *Marches, Waltzes, Airs, etc., Dedicated to the Officers of the 78th Highlanders* (T. Key, 1816).

Toeche-Mittler, Joachim, *Armeemärsche* (Kurt Vowinckel Verlag).

Wilson, Lt-Col L.M., *Music of the Queen's Regiment* (RHQ Queen's Regt., 1980).

The Bugle Horn Major's Companion (Henry Potter, 1822?).

The Drummers' Handbook (Defence Ministry, 1985).

The New Oxford Companion to Music (Oxford University Press, 1983).

Rifle Brigade Bugle Calls and Marches (JR. Lafleur & Son, 1882).

Trumpet & Bugle Sounds (War Office, 1893).

Trumpet & Bugle Sounds (War Office, 1902).

Trumpet & Bugle Sounds (War Office, 1909).

Trumpet & Bugle Sounds (War Office, 1927).

Trumpet & Bugle Calls (HMSO, 1966).

SELECT BIBLIOGRAPHY

Adams, Frank, *Clans, Septs and Regiments of the Scottish Highlands* (Johnston, 1934).

Ascoli, David, *A Companion to the British Army* (Harrap, 1983).

Baker, Anthony, *Battle Honours of the British Army* (Ian Allen, 1986).

Barnett, Correlli, *Britain and Her Army* (Allen Lane, 1970).

Binns, Lt-Col P.L,, *100 Years of Military Music* (Blackmore, 1959).

Blanch, Lesley, *The Wilder Shores of Love* (John Murray, 1954).

Blomfield, David (Ed.), *Lahore to Lucknow* (Leo Cooper, 1992).

Brett-James, Anthony, *Life in Wellington's Army* (Allen & Unwin, 1972).

Burns, Robert, *Poetical Works* (Gall & Inglis).

Carman, W.Y., *British Military Uniforms* (Hamlyn Group, 1968).

Caroe, Olaf, *The Pathans* (Papermac, 1965).

Chandler, David, *Art of War in the Age of Marlborough* (Batsford, 1976).

Childs, John, *The British Army of William III* (Manchester University, 1987).

Colburn, *United Service Magazine 1844* (Harrison & Co., 1844).

Cole & Priestly, D.H. & E.C., *An Outline of British Military History* (Sifton Praed, 1945).

Connell, Evan S., *Son of the Morning Star* (Picador, 1984).

Dalton, Charles, *The Scots Army 1661–1688* (Greenhill Books, 1989).

Davis, Brian L., *British Army Uniforms & Insignia of World War II* (Arms and Armour, 1983).

Duffy, Christopher, *The Military Experience in the Age of Reason* (Routledge & Kegan Paul, 1987).

Dunn, J.C. (Ed.), *The War the Infantry Knew* (Cardinal, 1989).

Edgerton, Robert B., *Like Lions They Fought* (Weidenfeld & Nicholson, 1988).

Elliot, Maj GenJ.G., *The Frontier 1839–1947* (Cassell, 1968).

Eking, John R., *Swords Around a Throne* (Weidenfeld & Nicholson, 1988).

Fairrie, Lt-Col Angus, *The Queen's Own Highlanders* (RHQ QO Hldrs, 1983).

Fawcett, William, *The Exercise of Riflemen* (War Office, 1811).

Featherstone, Donald, *Weapons & Equipment of the Victorian Soldier* (Blandford, 1978).

Forrest, G.W., *A History of the Indian Mutiny* (Blackwood, 1904).

Gates, David, *The British Light Infantry Arm* (Batsford, 1987).

Gleichen, Lord Edward, *A Guardsman's Memories* (Blackwood, 1932).

Glover, Michael (Ed.), *A Gentleman Volunteer* (Heinemann, 1979).

Greacen, Lavinia, *Chink* (Macmillan, 1989).

Grimble, Ian, *Clans and Chiefs* (Blond & Briggs, 1980).

Hallows, Ian S., *Regiments & Corps of the British Army* (Arms & Armour, 1991).

Hay, J., *The German Army from Within* (Hodder & Stoughton, 1914).

Hibbert, Christopher, *The Destruction of Lord Raglan* (Penguin Books, 1985).

Howarth, David, *A Near-run Thing* (Collins, 1968).

James, John, *The Paladins* (Macdonald, 1990).

Keegan, John, *Who's Who in Military History* (Weidenfeld & Nicholson, 1976).

Lachouque, Henri, *The Anatomy of Glory* (Lund Humphries, 1962).

Lehmann, Joseph, *The First Boer War* (Cape, 1972).

Lenman, Brian, *The Jacobite Risings in Britain* (Methuen, 1980).

Linklater, Magnus, *For King and Conscience* (Weidenfeld & Nicholson, 1989).

Livesey, Anthony, *Battles of the Great Commanders* (Tiger Books, 1990).

Longford, Elizabeth, *Wellington – The Years of the Sword* (Literary Guild, 1969).

Lummis, W.M. & Wynn, K.G., *Honour the Light Brigade* (Hayward, 1973).

MacMunn, Lieut-General Sir George, *The Armies of India* (Crecy Books, 1988).

MacMunn, Lieut-General Sir George, *The Martial Races of India* (Nisa Traders, 1982).

Malcolm, Charles, *The Piper in Peace and War* (John Murray, 1927).

Mason, Philip, *A Matter of Honour* (Jonathan Cape, 1974).

Maxwell, Sir Herbert, *The Life of Wellington* (Sampson Low, 1900).

Messenger, Charles, *A History of the British Army* (Bison Books, 1986).

Morris, Donald, *The Washing of the Spears* (Jonathan Cape, 1965).

Oman, Carola, *Sir John Moore* (Hodder & Stoughton, 1953).

Pakenham, Thomas, *The Boer War* (Weidenfeld & Nicholson, 1982).

Palmer, Roy, *The Rambling Soldier* (Peacock, 1977).

Prebble, John, *Glencoe* (Secker & Warburg, 1966).

Prebble, John, *The Highland Clearances* (Secker & Warburg, 1963).

Prebble, John, *Mutiny* (Secker & Warburg, 1975).

Prebble, John, *Culloden* (Secker & Warburg, 1961).

Prior, Melton, *Campaigns of a War Correspondent* (Edward Arnold, 1912).

Richards, Frank, *Old Soldier Sahib* (Faber, 1936).

Rider, Brian, *A More Expeditious Conveyance* (J.A. Allen & Co, 1984).

Robson, Brian, *The Road To Kabul* (Arms & Armour, 1986).

Schaumann, August, *On the Road with Wellington* (Heinemann, 1924).

Schofield, Victoria, *Every Rock, Every Bush* (Century, 1984).

Schwarzkopf, H. Norman, *It Doesn't Take a Hero* (BCA, 1992).

Scott, Sir Walter, *The Monastery* (Black, 1986).

Seton, Sir Bruce & Grant J., *The Pipes of War* (Maclehose Johnston, 1920).

Shand, Alexander, *Soldiers of Fortune in Camp and Court* (Constable, 1907).

Slim, Field Marshal The Viscount, *Defeat into Victory* (Cassell, 1956).

Stanhope, The Earl, *Conversations with the Duke of Wellington* (John Murray, 1889).

Stewart, Colonel David, *Sketches of the Highlanders of Scotland* (Constable, 1822).

Telfer Dunbar, John, *A History of Highland Dress* (Batsford, 1979).

Terraine, John, *The Smoke and the Fire* (Leo Cooper, 1992).

Terraine, John (Ed.), *General Jack's Diary* (Eyre & Spottiswoode, 1964).

Tsouras, Peter (Ed.), *Warrior's Words* (Cassell, 1992).

Walter, John (Ed.), *Weapons and Equipment of the British Army 1866* (Greenhill Books, 1988).

Walton, Peter (Ed.), *Scarlet into Khaki* (Greenhill Books, 1988).

Warner, Philip, *The Battle of Loos* (William Kimber, 1976).

Westlake, Ray, *Kitchener's Army* (Nutshell Publications, 1989).

Winstock, Lewis, *Songs & Music of the Redcoats* (Leo Cooper, 1970).

Wintle, Justin (Ed.), *A Dictionary of War Quotations* (Hodder & Stoughton, 1989).

Woodcock, Thomas, *The Oxford Guide to Heraldry* (Oxford University Press, 1989).

Woodham Smith, Cecil, *The Reason Why* (Constable, 1953).

INDEXES

Where it has been necessary to abbreviate regimental titles, the official form has been used. However, to avoid a long-standing source of confusion that continues to bedevil historians, 'Cameronians' has been spelled in full and 'Queen's Own Cameron Highlanders' has been abbreviated to Cameron Hldrs or QO Cameron Hldrs.

A and SH	=	Argyll and Sutherland Highlanders
BW	=	Black Watch
Gordons	=	Gordon Highlanders
KOSB	=	King's Own Scottish Borderers
QO Hldrs	=	Queen's Own Highlanders
Cameron Hldrs	=	Queen's Own Cameron Highlanders
QO Cameron Hldrs	=	Queen's Own Cameron Highlanders
RHF	=	Royal Highland Fusiliers
RSF	=	Royal Scots Fusiliers
HLI	=	Highland Light Infantry
RS	=	Royal Scots
Scots DG	=	Royal Scots Dragoon Guards
Greys	=	Royal Scots Greys
SG	=	Scots Guards
Seaforth	=	Seaforth Highlanders
TA	=	Territorial Army

Regiments have been indexed under their current amalgamated names as these are likely to be more familiar to the reader, e.g. under Royal Highland Fusiliers will be found both Royal Scots Fusiliers and Highland Light Infantry; and the Seaforth and Cameron Highlanders are indexed separately under the Queen's Own Highlanders. Where a regiment's precedence number has been mentioned in the text it has been indexed under its post-1881 or post-amalgamation title, e.g. the 25th (King's Own Borderers) Foot is indexed under the King's Own Scottish Borderers; and the 34th (Cumberland) Foot appears under the King's Own Royal Border Regiment.

BAND MUSIC

PIPE MUSIC

* Denotes a *piobaireachd* in the current list of known music.

? Denotes a *piobaireachd* not at present (2001) known.

REGIMENTS

TARTAN*

Buccleugh or Shepherd
Pipers of the 4th (Border) Battalion
King's Own Scottish Borderers
1881–1965, 72

79th or Cameron of Erracht
79th 1793–1881, 61
Queen's Own Cameron Highlanders
1881- 1961, 61
Pipes and Drums and Military
Band QO Hldrs 1961–94,[6] 132
Pipes and Drums The Highlanders
1994 to date, 132

Campbell of Cawdor[1]
91st 1864–81, 122

Douglas[2]
Pipers 26th Cameronians 1862- 81,
126, 131
The Cameronians 1891-1968, 65

Erskine
Pipers 21st 1928–58, 133
Pipes and Drums RHF 1958 to
date, 133

74th or Forbes
74th 1846–1881, 61
Liverpool Scottish 1900 to date[3]

92nd or Gordon
92nd 1793–1881, 61
Gordons 1881–1994, 61
The Highlanders 1994 to date, 132

42nd or Government
Worn by:
42nd[4] 1739–1881
71st[5] 1777–1799?
72nd 1778–1809
74th 1787–1809
75th 1787–1809
91st 1794–1809
93rd 1800–81
And by:
BW 1881 to date
Band BW 1873 to date
Pipers BW 1881–1890
The Cameronians 1881–1893
RS 1881- 1901, 131

RSF 1881–1958
KOSB 1881–1898
A and SH 1881 to date

Hodden Gray[8]
London Scottish (TA)[3] 1858 to date

Hunting Stuart
RS 1901 to date, 65, 133
Pipers 1st Bn 1901–1933, 131
Pipers 2nd Bn 1892–1933, 131

Leslie
KOSB 1899–to date, 65

MacGregor (Rob Roy sett)
Pipers 93rd 1826–1848, 127

MacGregor of Glengyle
Band 93rd 1826–1850, 134n

78th or MacKenzie[6]
71st[5] 1799–1809?
71st 1834–1881, 46
78th 1793–1881, 62
Seaforth 1881–1961[9]
HLI 1881–1958
RHF 1958 to date
QO Hldrs 1961–1994[6]

Royal Stuart[7]
'Musick Tartan', 111n
RS Pipers 2nd Bn 1881–1892, 131

Pipers 1933 to date, 133
Pipers 21st RNB Fusiliers 1830–
1881, 131

Royal Stuart
Band 42nd BW 1830–1873, 128
Pipers Black Watch 1890 to date,
128
72nd Highlanders 1823–1881, 46,
129
Pipers KOSB? to date, 122
Pipers Cameron Highlanders 1943–
1961, 133
Pipers Greys 1946 to date, 133
Pipers Scots Guards 1854 to date,
133
Band 93rd 1850–1862, 127

Notes overleaf

333

Notes

1 When the 91st Argyllshire Regiment became the 91st Argyllshire Highlanders – a non-kilted Highland corps – in 1864, the tartan known as the Campbell of Cawdor, a branch of Clan Campbell settled in north-east Scotland, was chosen because no one could positively identify the tartan worn by the 91st when it was raised by the Duke of Argyll in 1794. It was described as the 'green tartan with the blue line'. Later opinion accepts that the 42nd or Government tartan was intended, and it was to this tartan that the 91st reverted on becoming the 1st Bn Argyll and Sutherland Highlanders in 1881.

2 Although the 26th was authorised to hold three pipers within the establishment in 1862, the presence of pipers had been noted some thirty years earlier. It is believed they wore the Douglas tartan.

3 'V' (The Liverpool Scottish) Company, 5/8th (Volunteer) Bn, The King's Regiment, wore the Forbes tartan kilt and maintained the traditions of the Liverpool Scottish, but remained a unit of the Queen's Own Highlanders. Similarly, there was a London Scottish company that wore the hodden gray kilt in the London Regiment (Volunteers), which likewise remained part of the Gordon Highlanders. Both will became part of The Highland Regiment after the recent amalgamations.

4 The tartan was differenced at various periods by the addition of coloured overstripes, usually red.

5 It is possible that the 71st went into the 78th tartan on its return from India in 1799. Both had been raised in Ross-shire from the MacKenzie country. The Royal Highland Fusiliers wear the 78th tartan, except for the pipes and drums which wear the Erskine.

6 It has been suggested that the two white stripes in the 78th tartan were originally buff to match the 78th's – the Ross-shire Buffs – facings. The Queen's Own Highlanders wore the 78th tartan, except for the pipes, drums and band, which wore the 79th.

7 Described in one source as the 'musick tartan', the Royal Stuart is said to have been worn by the band of the 78th in 1793. The band of the 42nd was wearing a red tartan soon after the Waterloo campaign, apparently a variation of the regimental tartan, with scarlet substituted for black. This changed later to the Royal Stuart tartan.

8 Hodden gray was the colour of the homespun clothing worn by the Lowland Scottish peasantry in the eighteenth century.

9 The 5th (Sutherland) Bn, Seaforth Highlanders (TA), wore the Government tartan in the A and SH sett, which was sometimes called the Sutherland tartan. The 9th (Glasgow Highlanders) Bn, Highland Light Infantry (TA), wore Black Watch uniform and badges – but not the red hackle – until the kilt was restored to the HLI in 1948 when the Glasgow Highlanders went into the 78th or MacKenzie tartan in the HLI sett.

GENERAL INDEX